CONSCIOUSNESS AND REALITY :
HEGEL'S PHILOSOPHY OF SUBJECTIVITY

CONSCIOUSNESS AND REALITY : HEGEL'S PHILOSOPHY OF SUBJECTIVITY

by

JOSEPH L. NAVICKAS

MARTINUS NIJHOFF - THE HAGUE - 1976

To my wife ELEONORA-ALDONA
And to our children LEONAS
ARISTA
MARIUS
JONAS

Su meile

ISBN 90 247 1775 2

PRINTED IN BELGIUM

TABLE OF CONTENTS

PART FIVE : THE SPIRITUAL SUBJECT

EPILOGUE

FOREWORD

With the rise of analytical philosophy the criticism against Hegelianism has become increasingly shrill, and signs of an embarrassment that Hegel's philosophy should ever have arisen are noticeable in such influential works as those of Karl Popper and Hans Reichenbach, to mention but a few. However, many contemporary philosophers stress what is called subjectivity, conceiving reality as susceptible of methodical analysis only to the extent that it is in and for the subject. What is more, they not only insist on the importance of the subject for philosophy, but maintain that the subject must be conceived as the principal determinative of true objectivity. Since knowledge depends for its possibility on the inseverable correlatives of consciousness and reality, they would grant that a proper importance must be given to both subject and object. Still, exemplifying the relational principle within the unity of a dual structure, the subject serves as an exclusive agent that provides ingress into the meaning of the object.

To the extent that philosophy goes back to the very origins of consciousness, it belongs precisely to its nature that its cognitional effort move in the realm of subjectivity. Quite obviously, in this respect Hegel's shift to the subject has relevance and offers inspiration. Indeed, the most obvious reason for the revival of interest in Hegel's work is that the dialectical constitution (*Bildung*) of consciousness — as he calls it — makes more sense to modern mind than a purely factual one. It is true, too, that there are several other philosophical questions that Hegel made pioneering attempts to answer. As one of the first thinkers to study the historical setting of consciousness, he was the forerunner of modern critical scholarship on historicity. Convinced that immutability had outlived its usefulness, he was an embrionic methodologist and worked to achieve a merger between dialectic and history, between phenomenology and ontology. In brief, Hegel's thought is firm in defense of the subject as a dynamic agent articulating and specifying itself through gradual process and self-transcendence.

In this respect Hegel's effort is genuinely new, and no modern thinker can afford to neglect it.

My fundamental aim in this book has been to trace and to make intelligible the gradual constitution of Hegel's notion of subjectivity and objectivity. This is a topic to which any discussion of Hegel must constantly return. No issue is more important in Hegel's thought than the distinction and relation between subjectivity and objectivity. One might even say that a fully elaborated philosophy of Hegel coincides with his theory of subjectivity, consistently developed in all its ramifications.

In a problem so vast and intricate it has been necessary to make a somewhat rigid delimitation of the field. I have, therefore, taken as the object of my analysis Hegel's *Phenomenology of Spirit* which contains the principles of his philosophy of subjectivity. I have been impelled to focus my attention on the *Phenomenology* both because of its intrinsic interest and because of the light it throws on subsequent development of modern philosophy.

In this work I have adhered to the original division and sequence of the *Phenomenology*. This is not to suggest that I intend to offer a sort of paraphrase of Hegel's early work. The reason for this lies partly in the special character of the problem involved, partly in the rigorous architectonic of the work, which to my mind is not arbitrary but warranted by the dialectical growth of the subject. It seems obvious to me that any meaningful discussion of Hegelian subjectivity is not possible without reconstructing the tightly woven sequence of its phenomenological forms.

References to Hegel's original text in this work are all to the sixth edition of the *Phänomenologie des Geistes*, hereafter referred to as *Phän.*, edited by Johannes Hoffmeister (Hamburg : Felix Meiner, 1952). All references to the English text are to J. B. Baillie's translation of the *Phenomenology of Mind* (2nd rev. ed.; London : George Allen & Unwin Ltd., 1949), hereafter referred to as B.

One final word. It should be acknowledged that Chapters 1, 2, and 4 contain in slightly modified form several excerpts from my published article, "The Hegelian Notion of Subjectivity" (*International Philosophical Quarterly*, Vol. VIII, No. 1, 1968).

My sincere and special thanks go to Rev. Charles F. Donovan, S.J., Senior Vice President of Boston College, Dr. Donald White, Dean of the Graduate School, Rev. Joseph Flanagan, S.J., Chairman of the Department of Philosophy, and Prof. Thomas Blakeley for their constant encouragement, support, and suggestions in carrying out this project.

Part One : Introduction

CHAPTER I

THE SHIFT TO THE SUBJECT IN MODERN THOUGHT

The history of philosophy is the record of an arduous and diligent search for knowledge of reality. Not only is it a diligent search, but it is a continuous attempt to reconcile being and thought about being.[1] The depth of this search can be measured by the boldness of the craving with which thought seeks to represent in itself what lies outside of itself. But the deeper our thought penetrates reality, the more vehement is the opposition between subjectivity and objectivity and the more difficult becomes their reconciliation. The conflict between objectivity as externality and subjectivity as immanent consciousness has provided a fundamental problem in the unfolding of modern thought.[2]

In the history of modern philosophy there are few events of such decisive importance for the shaping of this problem as Hegel's radical examination of thought in its living performance and his discovery of the self-mediating process. Among the modern thinkers it was Hegel who tried hardest to reconcile subject and object, thinking and reality, and this attempt at reconciliation was one of the most immediate sources of criticism and misconception of his philosophy.[3] Subjectivity once was a pejorative notion,

[1] It might be well here to point out that this was also the view of Hegel : "The ultimate aim and business of philosophy is to reconcile thought or the Notion with reality". *Lectures on the History of Philosophy*, trans. E. S. Haldane and F. H. Simson (London : Routledge and Kegan Paul Ltd., 1896; Reprinted 1955), III, 545.

[2] Philosophy from Descartes to Hegel has been interpreted by Hegel himself as consisting of expanding Descartes' task, which was to correlate the occurrences of external reality with thinking.

[3] This criticism concerns Hegel's supposed radical identification of thought and reality. We are referring to the view implied in the well-known commentaries and critical works on Hegel, e.g. F. H. Bradley's *Appearance and Reality* (2nd ed.; Oxford : Clarendon Press, 1930), chap. XV; R. H. Lotze's *Logic*, trans. B. Bosanquet (London : Oxford University Press, 1884), bk. III, chap. i; J. McTaggart's *A Commentary on Hegel's Logic* (Cambridge :

denoting a violation of the authoritative demands of the mind. But in Hegel's philosophy this notion came to indicate a rejection of misconceived objectivity and a reaffirmation of the unconditional decision of the subject.

The possibility of objective knowledge was never more radically questioned than in the approach of modern thought generally characterized by its shift to the subject. The specific form in which this question was raised in modern times is to be sharply differentiated from the character of philosophical orientation in previous times. The Greeks were the first to make the initial and decisive affirmation that objective knowledge is possible to man, proceeding from the objective as from something immediately given. They were convinced that there is no sharp line separating thought from being, cognition from reality, that "the problem of being and the problem of knowledge are bound together in indissoluble unity".[4] Medieval philosophy, too, did not question the possibility of objective knowledge, for it accepted the Aristotelian definition of truth as a correspondence between a judgment and the external reality which the judgment intended to express. Even the early Renaissance did not make any serious change in this fundamental pressuposition of ancient and medieval thought, relying on independent reality as the principal seat of correspondence and intelligibility.

The shift to the subject set in with the reflections of Descartes on the *Cogito*, in which he found both the rational justification of knowledge and the evidence for the existence of a substantial ego. According to Descartes, everything which is not thinking itself must be doubted or placed between brackets. Since the subject can validly think only his own thinking and since

---

The University Press, 1910), p. 194; A. Seth's *Hegelianism and Personality* (London : W. Blackwood, 1887), pp. 133-134.

Hegel was misconceived as being a radical subjectivist, one who holds that to exist is to be perceived, or that objects exist only if there are conscious minds to apprehend them. Cf. J. N. Findlay, *Hegel : A Re-examination* (New York : Collier Books, 1962), pp. 15-18.

Last but not least, Hegel was misconceived as being a formal structuralist, one whose primary concern was the construction of symmetrical structures. Pierre-Jean Labarrière, whose doctoral dissertation has recently been published in France, has convincingly shown that Hegel's phenomenological structures and the gradual process are mutually implicative. The structures become significant only when they are related to the dialectical process itself, because the very essence of thought lies in its continuous movement. Cf. *Structures et mouvement dialectique dans la Phénoménologie de l'Esprit de Hegel* (Paris : Aubier, 1968), p. 55.

[4] Ernst Cassirer, *The Problem of Knowledge*, trans. W. H. Woglom and C. W. Hendel (New Haven : Yale University Press, 1950), p. 1.

he is primarily conscious of his own consciousness, the knowledge the subject has is nothing else than knowledge of consciousness. But as soon as knowledge is affirmed to be nothing but knowledge of consciousness, there seems to be no possibility of positing an autonomous reality of any kind. For Descartes, however, the *Cogito, ergo sum* meant a valid transition from thought to reality. He explained the *Cogito* as involving an apodictic evidence for the existence of a substantial subject : I am certain that I am because I think. Descartes has accepted uncritically the dualism of thought and reality but insisted on working from the very fact of thinking to the existence of a substantial bearer of consciousness. His method enclosed consciousness in self-sufficiency : consciousness was made entirely immanent and capable of living its life independently of the body.[5]

Descartes believed that there was an escape from the difficulties of subjectivism, for he had discovered a criterion of truth in the fact that "the things which we conceive very clearly and distinctly are all true".[6] This means that man can accept as objective whatever he conceives in clear and distinct ideas. In other words, every attempt to show that a certain reality corresponds to mental concepts rests upon the assumption that clear and distinct ideas are the objective expressions of reality.[7] However, with respect to material reality, Descartes was able to discern only one clearly distinct idea — the idea of quantity, thus limiting man's objective knowledge of reality to the experience of the physical sciences. Understanding that the argument based on clear and distinct ideas could not remove the principal difficulty, Descartes appealed to the *veracitas Dei*, although God's existence was previously placed between brackets. Therefore we can say that Descartes escapes subjectivism only by betraying his own methodical principles.[8]

[5] "... Sum tantum res cogitans, non extensa, et ex alia parte distinctam ideam corporis, quatenus est tantum res extensa, non cogitans, certum est me a corpore meo re vera esse distinctum, et *absque illo posse existere*". *Meditationes de Prima Philosophia* (Paris : Bibliothèque des Textes Philosophiques, 1964), p. 76. Italics mine.

[6] *The Philosophical Works*, trans. E. S. Haldane and G. R. T. Ross (New York : Dover, 1955), II, 102.

[7] According to Hans Reichenbach, "Descartes' proof for absolute certainty is constructed by means of a logical trick". *The Rise of Scientific Philosophy* (Berkeley : University of California Press, 1963; reprint), p. 34.

[8] "Descartes escapes subjectivism only by discerning, in the most intimate depths of his consciousness, the liberating presence of the Idea of God. But in reality there is no innate idea of God other than the movement of the mind itself towards the Absolute, which gives our affirmations their firmness and our idea of being its transcendence". Joseph de Finance, "Being and Subjectivity", *A Modern Introduction to Metaphysics*, ed. by D. A. Drennen (New York : The Free Press of Glencoe, 1962), p. 575.

According to Hegel, Descartes' insistence on subjectivity has brought about a "new epoch in Philosophy".[9] In his *Lectures on the History of Philosophy* Hegel interpreted Descartes as the real forerunner of modern thought, for in starting with consciousness without presuppositions he has inaugurated an idealistic approach in philosophy.[10] This was an innovation of great importance. However, for Hegel Cartesianism remained inadequate. He felt that the identity of being and thought, which constituted the most significant discovery in modern times, has not been worked out by Descartes.[11] Although Descartes has relied on thought alone, he failed to apply "himself to the deduction of all determinations from this culminating point of absolute certainty".[12]

It is very clear that Descartes tried to ground his philosophy in subjectivity. Still, it would be misleading to describe the entire system as idealistic or as a phase in the development of philosophy towards extreme idealism. For Descartes the *Cogito* was still related to autonomous reality, although the manner in which he established this relationship was hardly justifiable. His basic intention was to present an interpretation of extramental reality which he did not regard as reducible to the activity of pure consciousness.[13]

A radical shift to the subject occurred when Kant rejected the traditional proposition that objects disclose themselves to consciousness and claimed that consciousness itself is fully equipped to impose its own forms on objects prior to their being given. In the Preface to the second edition of the *Critique of Pure Reason* Kant describes his philosophical program in these words :

Until now it has been assumed that all our knowledge must conform to objects. But all attempts to establish something in regard to objects *a priori*, by means of concepts, and thus to extend our knowledge of them, have, on this presupposition, ended in failure. We must, therefore, make trial whether we may not be more successful in the tasks of metaphysics if we suppose that objects must conform to our knowledge ...[14]

---

[9] *Lectures on the History of Philosophy*, III, 223.

[10] *Ibid.*, III, 228.

[11] *Ibid.*, III, 230.

[12] *Ibid.*

[13] Cf. Frederick Copleston, *A History of Philosophy* (New York : Image Books, 1963), IV, 159.

[14] The original text runs as follows : "Bisher nahm man an, alle unsere Erkenntnis müsse sich nach den Gegenständen richten; aber alle Versuche über sie *a priori* etwas durch Begriffe auszumachen, wodurch unsere Erkenntnis erweitert würde, gingen unter dieser Voraussetzung zunichte. Man versuche es daher einmal, ob wir nicht in den Aufgaben der Metaphysik damit besser fortkommen, dass wir annehmen, die Gegenstände müssen sich nach unserem Erkenntnis richten ...". *Kritik der reinen Vernunft* (Berlin : Deutsche Bibliothek Verlagsgesellschaft, n.d.), I, 19.

Kant was the first thinker to institute the subjective *a priori* wherein intelligibility has its source. He was interested in "knowledge which is occupied not so much with objects as with the mode of our knowledge of objects insofar as this mode of knowledge is to be possible *a priori*".[15] Obviously, this question reaches back beyond knowledge of objects to the prior conditions of the knowledge of objects. It asks on what conditions there would be some objective element that corresponded to the rational affirmation of the subject. In other words, the transcendental inquiry of Kant is not concerned with the object itself but only and exclusively with the possibility of the precursory apprehension of it.

According to Kant, there are two sources of knowledge : the first is the capacity of receiving representations, the second is the power of knowing an object through these representations. Through the first (empirical or material) source of knowledge, objects are given to us; through the latter (formal or rational) they are thought.[16] Kant insists that without experience no object can be apprehended. This does not mean, however, that receptivity for impressions is the primary source of intelligibility and objectivity. The essential function of the empirical source of knowledge consists in setting the formal element in operation. In other words, the necessity and objectivity of phenomenal reality result from the operation of the *a priori* agencies of the mind. Therefore, the subjective element of knowledge, which is independent of experience, makes our judgments possible and objective. The Kantian *a priori* has a purely formal and determinative function in regard to a given experience : it merely awaits imposition upon the raw materials of sensible experience. Accordingly, it has no content that could be apprehended directly in itself, for it is given with the empirical object as its formal determination. Thus, the *a priori* can only be discovered when the transcendental reflection reduces the object to the conditions of its possibility.

Kant believes that he can guarantee the objectivity of the cognitive act

---

[15] Kant introduces this problem in his definition of transcendental knowledge : "Ich nenne alle Erkenntnis *transzendental*, die sich nicht sowohl mit Gegenständen, sondern mit unserer Erkenntnisart von Gegenständen, so fern diese *a priori* möglich sein soll, überhaupt beschäftigt." *Ibid.*, I, 53.

[16] "Unsere Erkenntnis entspringt aus zwei Grundquellen des Gemüts, deren die erste ist, die Vorstellungen zu empfangen (die Rezeptivität der Eindrücke), die zweite das Vermögen, durch diese Vorstellungen einen Gegenstand zu erkennen (Spontaneität der Begriffe) : durch die erste wird uns ein Gegenstand *gegeben*, durch die zweite wird dieser im Verhältnis auf jene Vorstellung (als blosse Bestimmung des Gemüts) *gedacht*". *Ibid.*, I, 86.

without really appealing to anything outside the subject.[17] The *a priori* categories are the only conceivable forms of objectivity, which, in conjunction with empirical material, penetrate the various quantitative, qualitative, relational, and modal concepts in terms of which phenomenal reality lends itself to understanding.[18] For Kant, the objectivity of the cognitive act is contained in the very necessity and inevitability of the act itself. Thus, the real is affirmed when the category of reality is employed by understanding, and this category is operative when there occurs an appropriate filling of the *a priori* forms of sensibility.[19] Therefore, the real in the full sense is merely a necessary imposition of the category of reality on the raw materials provided by experience.

What is so characteristically Kantian in all this is the separation of the material and the formal sources of knowledge. Martin Heidegger correctly observes that "this duality of the sources is not a simple juxtaposition, for only in a union of these sources prescribed by their structure can finite knowledge be what its essence demands".[20] But since the experiential source of knowledge lies outside the *a priori* action of the subject, there is a certain independence of the two sources.[21] Here lies the dualism of the Kantian philosophy which inspired Hegel to look for a consistent answer in the gradual dialectics of consciousness and reality.[22]

It will be sufficient for present purposes to indicate that Hegel was opposed to the Kantian separation of the realm of noumena from that of phenomena,

---

[17] "Kant's whole industry goes to prove that it is the categories alone which give objectivity and permanence to things; ..." Andrew Seth, *The Development from Kant to Hegel* (London : Williams and Norgate, 1882), p. 8.

[18] Cf. *Kritik der reinen Vernunft*, I, 100-107.

[19] "As there can be no objective experience without perception, space and time as the necessary conditions of perception are also the necessary conditions of objective experience". S. Körner, *Kant* (Baltimore : Penguin Books, 1955), p. 58.

[20] *Kant and the Problem of Metaphysics*, trans. James S. Churchill (Bloomington : Indiana University Press, 1962), p. 40.

[21] Since the material-empirical element of knowledge *is given* from without, the subject has no control over it. Evidently, the phrase "from without" may be misleading, since both sources of knowledge "perhaps spring from a common, but to us unknown, root". One has to agree with M. Heidegger that Kant's argument "does not lead to the clear and unconditional evidence of an axiom or first principle but in full consciousness proceeds into and points toward the unknown". *Op. cit.*, pp. 41-42.

[22] According to J. Maier, "His [Hegel's] contention is that since it is preposterous to say anything at all about an object that can have no relation to our consciousness, in other words, to speak of a reality apart from a subject, the mind (rational subjectivity) must itself be proclaimed the ultimate, unconditioned reality, the only true and real being". *On Hegel's Critique of Kant* (New York : Columbia University Press, 1939), p. 37.

drawing attention to the fact such a dualism is identical with the "unreconciled contradiction".[23] However, he agrees with Kant in asserting that only phenomena can provide a sufficiently firm basis for a philosophical knowledge of reality. For Hegel the appearances of reality in thought are adequately qualified to disclose all that is to be known. The realm of noumena is not another existential order, but an empty abstraction.[24]

We have to turn our attention now to another important aspect of Kantian thought which has determined the subsequent philosophizing of German idealism.[25] Kant in his *Critique of Pure Reason* postulated a synthetic unity of apperception as the *a priori* condition of the 'I think' (*Ich denke*)[26] accompanying all representations and cognitive acts.[27] Only insofar as the subject can be conscious of himself as the co-ordinating principle in which the variety of objects (*Mannigfaltigen*) is constituted, is it also possible for these objects to be unified in a single conscious center. It would be a mistake, however, to assume that the transcendental unity of consciousness is the generative principle of the categories, for the Kantian theory excludes the possibility of reaching behind the categories to their source. Therefore, the self of the *Ich denke* has no content whatsoever beyond the categorizing functions immanent in cognitive acts.

It is not surprising that the Kantian unity of apperception was transformed into the absolute Ego by Fichte, for he was always ready to admit that his own system was nothing but "the Kantian doctrine properly understood".[28] The Fichtean philosophy has the same viewpoint as the Kantian :

---

[23] *Lectures on the History of Philosophy*, III, 476.

[24] "But Being-in-itself is only the *caput mortuum*, the dead abstraction of the 'other', the empty undetermined Beyond". *Ibid.*, III, 472.

[25] We are referring to the influence of the Kantian doctrine of apperception on Hegel's notion of Spirit. J. N. Findlay writes : "The direct roots of Hegel's doctrine of Spirit lie, however, much closer to him in time. They are to be found in Kant's doctrine of 'transcendental apperception' or 'transcendental self-consciousness' as set forth in the *Critique of Pure Reason*, and in Fichte's doctrine of the self-positing Ego set forth in his Jena lectures and his *Groundwork of the Complete Theory of Knowledge* (published in 1794)". *Op. cit.*, p. 46.

[26] This is the very summit of human knowledge : "Die ursprünglich-synthetische Einheit der Apperzeption war für Kant die letzte Bedingung der Möglichkeit von menschlicher Erkenntnis überhaupt, ..." Herbert Marcuse, *Hegels Ontologie und die Grundlegung einer Theorie der Geschichtlichkeit* (Frankfurt : Klostermann, 1932), p. 30.

[27] "Das : *Ich denke*, muss alle meine Vorstellungen begleiten können; ... Ich nenne auch die Einheit derselben die *transzendentale* Einheit des Selbstbewusstseins, um die Möglichkeit der Erkenntnis *a priori* aus ihr zu bezeichnen". *Kritik der reinen Vernunft*, I, 124.

[28] J. G. Fichte, *Sämtliche Werke* (Berlin : Veit und Comp., 1845), I, 89. According

the ultimate is always subjectivity, as existent in and for itself. One thing, however, is sure : Fichte advanced beyond Kantian duality of cognitive sources and established the subjective being as the fundamental condition of all knowledge. While Kant claimed that the basic elements of knowledge are grounded in a common, but to us unknown, root,[29] Fichte formulated the notion of an irreducible starting point : the self-conscious Subject as a reality constituted by the very act in which it posits its authentic existence. Thus Fichte introduces the absolute Subject, the real-in-itself, the in-itself of the cognitive performance. Obviously, such a Subject is not primarily the in-itself of substantial content but an explicitly self-existent activity of thought. Fichte's Subject, we might venture to say, shines by its own light and posits itself in the very act by which its existence is apprehended.[30] On the other hand, the absolute Ego posits a resistant sphere of alien realities only because it needs this sphere to express its own infinite nature. Fichte's self-consciousness as such is independent, but still in this independence it retains a negative relation to what is outside consciousness. Therefore, the Ego remains fixed in its opposition to the non-ego and their reconciliation is never realized. In other words, Fichte does not attain to the idea of the Absolute as the real unity of subject and object, because his theory of knowledge, to use Hegel's expression, "regards the struggle of the ego with the object as that of the continuous process of determining the object through the ego as subject of consciousness, without the identity of the restfully self-developing Notion".[31] It should be remarked, however, that Fichte, by the immanent logic of his own rationalism, has been forced to admit that the absolute Ego is itself the synthesis of thinking and reality, of subject and object. According to this view, the unity of subject and object is demanded by the very essence of the Ego.[32] But in reality Fichte's subject

---

to Hegel, Fichte's philosophy is "the Kantian philosophy in its completion, and, as we must specially notice, it is set forth in a more logical way". *Lectures on the History of Philosophy*, III, 479.

[29] "Nur so viel scheint zur Einleitung oder Vorerinnerung nötig zu sein, dass es zwei Stämme der menschlichen Erkenntnis gebe, die vielleicht aus einer *gemeinschaftlichen, aber uns unbekannten Wurzel entspringen, ...*" *Kritik der reinen Vernunft*, I, [56]. Italics mine.

[30] "The principle [Absolute Ego] lives in the very act by which its existence is apprehended; here knowledge and existence are one in the fullest and most literal sense, ..." Andrew Seth, *op. cit.*, p. 19.

[31] *Lectures on the History of Philosophy*, III, 501.

[32] Fichte writes : "Welches ist das Band zwischen dem Subjekte, Mir, und dem Objekte meines Wissens, dem Dinge? Diese Frage findet in Absicht *meiner* nicht statt. Ich habe das Wissen in mir selbst, denn ich bin Intelligenz. Was ich bin, davon *weiss* ich, weil

remains preoccupied only with itself. The subject is nothing else than an immanent process which ever makes itself its own object. Therefore, Fichte accepts a subjectivity whose object-positing operation is merely an expression of the endless self-actualization and self-mediation.

From this position to Schelling's, it is an easy step. Like Fichte, Schelling is convinced that the subject is the indubitable *principium* of transcendental philosophy.[33] Like Fichte, he also claims that the subject is essentially preoccupied with itself, for in transcendental knowledge the object as object vanishes, leaving in its place consciousness immanent in cognitional acts.[34] Therefore Schelling's main problem consists in showing how to start from the subjective and to make the objective arise from it. In other words, his idealism is an attempt to vindicate and constitute the objective reality from the immanent principle of subjectivity. But here is a point at which Schelling's position differs from Fichte's. According to Fichte, the subject is an absolute reality having the capacity to establish the entire non-subjective reality. Thus, the absolute is described only from the subject's viewpoint, while the object loses its ontological independence and autonomy. Schelling tried to correct this view claiming that the real absolute must be apprehended as identity of the subjective and objective. He distinguishes himself from Fichte in denying that the objective reality is merely a condition for the subject to reveal and realize itself. Hence there is no need to break through the non-subjective barrier as in Fichte; rather consciousness can immediately conclude to all further cognitive contents from the absolute identity of subject and object in a straightforward and purely deductive manner.

Schelling discovered and verified the unity of thought and objective reality by means of intellectual intuition. In so doing, he suppressed the opposition between subject and object and asserted their unity *beforehand*, without

---

ich es bin, und wovon ich unmittelbar dadurch weiss, dass ich überhaupt nur bin, das bin *ich*, weil ich unmittelbar davon weiss. Es bedarf hier keines Bandes zwischen Subject und Object; mein eignes Wesen ist dieses Band". *Die Bestimmung des Menschen* (Hamburg : F. Meiner, 1954), p. 61.

[33] Like Descartes, Schelling insists that philosophy begins with the universal doubt. Schelling's doubt, however, aims exclusively at the objective reality, thus merely stressing the indubitable character of the subject. Cf. *Sämtliche Werke* (Stuttgart und Augsburg : J. G. Cotta, 1856-61), III, 343.

[34] Schelling inaugurated the notion of the absolute knowledge, as opposed to phenomenal knowledge, and began by supposing an immediate philosophical standpoint. This view implies that knowledge becomes philosophical immediately and not as a result reached by dialectical, self-mediating process as in Hegel. *Ibid.*, IV, 326.

tracing back in a reductive thinking process the cognitional experiences of consciousness to their original ground. Quite obviously, once the identity of subject and object is proclaimed by intellectual intuition, the methodical reconciliation of them becomes an arbitrary and superfluous task. It is precisely this point which Hegel chooses to evaluate in his *Lectures on the History of Philosophy*, denying the adequacy of an intellectual intuition and demanding a rational mediation by means of concepts.[35]

It was Schelling's theory of identity which permitted Hegel to explore the possibility of reconciling thought and being and at the same time to visualize the terminus of the whole cognitional process. Speaking in an anticipatory vein, we can say that for Hegel the possibility of reconciling being and thought about being lies in the gradual suppression of opposition between subject and object, that is, in the dialectical interplay of subjective and objective elements in thought about reality. Hegel's *Phenomenology of Spirit*, which entails a reformulation of the notions of "subject" and "object", was written precisely to clarify this basic insight.

---

[35] "In philosophy, when we desire to establish a position, we demand proof. But if we begin with intellectual intuition, that constitutes an oracle to which we have to give way, since the existence of intellectual intuition was made our postulate. The true proof this identity of subjective and objective is the truth, could only be brought about by means of each of the two being investigated in its logical, i.e. essential determinations; and in regard to them, it must then be shown that the subjective signifies the transformation of itself into the objective, and that the objective signifies its not remaining such, but making itself subjective". *Lectures on the History of Philosophy*, III, 526.

What Hegel is seeking to show here is that the responsibility for establishing a philosophical claim cannot rest on intellectual intuition. From the Preface to the *Phenomenology* we can gather that the same responsibility cannot rest on proof either, for the dialectical process eliminates all demonstration (*Beweise*). In other words, once the dialectical process is put into action, the verification of propositions by proof or demonstration becomes pointless and useless. Cf. B., p. 123. *Phän.*, p. 53.

CHAPTER II

HEGEL'S PREFATORY NOTION OF SUBJECTIVITY

The methodical problems raised by Descartes, the phenomenalism of Kant and his things-in-themselves, the notion of subjectivity proposed by Fichte, and the objective identity of subject and object established by Schelling, all serve to facilitate an investigation of the Hegelian theory of subjectivity.[1] Having described the views which insist upon the primacy of the subject as source of truth, we may begin our analysis by placing ourselves in the overall climate of thought that dominates Hegel's Preface to the *Phenomenology*.

Hegel's commentators from David Strauss to Jean Hyppolite have praised the *Phenomenology* as the most difficult, original, brilliant, and important work. Probably the main reason the work has won such extraordinary praise is that it is the most unique treatise in the history of philosophy. The work is laborious and surpasses all other philosophical treatises in abstruseness and complexity. The text is preceded by an equally original and difficult Preface, which presents a comprehensive view of Hegel's position as a whole. Hermann Glockner correctly remarks that "whoever has understood the Preface to the *Phenomenology* has understood Hegel",[2] for it belongs to the kind of summary intended to be read as conclusion instead of as foreword.

Hegel begins his Preface by declaring that a preliminary statement, which is designed to explain the author's aim, the conclusions to be arrived at, and the reasons why he wrote the book, is essentially unphilosophical. Yet this declaration is immediately followed by an exposition of the notion of *Wissenschaft* which alone has the right to the name of philosophical

---

[1] Cf. Nicolai Hartmann, *Die Philosophie des deutschen Idealismus* (2nd ed.; Berlin : Walter de Gruyter, 1960), p. 297.

[2] "Wer die Vorrede zur Phänomenologie verstanden hat, hat Hegel verstanden". *Hegel* (Stuttgart : Frommann, 1940), II, 419.

science. It seems, therefore, that Hegel throws "consistency to the winds"
and "proceeds to write the very preface he condemns".[3] The careful reader,
however, will come to the conclusion that Hegel can make such an assertion
without betraying consistency. One must bear in mind that authentic
philosophy, in the sense of dialectically organized knowledge, is not the
aim of the Preface. According to Hegel, it is not possible to philosophize
if the thinking does not consist in dialectical analysis. Therefore, the results
that are offered in a Preface of this kind do not claim to be philosophically
valid. Toward the end of the Preface, Hegel remarks that the nature of the
scientific method receives its valid exposition only in philosophy proper.
Accordingly, what has been said in the Preface expresses the conception of
the method, but cannot count for more than an anticipatory assurance,
for its complete justification does not lie in the narrative exposition.[4]

A summary exposition of the nature and function of Systematic Science
presupposes that dialectical research and discovery have already been carried
out by the philosopher. The Preface, written after the *Phenomenology*
had been completed, is a condensed statement about philosophy already constituted. It is not, then, a question of conducting an investigation along
routes yet to be discovered; rather it is a question of gradual exposition
of a familiar doctrine.

A foreword of this kind has a *pedagogical* function. It serves to focus
the attention of the reader on the issues and doctrines awaiting formal justification, and to offer a program to guide his expectations. Therefore in the
Preface Hegel makes no effort to vindicate his propositions and principles :
he simply describes the heuristic notion of the Systematic Science and takes
for granted that the dialectical analysis of the ensuing work will strike
an answering chord. For knowledge has philosophical value only when it
acquires the form of a Systematic Science.

It is not surprising, then, that in the Preface the theory of subjectivity is
presented in a fragmentary and programmatic manner. Although the preliminary statements have no validity prior to their dialectical elaboration,
they epitomize Hegel's position and characterize the manner in which he
approaches the problem of subjectivity. In this sense, the sketchy pronounce-

---

[3] J. Loewenberg, *Hegel's Phenomenology* : *Dialogues on the Life of Mind* (La Salle :
The Open Court Publishing Co., 1965), p. 2.

[4] "Das hier Gesagte drückt zwar den Begriff aus, kann aber für nicht mehr als für
eine antizipierte Versicherung gelten. Ihre Wahrheit liegt nicht in dieser zum Teil erzählen-
den Exposition ...". *Phän.*, p. 47. J. B. Baillie's translation of this passage is simply incorrect, for the term "historical" does not occur in the original text. Hegel uses the term
"narrative" instead. See Baillie's translation, p. 116.

ments may be regarded as constituting a sort of narrative introduction to Hegel's theory of subjectivity.

The most important epitome pertaining to Hegel's theory of subjectivity is the famous proposition that what is true must be conceived and expressed not only in terms of substance but in terms of subject as well. Hegel writes :

In my view — a view which the developed exposition of the system itself can alone justify — everything depends on grasping and expressing the ultimate truth not as Substance but as Subject as well.[5]

With this statement Hegel exalts the subject and declares that the notion of subjectivity is the key to his philosophy. Though one must admit that Hegel has not really elucidated the meaning of subjectivity by distinguishing it from substantiality, he clearly indicates that truth must always appear in the form of rational assertions the source of which is the knowing subject. It must be shown to be of the nature of reality to express itself, not only in terms of self-necessitating substance, but also in rational forms corresponding to the claims of the conscious subject. Since consciousness is essential to subjectivity, we can think of consciousness as positing an order of its own, and by its own operation wholly or in part determining the constitutive elements of that order.[6]

The use of the terms "subject" and "substance" by Hegel is quite remote from ordinary uses : they allude, respectively, to Fichte and Spinoza. By substance Spinoza means "that which is in itself, and is conceived through itself; in other words, that of which a conception can be formed independently of any other conception".[7] It was Spinoza who first formulated the notion of the substance as a being constituted by its own necessity. Since such a substance is by nature prior to its modifications and attributes, it is also prior to thought.[8] Thus, if there is an infinite being, it must be the self-necessitating being which in no way depends on thought or consciousness. It can be said, not without justification, that for Spinoza the ultimate truth belongs to the nature of substance, whereas for Hegel it is only through the medium of subjectivity that substance can be at all. To speak of substance is to speak of the activity whereby a subject is conscious of it. This does not necessarily mean that substance has no real existence except

---

[5] B., p. 80. *Phän.*, p. 19.

[6] Cf. G. R. G. Mure, *The Philosophy of Hegel* (London : Oxford University Press, 1965), p. 5.

[7] *Philosophy of Benedict de Spinoza*, trans. R. H. M. Elwes (New York : Tudor Publishing Co., n.d.), p. 39.

[8] *Ibid.*, p. 40.

such as it has in relation to the conscious subject. Hegel insists that the activity of the subject upon substance is not the imposition of arbitrary determinations or subjective categories on it, but the bringing out of what it implicitly is. Nor is this activity without any consequences for the subject itself. Like Fichte, Hegel believes that the subject is essentially the result of its own performance : its activity is transcending immediacy, negating it, and returning into itself.

Hegel emphasizes repeatedly that his subjectivity is nothing arbitrary and one-sided, but both active and conscious. By the subject he means that which makes itself what it becomes, what it is implicitly.[9] Yet the subject is active only insofar as it is the movement of positing itself, or the mediation between a self and its development into something different. Therefore, to speak of subjectivity is to speak of the self-mediating activity, which is constituted in accordance with its own principles.

To understand the role of mediation we must first try to grasp what Hegel conceived mediation to be. In order to accomplish this task we must begin by concentrating our attention on the following passage :

The living substance, further, is that being which is truly subject, or, what is the same thing, is truly realized and actual (*wirklich*) solely in the process of positing itself, or in mediating with its own self its transitions from one state or position to the opposite.[10]

According to Hegel, the subject should be envisaged as a living reality, which must realize itself through the affirmation of itself in a long process of distinct rational patterns.[11] That subjectivity must appear in the process of positing itself and that consciousness advances by dialectical necessity from position to counter-position are two propositions identical in meaning and significance. If this is so, then the subject should not be looked upon as something possessing an empirical content from which certain activities emerge. Hegel could not conceive of the subject existing in the form of an empirical being, nor could he conceive of it as being mere rational function of a substantial ego. For Hegel the subject had to be a conscious reality, and it had to have an object by contrast with which it could be aware of what it itself is. Hegel insists that it is essential to the subject that it not be conceived in isolation. As conscious, the subject is inseparable from its objects, for it

---

[9] Walter Kaufmann, *Hegel : Reinterpretation, Texts, and Commentary* (New York : Doubleday, 1965), p. 391.

[10] B., p. 80. *Phän.*, p. 20.

[11] This clearly alludes to Fichte whose theory of subjectivity insists upon the primacy of the mind.

constitutes itself only by being related to them. This means that the subject has the capacity of grasping itself in the other whose intrinsic purposiveness is subjectivity. Only within a notion thus understood can we describe the subject as a mediating process between becoming-other-than-self and self (*die Vermittlung des Sichanderswerdens mit sich selbst*). Mediation, Hegel claims, "is nothing but self-identity working itself out through an active self-directed process".[12] Therefore the constitution of subjectivity requires a system of positions and counter-positions related to each other by the mediating performance, for only as mutually related can they determine the sequential process of consciousness and the continuous development of the subject.

The meaning of mediation can obviously not be compressed within the framework of a single definition. To say that the notion of mediation refers to that process by which the self-restoring identity of the subject is reinstated is not to say all.[13] It is necessary to add that mediation is an operation wherein the subject, by exhibiting a synthesis of antagonistic positions grown mutually implicative, consciously realizes itself. In short, the self-realization of subjectivity depends on mediating performance. The subject, however, does not receive this mediation from outside itself but is itself this very mediation.[14] It is precisely for this reason that the subject is not only the source of the mediating process, but is indistinguishable from that process itself.

Hegel's notion of mediation makes it imperative that the subject be not static but dynamic, not passive but active, not immediate but mediating itself through a self-ordered series of partial and incompatible claims. The phenomenological analysis consists precisely in showing that these incomplete and antagonistic positions involve and depend on each other, that they are not cut off from one another, but indissolubly linked together. For Hegel that which is completely unmediated and undifferentiated has no meaning.[15] But the act of moving to and fro between subject and object

---

[12] B., p. 82. *Phän.*, p. 21.

[13] We are referring to Henri Niel's general definition of mediation : "Le résultat de l'idée de médiation est de montrer que le contenu de l'idée du sujet est constitué finalement par l'ensemble de ses relations à la totalité du cosmos". *De la médiation dans la philosophie de Hegel* (Paris : Aubier, 1945), p. 71. This relatedness of the subject to the totality of the real is always constituted by thought that mediates. Therefore, to speak of the mediating process is to speak of the subject as self-relating entity.

[14] "For mediating is nothing but self-identity working itself out through an active self-directed process; or, in other words, it is reflection into self, the aspect in which the ego is for itself, objective to itself". B., p. 82. *Phän.*, p. 21.

[15] Cf. W. T. Stace, *The Philosophy of Hegel* (New York : Dower, 1955), p. 344.

entails conscious differentiation, and conscious differentiation involves mediation.[16] Conceptual mediation is a movement which always goes beyond the stage already reached, and this process does not end until it is brought to the repose of absolute knowledge. It is the aim of the *Phenomenology* to exhibit the succession of rational attitudes in their proper order and development. And these, as consciously mediated, constitute Hegel's notion of subjectivity. Thus, with the theory of subjectivity Hegel had hit on the possibility of mediated apprehension of reality. However, what he has attempted with the mediating performance of the subject is not so much to establish a new theory of cognition as to reconcile being and variegated thoughts about being.

Despite its general and narrative character, the Preface contains another important hint as to the nature of subjectivity. For it is here that we first learn that negativity must be conceived as a distinct property of subjectivity. Of this attribute the essential outcome is dialectical movement, signifying both the reconstitution of the subject and the process whereby reality is reduced to unity.

In considering the nature of mediation, Hegel has come to realize that the subject as mediator is inconceivable without negativity. Being fundamentally the "process of its own becoming", the subject must possess an unconditional negativity for the achievement of real truth. But truth, says Hegel, is nothing but the self-restoring identity of the subject, the reflection-into-self-in-other-being : it is not an original unity as such and not the immediate as such.[17] Having once and for all rejected any possibility of immediate apprehension of truth, the only coherent thing to do was to rely on rational self-mediation. And this is possible only through the negative performance of the subject. Thus, the subject is what it accomplishes through its own negativity.

We can approach the problem of negativity under the propositions Hegel himself introduced, one proposition being that the distinction between subject and object is due to the negativity of consciousness.[18] This means

---

[16] "Als Substanz bezeichnet Hegel die Einheit, das Sein, den Inhalt, das Unmittelbare (unmittelbar ist das, was nicht durch die Vernunft vermittelt ist, d.h. was den 'vermittelnden' Weg der Vernunft nicht durchwandert hat)". Joseph Möller, *Der Geist und das Absolute* (Padernborn : F. Schöningh, 1951), p. 23.

[17] B., p. 80. *Phän.*, p. 20. The immediate is that which remains unrelated to thought. It is the massive, opaque, and substantial being, since it does not return to itself as thought does.

[18] "The dissimilarity which obtains in consciousness between the ego and the substance constituting its object, is their inner distinction, the factor of negativity in general". B., p. 96. *Phän.*, p. 32.

that the negative perfection of consciousness enables the subject to differentiate itself from the unconscious mode of existence and to consider the latter as an object. For Hegel as for Fichte, consciousness is that pure negativity, which splits up what is simple and opposes elements to one another, but which at the same time also negates this diversity and opposition.[19] This view implies that consciousness is not a determinate object or some distinct category, but a creative activity, capable of transcending every particular thing, concept, and viewpoint.[20] Being endowed with negativity, consciousness is compelled to go beyond itself and to transcend every determinate content.

Hegel gives evidence of having conceived consciousness as a source of the dialectical operation. He may be interpreted as saying that everything is immanent in consciousness, and it is precisely the formative and creative negativity of consciousness which enables it to engender the content of totality.[21] However, to say that pure negativity or self-transcendence constitutes the very nature of consciousness is simply to say that this same perfection — for perfection it is — exemplifies the essential property of the subject. That negativity is the bifurcation of the simple that denies this introduced diversity and that truth is the sameness (*Gleichheit*) which reconstitutes itself are two propositions epitomizing the Hegelian theory of subjectivity.

The notions of self-mediation and negativity are serviceable as offering general information about subjectivity. All this, however, is not enough for the elaboration of the theory of subjectivity Hegel had in mind; the subject thus understood is but an indeterminate and reconciliatory mediator. If we regard subject as having an active part in the "mediation of an immediacy", whose result is "mediated immediacy", we must ask this question : What does Hegel consider to be the major agency inherent in reconciliation of immediacy and mediation? Put more explicitly the question is this : Is the opposition of subject and object reducible to unity by some distinct operation of the subject? Fortunately, the Preface contains a hint as to the answer in its insistence that "philosophy has its being essentially in

---

[19] B., p. 80. *Phän.*, p. 20.

[20] B., p. 111. *Phän.*, p. 44.

[21] "Il faut à notre avis, pour comprendre ici le texte hégélien, admettre que le Tout est toujours immanent au développement de la conscience. La négation est créatrice parce que le terme posé avait été isolé, qu'il était lui-même une certaine négation. Dès lors on conçoit que sa négation permette de retrouver dans son détail ce Tout". Jean Hyppolite, *Genèse et structure de la Phénoménologie de l'Esprit de Hegel* (Paris : Aubier, 1946), I, 20.

the element of that universality which encloses the particular within it".[22]
This statement serves us to identify universality as a sort of medium in which
thought is reflected, but exactly what is meant by saying that the possibility
of philosophy presupposes the "element of universality" remains far
from clear. When, however, at the end of the Preface, Hegel speaks of universality as the "property of every self-conscious reason",[23] we begin to
grasp the significance of the newly introduced term.

We shall not, in the present chapter, attempt a complete explanation
of Hegel's concept of universality : this would be possible only when we
had followed the development of the concept throughout the *Phenomenology*.
There is, however, one major point that needs to be discussed at present.
What here does call for clarification is Hegel's drastic identification of subject
and universality.

According to Hegel, valid thoughts and insights "can only be won by
the labour of the notion", which means that the concept (*Begriff*) "alone
can produce universality in the knowing process".[24] What is really implied
in all this is that the concept is not a special category set over against other
categories, but a conscious process that determines its own content. Hegel
may be interpreted as saying that the "labour of the notion" is nothing else
than consciousness developing itself into pure self-consciousness or the I.[25]
For Hegel the movement of the notion exemplifies the universalizing function of consciousness, "determining itself to a particular, from which it

---

[22] B., p. [67]. *Phän.*, p. [9].

[23] B., p. 128. *Phän.*, p. 57.

[24] *Ibid.*

[25] Our interpretation of this point is somewhat similar to that of James H. Stirling :
"But the position of idealism is once for all held by Hegel, and the (universal) subject
accordingly is, in his eyes, self-determined; so that the absolute universal of the subject's
innermost or most characteristic movement, is the universal (himself), determining himself
to the particular (his state as object), and returning to himself from the same singular (the
notion, the knowledge gained, the reunion of the particular — the other, the negative of
the universal — with itself or with this universal). This is the nerve of self-consciousness;
and self-consciousness is the absolute — the dimensionless point that, though point and
dimensionless, is the Universe". *The Secret of Hegel* (London : Simpkin, Marshall and
Co., 1898), p. 160.
Evidently, little is explained by saying that consciousness is a dimensionless point.
One can argue that in the *Phenomenology* consciousness has a distinctly temporal dimension, for in this work Hegel wanted to show how consciousness develops in time. In any
case, what must be stressed is the activity of consciousness and its spiritual life, which
consists in the progressive explicitation of reality and in the gradual concretization of
thought.

returns again to itself".[26] The universalizing performance of consciousness consists in establishing the relation of subject to object, of concept to datum. In other words, the process in which an object yields up a universal meaning has its source in consciousness, for consciousness is an activity which disengages universality from particularity. Hegel makes plain that consciousness constitutes itself through the universal, that is, through its own universalizing performance. Thus, as J. N. Findlay says, "the Subject, which *is* conscious, seems to mean no more for Hegel than this same universalizing or unifying activity, described by a somewhat misleading substantival locution".[27]

Hegel's notion of universality is crucial, drawing attention to an intimate relationship between subjectivity and objectivity. Thus, the subject, as the universalizing agency, appropriates objects by bringing them into the category of universality which is the subject's own. Hegel, however, does not say that in the explicitation of the object its meaning is surrendered to the arbitrary decision of the subject. On the contrary, he claims that the subject relating itself in conscious manner to things, will reveal them as they really are. This sort of process we can qualify as "universalizing", not in the sense of abstraction that concerns itself with generic properties,[28] but in the sense of bringing objects into their proper form by the subject whose function is "to think universally of things, to range them under common characters in which their specific differences and crude individual immediacy will be submerged".[29] Since the unifying and universalizing action constitutes the relation of subject to objects, we can conclude that it is precisely this same act that guarantees the objective validity of knowledge. Foreshadowed here is the basic principle of Hegel's philosophy of subjectivity. For the subject is the agent that imparts universality into whatever it encounters, and thereby enables the object to be in and for itself. Hegel is fully convinced that the subject, as the conscious agent, unveils the object and lets this object be what it itself is. Thus, with the universalization as conscious operation, subjectivity emerges as the constitutive principle of all that lays claim to objective reality. For Hegel this kind of objectivity is more objective and more authentic than the so-called ontological objectivity spoken of by naive realism.

No matter how thoroughly investigated, the notion of subjectivity

---

[26] James H. Stirling, *op. cit.*, p. 160.

[27] J. N. Findlay, *op. cit.*, p. 38.

[28] "Das 'Allgemeine' darf bei Hegel nicht in dem Sinn des abstrakten Allgemeinen gefasst werden. Das Allgemeine ist das, was sich das Wissen selbst ist, ..." Joseph Möller, *op. cit.*, p. 23. footnote 52.

[29] J. N. Findlay, *op. cit.*, p. 227.

presented in the Preface remains a heuristic notion, which raises many questions but answers only very few. This fact is brought out by C. Nink in his outstanding commentary on Hegel's phenomenological thought. And so Nink will not recommend to the student of Hegel an analysis of the Preface or Introduction, but rather a gradual analysis of the text.[30]

However, in accordance with Hegel's original plan, the main issue of Introduction should not be regarded as irrelevant. There is, first of all, the question as to what exactly knowledge is. Thus, if attention is paid to the meaning of the subject, understood as conscious reality, one realizes that it does not occur except in fusion with consciousness of reality. For Hegel there can be no question of making knowledge the agreement of the consciousness with isolated reality. Such a knowing can never be affirmed, since this would mean the agreement of the object-as-known-to-the subject with the object-as-not-known-to-the subject. To maintain such an agreement is not possible, for it presupposes a comparison which cannot be established. Since we cannot know reality independently of consciousness, the question arises as to the nature of consciousness. It is for this reason that we have to devote a separate chapter to the examination of consciousness, for we can know being only by investigating its being-known.

---

[30] "Hegels *Vorrede* zur Phänomenologie und manche Gedanken seiner *Einleitung* sind so eng mit seiner ganzen Lehre verknüpft, dass ein Verständnis von ihnen sich erst dann erreichen lässt, wenn man das Hegelsche System in seinen Grundlinien kennt. Aus diesem Grunde wird eine Inhaltsangabe von ihnen nicht gegeben; es würde, bevor die Methode und Hauptrichtung des Gedankenganges der Phänomenologie bekannt sind, doch vieles rätselhaft bleiben. Später, wenn man die Grundgedanken der Phänomenologie beherrscht, wird man Vorrede und Einleitung ohne Mühe lesen, so dass dann ein Kommentar sich erübrigt". C. Nink, *Kommentar zu den grundlegenden Abschnitten von Hegels Phänomenologie des Geistes* (Regensburg : J. Habbel, 1931), p. 7.

CHAPTER III

CONSCIOUSNESS AND REALITY

Hegel's *Phenomenology of Spirit* can be described as the science of experience,[1] where the term "experience" signifies the dialectical process which perfects consciousness in itself, that is, both in its knowledge and in its object.[2] Now, since experience is essentially a subject-object relation, its meaning could be discovered in the determination of the real significance of that relation.[3] Therefore we may say that the main objective of the *Pheno-*

---

[1] The phrase "Wissenschaft der Erfahrung des Bewusstseins" [Science of the Experience of Consciousness] appeared on the title page of the First Part of the original edition. Cf. *Phänomenologie des Geistes* (6th ed.; Hamburg : F. Meiner, 1952), p. [61]. See also Baillie's translation, pp. 42, 144.

From the explanatory note, "Zur Feststellung des Textes", attached to the F. Meiner's edition, we gather that there exists a puzzling situation concerning the diversity of titles of the *Phenomenology* : *op. cit.*, p. 577.

In his long and profound essay on Hegel's conception of experience in *Holzwege*, Martin Heidegger assumes that the originally selected title was omitted during the publication of the *Phenomenology*. See "Hegels Begriff der Erfahrung", *Holzwege* (Frankfurt : Vittorio Klostermann, 1950), p. 183. Heidegger, approving Hegel's "first sailing", as he has approved the first edition of Kant's *Critique of Pure Reason*, seems to regret that Hegel gave up the original heading and thus has failed to include in the new title such important terms as "consciousness" and "experience". But, then, no less important is the term "dialectics", and yet it never appeared even in the subtitle. We can only surmise that Hegel was not very anxious to announce his fundamental concepts on the title page.

[2] "This dialectical process which consciousness executes on itself — on its knowledge as well as on its object — in the sense that out of it the new and true object arises, is precisely what is termed Experience", B., p. 142. *Phän.*, p. 73.

[3] Gottfried Stiehler writes : "Erfahrung besteht für Hegel in einem ständig tieferen Eindringen in die Objektwelt vermittels der fortlaufenden Überwindung der entstehenden Widersprüche zwischen Wissen und Gegenstand". *Die Dialektik in Hegels Phänomenologie des Geistes* (Berlin : Akademie, 1964), p. 62.

For Martin Heidegger, however, experience is primarily a *dialogue* between the natural consciousness and the absolute knowledge : *op. cit.*, p. 186. Heidegger's conception of natural consciousness does not create any problems and ambiguities. The situation,

menology consists in the progressive exposition of the significance of subject-object duality within experience.[4]

If we continue to consider Hegel's notion of experience, we will see that it
involves much more than the distinction between subject and object. J. B.
Baillie correctly remarks that "Hegel takes experience to mean the inseparable and continuous interrelation of subject and object".[5] What we wish
to stress at this point is the importance of the term "continuous", because
Hegel's *Phenomenology* exhibits continual shifts of position with respect
to the subject and object of knowledge. Every cognitive situation or experience involves a meaningful relation between some given object and the
concept formed of it. However, "about the real nature of the relation and
of the terms in that relation no true statement is initially possible",[6] for
experience involves a process of dialectical transition in which subject
and object become progressively modified. In Hegel's own words, stated
in the *Lectures on the History of Philosophy*, the dialectical process has to
show that "the subjective signifies the transformation of itself into the objective, and the objective signifies its not remaining such, but making itself
subjective".[7] What is contained in this statement, is that knowledge entails
a process of rational growth, in which subject and object become radically
altered in accordance with the dialectical method. Thus, the object presents
itself to consciousness as a vanishing element. The cancelling of the object,
however, has a positive significance for consciousness, for in apprehending
this fact consciousness establishes itself as object, or sets up the object as
its self. It seems clear enough that Hegel's notion of consciousness is a new

---

however, is different with regard to the absolute knowledge, which is defined as the
'organizing' exposition of the appearing and of the historically objective spirit. Evidently,
without *die Darstellung* and *die Organisation* the absolute knowledge cannot and could
not be constituted, but the constitutive function of these activities is not the same thing as
the absolute knowledge itself. Though the organizing performance springs from the active
subject and though the subject's negative, mediating, and universalizing capacities are
truly unconditional powers, the knowledge possessed and enjoyed by the subject *is never
absolute* at any stage of the phenomenological process. In Hegel's eyes, the last stage of
the process is categorically indispensable for the constitution of the absolute knowledge.
Phän., p. 556. B., p. 797.

[4] "Grundsatz der Phänomenologie ist von Anfang bis Ende die Vermittlung des
Denkens mit dem Sein, des Ichs mit dem Nicht-Ich". Ernst Bloch, *Subjekt-Objekt* (Berlin :
Aufbau, 1951), p. 54.

[5] *Op. cit.*, p. 43. See also J. B. Baillie, *The Origin and Significance of Hegel's Logic*
(London : Macmillan, 1901), chap. VI.

[6] J. Loewenberg, *op. cit.*, p. 14.

[7] *Lectures on the History of Philosophy*, III, 526.

and very intricate one. Detailed and careful analysis is needed if one is to grasp properly the precise meaning of the cognitive process and appreciate its originality. Not only does Hegel give the word "consciousness" a distinct meaning, but he makes a further distinction between consciousness, self-consciousness, reason, and spirit. These four terms, which in traditional philosophy are roughly synonymous, are not at all synonymous for Hegel.

Despite all the intricacy involved in describing subjectivity from the viewpoint of consciousness, self-consciousness, reason, and spirit, one thing stands out clearly : no one can understand Hegel's philosophy of subjectivity who has not first seen it traversing a series of phenomenological forms. In other words, the full meaning of subjectivity can be grasped only in the course of gradual analysis.[8]

From the standpoint of knowledge, the *Phenomenology of Spirit* can be considered as the whole of the Hegelian system, for it discloses all important changes that take place between subject and object as the cognitive experience is traced through the various stages of consciousness.[9] Since "in the alteration of the knowledge, the object itself, in point of fact, is altered",[10] the *Phenomenology* is not only a theory of knowledge but also a theory of object.[11] In other words, being concerned with the essential correlatives of consciousness, Hegel's *Phenomenology* entails epistemology as well as ontology.[12] The point of interest in the work is the transition "from one rela-

---

[8] Hegel makes no effort to demonstrate his assertions and conclusions, since he assumes that the dialectical exposition itself shall validate them in the process. We have alluded to this fact before, but the emphasis will not be misplaced by reiterating Hegel's position. According to him, when dialectic "has been separated from proof, the idea of philosophical demonstration as a matter of fact has vanished altogether". B., p. 123. *Phän.*, p. 53.

[9] "The experience which consciousness has concerning itself can, by its essential principle, embrace nothing less than the entire system of consciousness, the whole realm of the truth of mind, ..." B., p. 144. *Phän.*, p. 75. R. Haym, however, ignoring the distinction between phenomenology and methaphysics, that is, between phenomenal knowledge and notional knowledge, claims that Hegel's *Phenomenology* is really his whole system. Cf. *Hegel und seine Zeit* (Berlin : R. Gaertner, 1875), p. 255.

[10] B., p. 142. *Phän.*, p. 72.

[11] "Hegel weitet den Begriff der Erkenntnistheorie zu dem einer *Theorie des absoluten Erkennens*; indem das Erkennen sich selbst prüft, prüft es zugleich seinen Gegenstand; die Erkenntnistheorie ist zugleich Gegenstandstheorie". R. Kroner, *Von Kant bis Hegel* (2nd ed.; Tübingen : J. C. B. Mohr, 1961), II, 365. See also B. Croce, *What is living and what is dead of the Philosophy of Hegel*, trans. D. Ainslie (London : Macmillan, 1915), p. 117.

[12] "La Phénoménologie de Hegel est donc 'existentielle' comme celle de Heidegger. Et elle doit servir de base à une ontologie". Alexandre Kojève, *Introduction à la lecture de Hegel* (6th ed.; Paris : Gallimard, 1947), p. 29.

tion of consciousness to the entire world of being, to another such relation",[13] provided that "with change in the knowledge, the object also becomes different",[14] since such alteration renders experience dialectical. The subject, as the conscious term of the cognitive relation and insofar as it has risen to the level of consciousness, distinguishes itself from the substantial and unconscious mode of existence and looks on the latter as an external object. For the observing consciousness, the different forms of its self-recognition appear as a gradual change in the object itself. However, the growing self-recognition of the subject is merely the discovery in the object of those properties which characterize consciousness itself. According to Hegel, this development in consciousness will reach a terminal stage when the subject recognizes its own unfolding and raises its primary certainty to absolute truth. All this, however, is merely an anticipation.

Hegel accepts the initial cognitive experience as it is accepted by common-sense, that is, as it flourishes spontaneously, and then develops its implications. He remains within the realm of phenomenal knowledge, observing, examining, and testing such knowledge by its own criteria. Unlike Fichte and Schelling, who believed in the immediate emergence of the philosophical viewpoint and self-consciousness, Hegel starts from naive and prereflective consciousness, supposing that knowledge becomes philosophic only when it appears as result reached by a dialectical process.[15] As soon as it is recognized that Hegel assumes nothing except what the phenomenal knowledge itself produces, it becomes evident that the subject matter of the *Phenomenology* is knowledge such as it appears to consciousness. According to Hegel, this phenomenal and seemingly obvious knowledge transforms itself into absolute knowledge, for the latter is but another name for apparent knowledge purged of relativity and transfigured into a purely scientific cognition. Passing dialectically from sense-certainty, sense-perception, and understanding, through self-consciousness, reason, spirit, and religion, Hegel arrives at what seems to him to be the ultimate cognitive attitude. This final attitude of consciousness, which Hegel calls absolute knowledge (*das absolute Wissen*), is not only his expression of the scientific nature of knowledge, but also his final view of the significance of the subject-object relationship. Absolute knowledge represents the conclusion of a dialectical process of which the analysis of sense-certainty constitutes the beginning.[16]

---

[13] G. W. Cunningham, *Thought and Reality in Hegel's System* (New York : Longmans, Green, and Co., 1910), p. 3.

[14] B., p. 142. *Phän.*, p. 72.

[15] Cf. Gottfried Stiehler, *op. cit.*, p. 7.

[16] "Absolute knowledge, as Hegel manipulates the expression, is alleged to be the

This ultimate form of cognition expresses the most adequate relation of thought and being, finding in the identity of subject and object the very essence of that relation. The career of knowledge thus culminates in the absolute knowledge where the original certainty of consciousness (subjectivity) is posited as truth and the truth (objectivity) is affirmed as self-consciousness.

Hegel's treatment of the absolute knowledge will become clearer to us only after we become familiar with his doctrine of consciousness presented in the Introduction to the *Phenomenology*. In this Introduction, designed to reformulate the problem of knowledge without prior assumptions about its nature and structure, Hegel describes the phenomenal consciousness, preparing the ground for its detailed analysis. According to Hegel, the fundamental act of consciousness consists in distinguishing an object, to which it constantly relates itself. The actual performance "of this process of relating, or of there being something for a consciousness, is knowledge".[17] When Hegel insists that consciousness recognizes the presence of an object, he simply means that there is something *for* consciousness (*etwas für ein Bewusstsein*). In consciousness thus we discover a distinct element which deserves to be called knowledge of something. To be conscious is to be-with-objects. But through this being-with-objects in consciousness both the subject and the object begin to become themselves. Consciousness is sensitive to objects, but it unveils them only through the subjective performance. Perceiving consciousness and perceived object constitute a dialectical unity. Therefore the objectivity about which Hegel speaks is not objectivity-without-subjectivity.

If phenomenal consciousness is said never to be consciousness of consciousness itself but of the object, it is no longer possible to ask the question whether or not perceiving consciousness grasps reality. Still, the reality which the subject immediately perceives is never being-in-itself, but being for consciousness, or being for another (*Sein für ein anderes*). Just because consciousness has knowledge of an object, it can ask what that object is in itself, and this it thinks of as an independent being. The act of cognition is knowledge of this or that object, which is "to consciousness not merely *for it*, but also outside this relation, or has a being in itself".[18] Therefore, from the object for consciousness Hegel distinguishes being in itself (*Ansich*)

---

outcome of phenomenology, thus undeniably coming within its definable range. It serves, as it were, as a sort of finale or coda". J. Loewenberg, *op. cit.*, p. 355.

[17] B., p. 139. *Phän.*, p. 70.
[18] B., p. 140. *Phän.*, p. 71.

or the independent reality, existing, as it were, outside cognitive relation. For Hegel, this "aspect of being *per se* or in itself is called Truth".[19] One might think, not without justification, that this conception of truth expresses Hegel's intention to seek anchorage in the traditional position that regards truth as a property of being. One might even go as far as to assert that it constitutes the realistic principle of his philosophy. However, the statement merely expresses the actual cognitive situation : consciousness knows something with an unmistakable certitude and yet lays claim to a truth which is independent of this certitude. It takes but little effort to realize that the distinction of which Hegel speaks has been inaugurated by consciousness itself. To say that consciousness lays claim to a truth which lies outside its own certitude is to say that the basic performance of consciousness consists in distinguishing the element of truth (being *per se*) from the element of knowledge (being for another). This distinction is as essential and natural to consciousness as are the efforts to remove it. Just as consciousness finds that there is an opposition between the object as it is for consciousness and the object as it is in itself, so too it cannot rest content with an opposition so radical and unreconciled, but must go on to reduce it to unity. Hegel is here forecasting his basic insight that there is an intimate relation between reality and the conscious procedures which constitute such a reality. This clearly implies that the reality about which Hegel speaks does not have the objectivistic meaning which naive realism and empiricism want to assign to the term. This point, however, calls for clarification.

Since Hegel's *Phenomenology* starts from cognition as natural phenomenon, the distinction between "being for another" and "being in itself" falls within the same knowledge which is under investigation. This means, however, that "consciousness furnishes its own criterion", comparing "itself with its own self".[20] Thus, by declaring that being in itself should be called Truth, consciousness sets up a criterion by which it measures its own knowledge. Now, if cognition deserves to be called notion or conception and the Truth an object, then the investigation will consist in determining whether the notion corresponds with the object. But we find a considerable significance in the fact that Hegel regards this process as reversible. According to him, the Truth can be called concept or notion and the knowledge may be termed object. Now, if this be the case, the phenomenological investigation will consist "in our seeing whether the object corresponds to its own notion".[21] If we wish to understand Hegel correctly,

[19] B., p. 139. *Phän.*, p. 70.
[20] B., p. 140. *Phän.*, p. 71.
[21] B., p. 141. *Phän.*, p. 72.

we have to remember the fact that "object for consciousness" and "object in itself" are within and for the same consciousness. We can say that consciousness is on the one hand consciousness of the object, on the other hand consciousness of itself, that is, consciousness of that which is for it the True, and consciousness of its own knowledge of this.[22] This definition should not give rise to any ambiguity. The truth regarding objects results from the encounter with the objects in consciousness. That is, through consciousness subject and object enter into a dialectical dialogue, and in this dialogue truth reveals itself both in the form of the notion and in the form of the object. Thus, notionally considered, the essence of truth lies in the conscious unveiling of the meaning of the object and, objectively considered, the essence of truth lies in the revelation of the unveiled object itself. This means that the truth explicitated is always a truth of consciousness. Obviously, such a view removes the very basis of the controversy between extreme idealism and naive realism. For it is not possible to ask whether something which in consciousness has a certain meaning possesses this same meaning also outside consciousness. Hegel insists that consciousness is neither "the instrument by which to take possession of the Absolute" nor "a kind of passive medium through which the light of the truth reaches us".[23] Conscious argument is the arbiter on every issue, for it expresses a complete coincidence of the rational and the real. However, the difficulty here is that, since consciousness has not effectively conquered its essential immanence, the subject cannot lay claim to a truth existing independently of the actual cognitive act which discloses it.

Hegel is anxious to emphasize that consciousness presents itself as implying a relation to an object, and the knowledge of the object constitutes its self-recognition. This is but another way of saying that every object will be discovered on dialectical analysis to have contributed to the self-realization of the subject. Here lies the main reason why the distinction what a thing is for consciousness and what it is in itself must be preserved throughout the *Phenomenology*. Although the object is *really* apprehended, consciousness seems to be unable to know it as it *is*, not for consciousness, but in itself. Thus, what the thing is in itself is one thing for consciousness, while the existence of the object for consciousness is another thing. Consciousness has knowledge only to the extent it recognizes and posits an element of Truth. However, this knowledge of the True is not immutable

---

[22] "For consciousness is, on the one hand, consciousness of the object, on the other, consciousness of itself; consciousness of what to it is true, and consciousness of its knowledge of that truth". *Ibid.*

[23] B., p. [131]. *Phän.*, p. [63].

but entails modification, once an inadequacy is discovered between conception and object.[24] In other words, the phenomenological investigation turns upon the distinction between conception and object. When they do not correspond, consciousness is forced to alter its knowledge in order to make it fit the object. But in the alteration of the knowledge, the object itself is altered, for the knowledge which existed in consciousness "was essentially a knowledge of the object".[25]

In investigating consciousness Hegel always begins with a consciousness which already manifests a certain comparison of consciousness with itself. It is precisely this same comparison which leads consciousness to the realization that "what was *per se* was only *per se for consciousness*".[26]

So it happens that Hegel's problem is to lay the foundations of knowledge in consciousness. He moves in the line of Kant and Fichte, with this difference, that he regards the acts of the subject as dialectical. Although consciousness depends for its possibility on the inseparable correlatives of subject and object, the subject retains a real priority over the object and emerges as the principal determinative of all that lays claim to objectivity. In Hegel's philosophy, as we have pointed out before, everything depends on grasping and expressing that which is objectively true not only in terms of substantial being but in those of subject as well. In saying that truth has its roots in the consciousness of the self Hegel is simply expressing in succinct fashion the fundamental feature of his notion of subjectivity. This is the crucial point, Hegel's phenomenological analysis having no other purpose than to bring this idea into clear focus.

What we have said above may not bring about any insight into Hegel's theory of subjectivity, for we have derived our initial and general views from his prefatory and introductory remarks. In accordance with Hegel's original plan, it has seemed necessary to make these few descriptive remarks before entering into the text, which sets forth a line of argument to be followed by the individual consciousness in rising from the certainty of sense to the philosophical awareness of its own unconditional rationality. We are now prepared to examine Hegel's phenomenological procedure whereby we can arrive at the philosophically conscious subject. This attempt at detailed investigation, however, will be the main issue of the subsequent chapters.

---

[24] "La conscience éprouve son savoir dans ce qu'elle tient pour le vrai, et, en tant qu'elle est encore conscience finie, une figure particulière, elle est contrainte de se dépasser elle-même. Son savoir du Vrai se change quand elle découvre l'inadéquation qui est présente en lui". Jean Hyppolite, *op. cit.*, I, 28.

[25] B., p. 142. *Phän.*, p. 72.

[26] *Ibid.*

Part Two : The Conscious Subject

CHAPTER IV

THE INITIAL TRANSACTION BETWEEN THE
SUBJECT AND ITS OBJECT

Hegel's phenomenological analysis is, at bottom, nothing but the retrospective device by means of which he attempts to describe what the subject really is. Essentially, it is a development of the subject, and this sums up the general aim of the work. However, the being of the subject is not an isolated being. The *Phenomenology* is thus concerned with subjectivity and objectivity, and these notions take on different meanings as consciousness shifts from one form of experience to another. Now, to say this implies saying that the phenomenological analysis cannot disclose what the subject is without first applying the dialectical method, which, as E. Coreth puts it, constitutes the "beginning and the end of Hegel's philosophy".[1] Thus, in principle, his philosophy is self-grounding : the process by which he presents the theory of subjectivity is the very process which unfolds the life of consciousness itself.

Unlike Fichte, Hegel refuses to start his genuine philosophizing from the self-conscious subject, since initially there is no consciousness of the self. According to Hegel, the subject knows an object, but in this cognitive experience the self-consciousness of the subject is omitted. Hegel is convinced that there is nothing contradictory is saying that the primary cognitive act lacks self-awareness, or that the act of self-reflection is initially unnecessary and impossible. Perhaps it is not at all strange to insist that the perfection of self-consciousness cannot occur in a single and direct leap, for to be conscious of something is a different kind of act from being conscious of one's consciousness. Obviously, all this is very different from the traditional idea that self-consciousness and the consciousness of objects are originally only two aspects of one and the same act.

It is noteworthy that Hegel does not look for some first principle on which to base his phenomenological analysis. Instead, he points to the imme-

---

[1] Emerich Coreth, *Das dialektische Sein in Hegels Logik* (Wien : Herder, 1952), p. 18.

diate knowledge and promises to proceed "in an immediate way". This
does not mean, of course, that Hegel's analysis is radically presuppositionless. As a matter of fact, he begins with several presuppositions : one,
that consciousness "is at the start or immediately our object"; the other,
that we can keep "mere apprehension (*Auffassen*) free from conceptual
comprehension (*Begreifen*)".[2] In other words, Hegel assumes that only
acts of consciousness can really constitute the subject matter of philosophical
activity and that sense-certitude can function productively in isolation.
Although Hegel was not the first thinker to start from the cognitive factors
and to reject everything which does not bear the credentials of that which
is immediately given, he is the first to speak of sense-certitude as the most
elementary mode of consciousness, capable of making an existential claim
that something exists. And to this mode of cognition and all that it implies
we must now turn.

There can be no doubt that Hegel wants to begin his phenomenological
investigations from the very beginning, for already in the Introduction he
has suspended all theories concerning the cognitional process. If knowledge
is neither an instrument which we actually employ nor a passive medium
through which we have a glimpse of truth, then it must be treated as a
generic phenomenon, "which is traversing the series of its own forms of
embodiment".[3] Now, since consciousness does occur, the first point demanding phenomenologist's attention is the discovery of the initial cognitive
act which constitutes the starting point of conscious development and the
fount of subjectivity. In other words, the first task confronting Hegel is
the detection of the act of awareness which takes precedence over conceptualization, understanding, and reflection. Hegel is convinced that in investigating phenomenal knowledge it is indispensable to begin with a conscious
act which enjoys primacy and sets the dialectical process in motion. It is
not surprising, then, that the *Phenomenology* begins with a mode of cognition
first in the order of sensuous apprehension from which judgment, reflection,
and rational formulations are excluded.

What has always been characteristic of the Hegelian position is that it
has retained the distinction between subject and object. It cannot be repeated
too often that this contrast reappears in different forms throughout the
Phenomenology. No wonder then that the same contrast and structure
should arise within purely sensuous certainty (*die sinnliche Gewissheit*).
Here the knowable datum (object) and the act of knowing (sensing

___

[2] B., p. [149]. *Phän.*, p. [79].
[3] B., p. 135 *Phän.*, p. 67.

subject) are distinct but mutually implicative. Both of these terms, however, are essentially obscure, vague, and unspecifiable. Thus, the indeterminateness of the subject imitates the indeterminateness of the object. Whatever the indeterminateness may be said to signify, it certainly does not exclude the movement of shifting positions with respect to the subject and object. That is to say, since the primary cognitive experience rests on the duality of subject and object, it gives rise to the problem of the seat of truth : should consciousness look for the truth in the object sensed or in the act of sensation? The dialectical procedure which Hegel grafts upon the sense-certainty seems quite natural and logical. This means that the first phase of the dialectic hinges on two ways of approach to certainty. The first accentuates the object sensed, the other has to do with the subjective act of awareness.

According to Hegel, the first approach to certainty is one in which the object is represented as if it could exist by itself and enjoy complete autonomy. Therefore, the object is put forward as existing in itself and as something absolutely essential. The stubborn fact that the object sensed is the real truth allows consciousness to conclude that the existence of the object is quite independent of the knowledge it causes. It is natural for naive consciousness to insist that the real "substance" of knowledge is not to be found in the conscious act; it is to be found in the particular object existing independently of consciousness. In other words, the truth-accent first falls on the object, which is taken to be indifferent to the manner in which the subject is conscious of it. However, all that naive consciousness knows about its object is that this object *exists*. Thus, the entire content of the objective sense-certainty can be described by the verb "to be" employed in its present tense : it is.[4] Although the object encountered seems to display an extremely rich and meaningful content, to say anything more about it is to introduce reflection and destroy immediacy. In form, "it is" is an existential judgment, because it expresses the existence of the thing known (*das Sein der Sache*), but as far as its real significance is concerned, it denotes prereflective certainty which does not originate in an appraisal subsuming a rational viewpoint. "It is" is not an answer to any rational question but rather refers to the first assertion of awaking consciousness.

Recalling the peculiar manner in which phenomenological knowledge functions as its own criterion, we may now give a more precise meaning

---

[4] "This bare fact of *certainty*, however, is really and admittedly the abstractest and the poorest kind of *truth*. It merely says regarding what it knows : it *is*; and its truth contains solely the *being* of the fact it knows". B., p. [149]. *Phän.*, p. [79].

to the claim that the whole truth of sense-certainty lies in the object. Central here is the fact that the attribution of truth to some object is one thing, whereas the expression and specification of that which is endowed with truth is another thing. In other words, since sense-consciousness claims that it grasps its object as it is, an attempt must be made to specify what it endows with the objective truth value. However, when this task is carried out, the truth of the object disappears in the course of the search for clarification. Let us briefly follow this process of consciousness, where the crux of the matter lies in the subject's capacity to discover universal meanings.

Hegel is convinced that sense-certainty hinges on particularity.[5] Therefore it is necessary to make an attempt to express the particular by a demonstrative term like "this", "here", or "now". These terms, however, can be applied to ever new objects and events. More than that, the object sensed at one particular moment will not be identified at another. Thus, what started out to be a definitive expression of the particular now appears to be quite the reverse, a pure universal. The universal is what comes to light in sense-consciousness as soon as this mode of cognition is necessitated to express in words what is meant when it speaks of any particular being. Since the particular object resists all formulation and expression, it has no other meaning than that of universality. Thus, the apprehension of the particular object is possible only to the extent that it is subsumed under the category of universality, whose source is the conscious subject. However, precluded from expressing its object, the original certitude is banished from it, for it turns out to be a certitude of nothing particular. But for the object to change in this manner is for consciousness to pass over from the object sensed to the act of sensation. In other words, because the object is inexpressible, the position of sense-certainty must be shifted to the subject and the acts of the subject.

If there is an awareness of an object, it must be through the conscious act of the subject, since certainty by definition lies "in the I, in the immediate fact of my seeing, hearing, and so on".[6] And so, the truth-accent falls on the subject, and sense-certainty becomes contingent upon the sensing consciousness and not the object affecting it.

The interest in the fact of sensation acquires priority over the interest in the object sensed for one obvious reason. For as soon as there is question of certitude, the objective form of truth falls short of what is needed. It

---

[5] Cf. Wilhelm Seeberger, *Hegel, oder die Entwicklung des Geistes zur Freiheit* (Stuttgart : Ernst Klett, 1961), p. 279.

[6] B., pp. 153-154. *Phän.*, p. 83.

is clear that the object is really meaningless unless it is known by the subject. Every meaningful apprehension is essentially subjective. Which is another way of saying that the ego can find truth only in what he means,[7] for certainty is a property of the cognitive act. Meaning is correlative with the immediate certitude which lies primarily in consciousness. There is meaning, therefore, as soon as there is a conscious subject to whom truth appears as truth. In other words, what the subject recognizes as true is but the content of the conscious act. Since one can attach meaning only to one's own conscious experiences, the certitude which was banished from the object is forced back into the subject. However, it is permissible to question whether the dialectic of prereflective consciousness would have taken precisely this course without a thoughtful and rational consideration.[8]

According to Hegel, the subjective form of sense-certainty, like the objective, should be asked to specify its claim. As a matter of fact, the subject may not and cannot even try to avoid such a process of specification, for it erupts naturally and necessarily. However, as in the case of the object, the particular subject resists all specification and explicitation. It is impossible to express a particular cognitive act or an individual subject, for the pronoun "I" simply does not mean the individual as such. Being essentially universal, the pronoun "I" is powerless to individuate a specific and singular ego. In Hegel's own words, "when I say 'I', 'this individual I', I say quite generally 'all I's', every one is what I say, every one is 'I', this individual I".[9] In other words, I mean an individual I, but I am unable to say what I mean by "this individual I". Thus, as in the case of objective sense-certainty, it becomes impossible to express a concrete subject without appealing to a universal meaning.

Here we should interrupt our exposition in order to clarify one important issue. While examining Hegel's dialectical shift to the subject, Wilhelm Purpus has remarked that the most significant aspect in this transition is the emergence of the subjective idealism, where all I's stand in the relationship of identity and distinction.[10] Admittedly, it seems safe to say that Hegel

---

[7] "The certainty is now found to lie in the opposite element, namely in knowledge, which formerly was the nonessential factor. Its truth lies in the object as my (*meinem*) object, or lies in the 'meaning' (*Meinen*), in what I 'mean'; it *is*, because *I* know it". B., p. 153. *Phän.*, p. 83.

[8] Cf. James Collins, *A History of Modern European Philosophy* (Milwaukee : Bruce, 1954), p. 616.

[9] B., p. 154. *Phän.*, pp. 84-83.

[10] "Wesen und Erfahrung des subjektiven Idealismus sind hier in unübertrefflicher Weise gekennzeichnet. Dieser Idealismus, der in seiner Konsequenz auch das ihm gegen-

is impersonating here the position of Protagoras that "man is the measure of all things", or that "truth is what appears to each one".[11] We must remember, however, that at this stage it is difficult to give "subjective idealism" any content save that of a personal and unsophisticated certitude. Without considering whether or not any conscious act can ever break the reflexive circle, the fact remains that here we are dealing only with naive and artless idealism, which, in recognizing *another* subject, excludes the position of radical solipsism.

Hegel's subjectivism comes out most impressively in his reflections on universality. As we have seen, sense-certainty holds fast to the mere reality of particular objects. However, no object of immediate certainty can ever be reached by words or gesture. For, as soon as the attempt is made to grasp the particular as particular, one discovers that it can be expressed only as the universal. Whenever I sense something, it is always primarily a particular something which is for me. But at the same time I have to admit that the explicitation of this something is shrouded in universality. Now, this contradiction between sensuous certainty and language is interpreted by Hegel as a contradiction in sense-certainty itself.[12]

From all this it should be clear that the initial mode of cognition is struck with inadequacy. But the question could be asked how such a statement can be made. The assertion that particularity is ineffable, that individual objects and subjects are unspecifiable can be made only because "the unspoken has no meaning and speech is the medium of the universal".[13] To be sure, for Hegel language is not merely a set of abstract and conventional symbols, but a medium in which the nature of consciousness itself is revealed. No one can deny that Hegel has the merit of having recognized that without language knowing remains implicit, even though his preoccupation with contriving a dialectical structure blinded him to the inadequacy

---

überstehende Ich als *blossen* Schein, als *blossen* Meinen bestimmen müsste, scheitert an der Sprödigkeit des anderen Ich, das für sein Hier dasselbe Recht in Anspruch nimmt, seinen Bestimmungen dieselbe Gültigkeit zumisst; beide Ich sind wohl das eine in des anderen Idealität aufgehoben und stehen so in der Beziehung der Identität, der Attraktion, beide erhalten sich aber auch in dieser Beziehung als unterschieden von einander — die Repulsion". Wilhelm Purpus, *Zur Dialektik des Bewusstseins nach Hegel* (Berlin : Trowitzsch & Sohn, 1908), p. 45.

[11] Cf. Jean Hyppolite, *op. cit.*, I, 94.

[12] J. Loewenberg correctly remarks that "the contradiction is not *in* sense-certainty but only *between* it and speech". *Op. cit.*, p. 39.

[13] *Ibid.*

of the conceptual mode of explicitation. Quite obviously, the primary knowing of the object is immediate. However, its immediacy is not explicit, and it cannot be made explicit by any gesticulatory procedures, such as showing, indicating, and pointing out the particular. Rather an act of meaningful utterance is demanded. Yet, as can be expected, this act terminates immediacy, because the subject never expresses particularity exhaustively by forcing it into universal categories. Thus, Hegel sacrifices the lived experience to the universal articulation, for he is convinced that the word alone can reveal the true essence of the object.[14] However, this does not involve a radical refutation of sense-certainty; instead, it involves, as G. A. Gabler has remarked, modifying the character of the initial mode of cognition.[15] The modifications which have been introduced are, first, a cancellation of one-sided claims, for sense-certainty is certainty only within the unity of reciprocal interaction between subjectivity and objectivity, and, secondly, an elevation of cognitive experience up to the level of oral discourse. The importance of all this, of course, is not so much in the suppression of the immediate certainty as in the emergence of universality, which, needless to say, has a subjective origin. If we examine the matter closely, we find that the subject is going through a turning point in its growth. Universality is discovered by the subject, but only because the object contributes what can be universalized. In observing and describing the object, however, the subject seeks nothing but its own nature, reflecting chiefly its universal, negative, and mediating features. To these features we must give special attention, for on their activity hinges the constitution of subjectivity.

First of all, the dialectical nature of sense-certainty provides a satisfactory clarification of the meaning of universality. As we have seen, it is essential to the object that it be apprehended as universal. It is always a universal meaning which characterizes the object encountered. Furnishing the categ-

---

[14] "Mais, quand nous allons jusqu'au fond du langage, il n'en est pas moins vrai que, pour Heidegger comme pour Hegel, il nous fait atteindre le vrai. Car dans le langage, dans le mot, c'est la chose elle-même qui s'ouvre à nous. L'essence des mots vient dans la parole". Jean Wahl, "Hegel et Heidegger", Angèle Marietti, La pensée de Hegel (Paris : Bordas, 1957), p. 186. See also the following works : Theodor Bodammer, Hegels Deutung der Sprache (Hamburg : F. Meiner, 1969), Josef Simon, Das Problem der Sprache bei Hegel (Stuttgart : W. Kohlhammer, 1966).

[15] "Hiermit aber ist das Sinnliche selbst noch keineswegs verschwunden, da im Gegenteil das ganze Wahrnehmen das Sinnliche noch zur Grundlage hat und von ihm ausgeht. Was sich aber geändert hat, ist der Charäkter des Sinnlichen, oder die Art und Weise 'Wie' es für das Bewusstsein ist." G. A. Gabler, Kritik des Bewusstseins (New ed.; Leiden : A. H. Adriani, 1901), pp. 85-86.

ory of universality, the subject guarantees not only articulate consciousness but objectivity as well. The distinguishing mark of sense-certainty regarded as a valid mode of cognition lies in the subject's ability to disengage universality from particularity. Accordingly, explicit consciousness depends for its possibility on the universalizing performance of the subject. Whenever there is articulate cognition and discourse, there is a universalizing activity of consciousness, although this activity is not perfect except in a framework of progressive development. In the transition from sense-certainty to perception, there is suppression but also preservation, because the whole transition is from universality implicit to explicit universality. Thus, when the subject turns cognitively to an object, which is no longer a particular (*ein einzelnes*) but a Here which "is itself simply many Heres together",[16] we are witnessing the transition from immediate awareness of universality to perceptual cognition of universality. The universality of perceptual cognition satisfies more adequately the demands of true knowledge, although it is still effected under conditions of sense. In all this the object has been changed; it has been transformed into a recognizable *thing*. Taken, then, as its point of departure the thing which is itself an ensemble of universal categories, the subject can turn its attention to the sensuous datum as it truly is.

Secondly, as in the case of universality, the initial mode of apprehension provides a satisfactory explanation of the meaning of negativity. As has been pointed out before, sense-consciousness is refuted by the fact that the particular object is inexpressible and incommunicable. This sort of conclusion we can qualify as "negative", for immediate consciousness has reached an impasse. According to Hegel, however, the matter can be turned around, for the refutation of sense-certainty includes essentially a positive aspect. Thus, the negative result reached by consciousness should not be interpreted as a predicament affording no escape. The negative conclusion implied in sense-certainty has a positive significance precisely because it contributes to the acquisition of new knowledge.[17] For the initial certainty to break down dialectically is for consciousness to pass over from sensuous awareness to perceptual cognition. It is Hegel's contention that "in the negation the transition is made by which the progress through the complete succession of forms comes about of itself".[18] To put it differently : it is only through the negative function of the subject that a new phenomeno-

---

[16] B., p. 160. *Phän.*, p. 89.

[17] This is well explained by Martin Busse : "In der Entwicklung der Phänomenologie wird das Negative als Resultat und darum als neuer Inhalt aufgefasst". *Hegels Phänomenologie des Geistes und der Staat* (Berlin : Junker und Dünnhaupt, 1931), p. 6.

[18] B., p. 137. *Phän.*, p. 69.

logical form can arise at all. Therefore, there is a great advantage to be gained from the negative performance of the subject. Here, then, it is not a question of arresting the subject's growth; rather, it is a question of developing a richer mode of subjectivity. New perspectives suddenly arise here, which Hegel did not fail to consider. To speak of negativity is to speak of cognitive transitions in the subject's gradual advance from natural to philosophical knowledge.

Thirdly, before we take up the task of discussing the nature of perceptual cognition, something must be said regarding the subject's mediating performance. It cannot be reiterated too often that in the first phase of phenomenal cognition the relation of subject to object is an immediate relation.[19] This means that "neither the I nor the thing has here the meaning of a manifold relation with a variety of other things, of mediation in a variety of ways".[20] Although the immediate knowledge presents itself as naive confidence, the very essence of consciousness demands that this immediate condition should be superseded (*aufgehoben*). The object as the object is unconcealed from the subject, however, it is not conceptually transparent to the subject. That is, the object never appears to the subject in perfectly rational clarity. This should not be surprising, for not even the subject is transparent to itself. This "not even" indicates the inadequacy of the immediate type of cognition. Reality can be made explicit only through a mediating thought process, which is but another way of saying that the knowledge of reality can be expressed only in grasping the cognitive performance of the subject. As was mentioned before, Hegel distinguishes himself from other German idealists in rejecting the immediacy of an intellectual insight and demanding a dialectical mediation by means of universal notions. According to Hegel, so long as consciousness is immediately aware of an object it cannot be properly philosophic; to be philosophic it must become consciousness itself, that is, "it must be its own object in which it finds itself reflected".[21] Therefore, to speak of knowledge is to speak of self-mediating activity of the subject.

When sense-certainty is examined for the conditions of its possibility, it breaks up into two "thises" : one this is the subject, the second is the object. This distinction is due to the negative act of the subject. Still, it is not sufficient to establish a contrast between subjectivity and objectivity; Hegel demands an active mediation, in which the unity of contradictories is achieved. He writes :

[19] Cf. W. T. Stace, *op. cit.*, p. 341.
[20] B., p. 150. *Phän.*, p. 80.
[21] B., p. 86. *Phän.*, p. 24.

When *we* [the external critics] reflect on this distinction, it is seen that neither the one nor the other is merely immediate, merely *is* in sense-certainty, but is at the same time *mediated* : I have the certainty through the other, viz. through the actual fact; and this, again, exists in that certainty through an other, viz. through the I.[22]

The notion of mediation makes it clear that the subject is not only the principle of the mediating process, but is indistinguishable from that process itself. It is not astonishing, then, that Hegel should describe the mediating process involved in knowledge as the history of the subject's own inner development.[23] This sort of procedure is extremely important, for it permits Hegel to explain that the subject is both one term of the cognitive relationship and also the whole relationship. *Objekt ist aufgehoben im Subjekt* — such is Hegel's general principle of mediation. The negative meaning of the term "*aufheben*" indicates that an isolated object cannot be affirmed, for the affirmation itself signifies the very relation which the subject would have to negate to speak of the autonomous object. Although the object is other than the subject, it simply does not occur except in fusion with the subject.[24] Thus, pure objectivity or the thing-as-not-known-to-the subject must be excluded. But we can speak of the object as "*aufgehoben*" in a positive sense. Viewed thus, the object is preserved, elevated, and promoted to the rank of conscious actuality; the other of the subject is its own other.

In Hegel's view there can be no radical either-or between subject and object. Considered as correlatives, subject and object are so intimately connected that each depends on the other for its intelligibility. Still, these two conjoined elements do not carry the same weight and importance. For Hegel, the subject ranks higher than the object. The distinguishing mark of the subject lies primarily in the subject's priority over the object. It is evident that the subject's supremacy derives from the universalizing action, negativity, and self-mediation of consciousness. Strange as it may seem, the universalizing performance, negativity, and self-mediation of the subject supply the link connecting subjectivity and objectivity.

[22] B., p. 150. *Phän.*, p. 80.
[23] Cf. B., p. 158. *Phän.*, p. 86. The historicity of the subject comes to the fore in sense-certainty. However, what is true of sense-certainty is true of every subsequent phenomenological form. The following works contain substantial information regarding Hegel's conception of history and historicity : Jean Hyppolite, *Introduction à la Philosophie de l'histoire de Hegel* (Paris : M. Rivière, 1948), Michael B. Foster, *Die Geschichte als Schicksal des Geistes in der Hegelschen Philosophie* (Tübingen : J. C. B. Mohr, 1929), Gaston Fessard, "Attitude ambivalente de Hegel en face de l'histoire", *Archives de philosophie*, 24 (1961), 207-241.
[24] "No object unless it be the subject's own". J. Loewenberg, *op. cit.*, p. 361.

If described in an anticipatory vein, the ultimate goal of the subject-object dialectical movement lies in the achievement of philosophical consciousness or absolute knowledge. On that level, the subject and the object undergo final transformation and emerge as equatable, as producing an identity from themselves. If we insist on this point, it is because the contrast between subject and object does not disappear by conscious absorption of the objective externality into the subject. According to Hegel, the independent and externalized object presents itself to the subject as a vanishing element, as "cancelling its own existence". However, the gradual disappearance of the independent object occurs simultaneously with the process by which consciousness objectivizes itself. To be conscious of the object is to act on the first level of cognitional process; it is to be on the way towards an objectivization of consciousness; but it is not to have reached anything more than an initial objectivization. When one merely senses without as yet perceiving, one is impersonating the subject's struggle with the inexpressible; when one perceives without as yet understanding, one is depicting the subject's effort to take truly the sensuously given. Perception, like the act of sensation, is not a simple act. It has a long and complicated career, and to this dialectical career of the perceiving subject we must now turn.

CHAPTER V

THE PERCEIVING SUBJECT

The first point to be made is that perception is a cognitive act in affinity with sensation. Like sensation, perception is related to sensible objects and their various attributes. But if there is a parallel between a sensuous attitude and a perceptive attitude, there also exists a difference. Where the sensuous consciousness seeks to grasp the ineffable individual, the perceiving subject is concerned with the specification of the sensible universal. To the perceiving consciousness the most pressing question is the determination of universality.[1] Such a question clearly cannot be answered by perception, unless it is transformed into understanding. According to Hegel, in perception consciousness finds itself in a state of contradiction that has to be overcome. Thus, as the dialectic terminates, the subject discovers two opposed features in the object and two opposed functions in the perceiving mind. Since it is not within the capacity of perception to solve this major difficulty, it faces the alternative either of returning to sensation or of performing the conceptual act. It is Hegel's contention that the percipient accepts the conceptual role, and it is precisely the performance of the conceptual act which constitutes the basis of the scientific understanding. This, however, is a subtle and complicated process, demanding a careful analysis and consideration.

The analysis of sense-certainty has disclosed that its real truth is not the particular but the universal. A simple entity "which is neither this or that, which is *not-this*, and with equal indifference this as well as that — a

---

[1] "Perception, on the other hand, takes what exists for it to be a universal. Universality being its principle in general, its moments immediately distinguished within it are also universal; *I* is a universal, and the *object* is a universal". B., p. [162]. *Phän.*, p. 89.

It should be noted here that Hegel's *Wahrnehmung* is not easily translated by one single English term. What is more, Hegel's *Wahrnehmung* does not have the same meaning as the cognitional act of perception of the traditional philosophy.

thing of this kind we call a Universal".[2] Sense-certainty, as a consciousness claiming to give us knowledge of that which exists, proves itself invalid, but its "element" of universality survives as the constitutive "principle" of perception.

Though it is difficult to understand how the sensuous consciousness can invalidate itself and turn into perception, Hegel insists that perception and sensation are dialectically related, for the first grows out of the latter. Viewed thus, perception is a corrective act, accomplishing what sense-certainty tried but failed to do.[3] Quite obviously, the perceiving subject does more than attend to incommunicable impressions of sensation. It looks for distinctions within the same object. To do this the subject relies upon a power of the mind to discern a thing and its properties. Thus, the percipient embarks on incessant struggle with the thing's unity and diversity. This, for Hegel, represents a higher stage in the phenomenology of consciousness, basic here being the singleness of the thing and the multiplicity of its properties.

To say that perception grows out of sense-certainty is to say that the object of the emerging mode of consciousness is the *experience* of the previous one. Now, the factor that determines the course of perceptual experience is the new relationship between the subject and its object. If the percipient adheres to his objects and lets himself be governed by them, he will realize that the distinction between the unity of the object and the multiplicity of its properties is the basic issue of perception. This is but another way of saying that perceptual experience contains within itself all that can be known about the object. When perceptual experience begins, the object seems an isolated *"thing with many properties"*.[4] As in the case of sense-certainty, the subject first gathers the cognitive information from the object. This clearly implies that the cognitive attitude in becoming a perceiving subject is essentially receptive, the subject being acted upon by the object. But as the dialectical process proceeds, it becomes evident that the objectivity of the thing must be constituted by the subject. For when the percipient attempts to apprehend what the thing really is, he plunges into a series of unavoidable contradictions. This, of course, means that the experience gathered directly from the object is struck with inconsistency. Fluctuation in the apprehension of the object is a

---

[2] B., p. 152. *Phän.*, p. 82.

[3] Cf. Nicolai Hartmann, *Die Philosophie des deutschen Idealismus* (2nd ed.; Berlin: Walter de Gruyter, 1960), p. 325.

[4] B., p. 163, *Phän.*, p. 90.

clear indication that every attempt at purely passive reception of truth cancels its own meaning. This major difficulty cannot be avoided by assigning the two opposed characteristics to each of the two constituents of perception, so that the singleness of the object is attributed to the subject and the diversity of its properties to the object. Nor does it help to maintain that the thing is really a unity and that the diversity of qualities is due to its relation to other things. In short, all attempts to escape the difficulties of perception only serve to demonstrate that the thing is a "tissue of contradictions" and that perception alone cannot cope with its problems.

Assuming that perception presupposes an interplay between subject and object, it is natural to look for the essence of perceptual experience first in the thing itself, because the object, to use Hegel's expression, is "quite indifferent as to whether it is perceived or not".[5] All intelligibility and all truth ultimately go always back to the object itself. This fact cannot be denied. Therefore, the initial assumption of the perceiving subject is that perception is an act of passive receptivity and its object independent of consciousness. The subject, says Hegel, has merely to take the object "and assume the attitude of pure apprehension".[6] If perceiving consciousness is passive, then the thing itself decides the veridicality of any proposition regarding what is perceived. Thus, being convinced that the occurrence of perception is contingent upon some independent thing, the subject invests with fundamental truth only the thing perceived.

It takes but little effort to realize that the initial attitude of perception intimates the doctrine of empiricism. For empiricism always emphasized the passivity of consciousness and assumed that true knowledge was the veridical, purely passive mirroring of an external reality whose object did not depend in any way on the knowing subject. The basic presupposition of this theory is that the perceptual act resembles a photographic film which might be said to react to external impressions. Thus, consciousness has to be conceived as pure passivity on which an object that is completely in-itself imprints itself.

With such an attitude to hand, the subject is invited to perceive an object and "see what sort of experience consciousness forms in the course of its actual perception".[7] We must remember, however, that the object of perception is in its essential structure the same as the process of perceiving. There-

[5] *Ibid.*
[6] B., p. 166. *Phän.*, p. 92.
[7] B., p. 167. *Phän.*, p. 93.

fore, to speak of the object is simply to trace the course of perceptual experience. Still, since these two moments can be posited as distinct and "since they are related as opposites", only one can claim priority in constituting perception. Hegel insists that perceiving, being contingent upon some prior object serving as stimulator, is the nonessential, secondary moment. To establish the priority of the object, Hegel resorts to the "insubstantial" character of perceiving and modifies its meaning with the qualification, "which can be as well as not be".[8] Now, the object perceived is given to the passive subject as purely single, "which consists in *excluding* properties of an opposite character".[9] But the same object is likewise given as having many distinct properties determinative of the object's singleness. The unity of the thing is an expression of determination and negation : by relating itself to itself, the "one" excludes an "other" and determines the thinghood of the Here. However, this single Here is *also* manifold : it is colored, *also* of a specific shape, *also* of a peculiar weight, and *also* of a distinct flavor. All these properties lie in a single Here; each and every property "is everywhere in the same Here where the others are".[10] Since every property exhibits a univocal identity, it leaves the others undisturbed and "is related to these by being *also* along with them, a relation of mere indifference".[11]

However, there is still another aspect which must be taken into consideration. Namely, if these properties were related to themselves alone, they could not be determinative of the object's excluding unity. Being indifferent to each other, they merely participate in the abstract universal medium. Therefore, viewed as belonging to a medium, the diverse properties are not affecting each other or thing's unity. However, the determinateness of a specific thing must lie in its own properties and nowhere else. But the properties of the thing can determine its unity only by being distinguished and related to others as their opposites. Thus, viewed as belonging to the negative unity, they affect each other and mutually exclude one another.

In summarizing, we can say that there are three major factors constituting the nature of the thing : (1) the "also", which establishes the connection between the qualities of the thing; (2) the "one", which expresses the moment of negation and exclusivity; and (3) the many properties themselves, exhibiting an isolated existence apart from the "also" connecting them.

According to Hegel, this merely describes the development of the object

---

[8] B., p. 163. *Phän.*, p. 90.
[9] B., p. 166. *Phän.*, p. 92.
[10] B., p. 164. *Phän.*, p. 91.
[11] B., p. 165. *Phän.*, p. 91.

itself. The next point demanding our attention is the attitude of consciousness towards this same object.

Since the whole truth is attached to the object, while consciousness assumes a passive attitude, it seems that the percipient can rightly expect a consistency in the manner of apprehension and a certain constancy in the content perceived. According to Hegel, however, this does not preclude the subject from being aware of the possibility of deception, for consciousness was given only the variable and non-essential function. In other words, the acceptance of the purely receptive role leaves the subject totally unconvinced as to the validity of perception.

The emerging suspicion invites the subject to look for the criterion of truth without abandoning the passive approach. Since this sort of attitude does not allow it to impose any external criterion, the subject is forced to admit that it lies in the self-sameness (*Sichselbstgleichheit*) of the object.[12] Since the percipient is content to know that the self-sameness of the object constitutes the standard of truth, then an objective evaluation and critique of perception seems possible. For such a critique nothing need be consulted except fluctuations in the consciousness of the object. Quite obviously, the presence of fluctuations in the apprehension of the object is an unmistakable indication that the object became modified as a result of being perceived. It is for this reason that the subject compares the diverse moments of apprehension with one another. If in this comparison the self-sameness of the object is contradicted, this is not an error on the part of the object, but on the part of perception.

Thus, the first concern of the suspicious subject is to disclose the contradictions contained in the experience of the object. It is very doubtful, however, whether Hegel could have offered this explicitation, if he himself had not confused the perceptive mode of apprehension with reflection. The act of perception asserts of itself neither that the thing is perceived objectively nor that it is mistaken; only reflection can affirm one or the other. Although Hegel reports only what is known by perception, it is evident that the act of reporting involves judgment and thought. All this becomes very clear in the development of erroneous views already expressed in the description of the actual perception. Let us describe this briefly.

As we have seen, the object perceived presents itself as purely one, in the sense of possessing particularity or singular unity. Since the subject is also aware of the property in it, a property which is universal, the original mode of apprehension must be revised, reporting that the error is due to

---

[12] See *Phän.*, p. 93.

the agency of the subject. On account of the universality of the property, the object perceived must be taken as a community as-such (*Gemeinschaft überhaupt*).[13] However, this position is untenable. The property perceived is given as "determinate, opposed to another and excluding this other".[14] What is presented as determinate must be understood as opposed and exclusive. This fact only confirms the truth that properties can perform their determining function only when apprehended as specifying a particular thing. Thus, we may say that the percipient did not apprehend the object correctly when he defined it as a "community with others". If we take acount of the determinateness of the property and set aside its assertable universality, we note that perception must be revised, for the object emerges as a unity that excludes. To be conscious of the determinateness of the property is an invitation to ascribe to the object an exclusive unity. However, in this isolated "one", the subject finds many properties, which are indifferent to one another without affecting one another. Thus, the specific color of the object does not affect its particular form, and neither property determines its weight or the flavor. Since all these properties are not perceivable as interdependent, the subject can no longer say that the specific nature of the thing lies in reciprocal interdependence of its properties.

However, the percipient did not perceive the object correctly when he took it for something that excludes. One decisive reason for this is that one property emerges after another, each being related to the next merely by an abstract "also". Therefore, if properties are given as indifferent to one another and excluding each other, the object must be viewed as a universal medium or the "also". But this position is evidently erroneous, for it suggests that the thing is merely a collection of independent attributes. The thing is what its properties are, and its properties are given "in the form of sense universals".[15] But sense universals without being proper properties of an individual thing lose their function as specifying determinants. Therefore, what is given as universal medium is merely an incorrigible image of the concrete thing.

It does not require much effort to see that perception thus explicitated is facing its own dissolution, while the subject is "thrown back on the beginning". This outcome, of course, would be without positive significance if it were not aimed at establishing the transition from passive perception

---

[13] *Ibid.*
[14] B., p. 167. *Phän.*, p. 93.
[15] B., p. 168. *Phän.*, p. 94.

to reflective perception, or, as Roger Garaudy puts it, from empiricism to Kantian criticism.[16]

To get back to the last perceptual attitude : the subject, despite successive modifications, fails to reconcile unity and multiplicity. If attention is paid to the thing's unity, whose place in perception is central, the subject is forced to admit that a single object is not really in possession of specific properties. And this is so for two reasons. First, because in this case the specificity of the thing seems to lie in an original combination of determining properties. However, these properties are not actually perceivable as interdependent. Secondly, because properties can function as specific determinants only when apprehended as belonging to the thing itself. But in perception they are given as common properties, for they are found in other particular things as well.

Let us shift our approach now and look at perception from the point of view of multiplicity. Thus, if attention is paid to the multiple character of the thing, what is lost sight of is the individuality of the thing. One can only say that the thing is merely a sort of abstract medium in which properties appear in a succession of sensuous universals. The term "sensuous" is here all important, for it permits Hegel to introduce the first alternative of perceptual dilemma : the return to the original starting point. However, being aware of the fact that sense-certainty is destined by its very nature to pass over into perception, the subject refuses to be dragged into the same dialectical circuit and chooses the second alternative : the active participation in the act of perceiving.

It is natural that Hegel's exposition of purely passive perception should be followed by a critical analysis of it, for the dialectic requires that the transition to the new form of perception be a transition from one extreme to another. Once we have grasped this guiding thesis of Hegelian doctrine, it becomes possible to understand why Hegel commits himself to an objectivistic notion of perception, only to end up proposing a criticism of objectivistic perception. At this stage, therefore, he assigns to the percipient a reflective function. "In this way consciousness becomes definitely aware of how its perceptual process is essentially constituted".[17] Consequently, if the percipient does in fact assert his ability to reflect upon the act of perception, there is at least one fact he certainly recognizes. He knows that reflection is indispensable to perception.

It cannot be doubted that radical passivity belongs to the mirror, in which

---

[16] *Dieu est mort* : *Étude sur Hegel* (Paris : Presses Universitaires de France, 1962), p. 215.
[17] B., p. 168. *Phän.*, p. 94.

there is no longer any question of cognition. The passive mirroring of reality may resemble perception, but it is not perception, and there is hardly any need to impersonate such a doctrine. Accordingly, to speak of the distinction between subjectivity and objectivity is to express oneself as if they were two opposed things. But it is never possible for the knowing subject to ask whether there is a thing in the objectivistic sense, because this question presupposes that man withdraws from the act of perceiving the cognitive attitude which he himself is. An act of perception without subjectivity is inconceivable, because it is meaningless to speak of a perceived object without the presence of a conscious subject.

The first condition for perception to be possible is that the subject too participates in some measure in cognition. This fact is expressed by the statement that perceptual process "is not a simple bare apprehension".[18] Accordingly, Hegel avails himself of the phrase "dissolution of perception" to indicate the absurdity of regarding perception as a passive reception of the object. The subject not only perceives, "but is also conscious of its reflection into self, and keeps this apart from the simple apprehension proper".[19] For this proposition to make sense, we must remember that the object cannot be apprehended except as presented to consciousness. Still, we must be on our guard lest an equivocation conceals from us the precise sense of Hegel's words. An urgent issue is raised by the question : Is there a way in which the subject could creep into perceptual activity? Hegel is convinced that the subject, relying on its reflective capacity, can easily distinguish between the object's real nature and the modification installed in it as a result of cognitive performance. By recognizing as its own certain features formerly attributed to the object, the perceiving subject can "get the true object bare and naked".[20] It might be asked, perhaps, whether by this reflective procedure Hegel hopes to arrive at complete and univocal knowledge of the object. His answer to this is : No. Even though the reflective activity of the subject perfects perception, it is powerless to reconcile the contradictory aspect of perception. And we shall see issuing from the performance of the subject consequences parallel to those we have previously discovered concerning purely passive perception.

The initial step in reflection occurs when the subject ascribes unity to the object and assumes full responsibility for its diversity. Since the thing is taken as a unitary entity and since unity and multiplicity are assumed to

[18] B., p. 169. *Phän.*, p. 94.
[19] *Ibid.*
[20] *Ibid.*

be two mutually exclusive factors, we must not be surprised that the subject makes itself responsible for the object's multiplicity. This conclusion is still more evident if we envisage the actual argument presented by the subject. And it is from this argument that Hegel sets out to establish the plausibility of regarding the subject as the source of diverse properties.

The subject *knows* that the object is reached through the channels of many different sense organs. "This thing, then, is, in point of fact, merely white to *our* eyes, *also* tart to *our* tongue, and *also* cubical to *our* feeling, and so on".[21] Since these different qualities are produced by different sense organs, it is reasonable to say that the diversity of a thing's properties "comes not from the thing, but from us". The subject perceives the object only from a standpoint which is determined by the anatomical structure of the body. The qualitative aspects of the thing have their origin in a subjective operation, precisely because the object perceived affects not one but many anatomical units and each unit produces a distinct sensation, which we, as subjects, have previously ascribed to the thing itself. But this, of course, is not all. In analyzing this conclusion, we see one major consequence issue out of it : The subject's involvement in perception removes inconsistency and strengthens the unitary character of the thing.[22]

At first sight, this view may sound consistent and plausible. But then a new problem arises. If the thing we perceive is given as a unitary entity, how can we identify it through its unity since the unity of the thing does not determine its specificity? The diversity of the thing has been explained; the unity of the thing has been explained too. But what has not been explained is the thing as a specific and distinct entity, "for to be 'one' is to be in a universal relation of self to self, and hence by the fact of its being 'one' it is rather like all".[23] If it is true that the thing's discriminable sensuous properties have existence only in us, it follows that the object as such is unrecognizable. The object cannot be a specific object unless its qualitative aspects are apprehended as belonging to the object itself. To say that the object's properties are construed by the subject is to say that there is no objective criterion which would enable us to distinguish one perceived thing from another. Thus, if we adopt the subjectivistic point of view,

---

[21] B., pp. 169-170. *Phän.*, p. 95.

[22] "We are, consequently, the universal medium where such elements get dissociated, and exist each by itself. By the fact, then, that we regard the characteristic of being a universal medium as *our* reflection, *we* preserve and maintain the self-sameness and truth of the thing, its being a 'one' ". B., p. 170. *Phän.*, p. 95.

[23] B., p. 170. *Phän.*, pp. 95-96.

we thereby jeopardize the specific nature of the object. It is not surprising, therefore, that this position is essentially one-sided and untenable.

As he is following the dialectical procedure, Hegel does not hesitate to say that the determination of the thing by its own specific properties implies the revision of the previous view. In order to understand the position of Hegel on this point, we must first remember the privileged role he attributes to the notion of specification : "It is through the determinate characteristic that the thing excludes other things".[24] Since "things themselves are thus determinate in and for themselves", their specific properties must be taken as objective, self-contained, and indifferent to one another. Which is but another way of saying that the view of their subjective origin must be cancelled once and for all. Still, the above cancellation should not be construed as a complete suppression of the subject's intervention in perception. The new position must preserve the subjectivistic standpoint, for it has to meet at all points the basic requirement of Hegel's assumption that unity and multiplicity are not only distinct but mutually exclusive. What is now depicted as subjective is the putting of specific properties into the "one". In the new context, therefore, the dialectic of perception is made to exhibit that the unity of the object is deprived of its objective status and deteriorates into a mere "also". "It is, then, in truth the thing itself which is white, and *also* cubical, and *also* tart, and so on; in other words, the *thing* is the "also", the general medium, wherein the many properties subsist externally to one another, and without cancelling one another; and, so taken, the thing is taken as what it truly is".[25] But, as has been pointed out before, the act of putting (*das Ineinssetzen*) these properties into the "one" originates in the subject, which must keep them apart by means of a qualifying "insofar". Thus we say of the thing : so far as it is white it is not cubical, and so far as it is cubical it is not sharp.

If we look back, says Hegel, on what consciousness previously took upon itself, and now takes upon itself, we realize that this cognitive agency alternately makes itself and the thing into both a pure "one" and an "also" resolved into many independent aspects. Let us put the problem as bluntly as possible. When this twofold interpretation is acknowledged to be possible, what becomes of perception? It is not without interest for the understanding of what this result means to inquire whether one of these positions is more reasonable or adequate than the other. First of all, to describe perception from one of these two complementary viewpoints and to neglect

---

[24] B., p. 170. *Phän.*, p. 96.
[25] B., p. 171. *Phän.*, p. 96.

the other, is to get involved in inextricable difficulties. Secondly, these two reflective attempts to install into perception a subjective factor are dialectically related : the first cognitive performance constitutes the subject matter of the second.[26] Thirdly, the subjective agency "thus finds through this comparison that not only *its* way of taking the truth contains the diverse moments of apprehension and return upon itself, but that the truth itself, the thing, manifests itself in this twofold manner".[27] In other words, since the percipient can alternately attribute to himself the object's unity and multiplicity, he must alternately regard the object as containing within itself the "opposite aspects of truth". Now, the recognition that the object "manifests itself in this twofold manner" is an invitation to abandon the attempt to make the subjective performance the seat either of the object's unity or of its multiplicity. And thus the endeavor to show that the object is what the subject takes it to be after excluding the elements contributed by the cognitive activity comes to nought.

According to Hegel, however, the subject can get away from this difficult situation by taking as its object the entire perceptual process "which was previously shared between the object and consciousness".[28] Let us note that the idea of the process, applied to perceiving consciousness, includes more than the thing for itself (*an sich*) and the subject responsible either for unity or multiplicity. It implies the notion of relation and the notion of perspective. Therefore, it is characteristic of the new position that all our statements referring to objects and their properties should be modified with the qualification, "insofar as relation and perspectives go". But what is here at stake is the explicitation of the mutual implications of universality and singleness.

When the object is considered from the viewpoint of the entire process, all previous claims and antithetical moments crop up, forcing the subject to accept a sophistical attitude. In other words, the final performance of the perceiving subject consists in an attempt to inject into perception a specious and evasive reasoning. Hegel offers an explanation of why he does this, and thus the interpreter is not left to his own surmises : "The sophistry

---

[26] "Réfléchissant sur cette double expérience, c'est-à-dire sur notre première réflexion dans l'appréhension de la chose, nous découvrons que nous faisons alternativement aussi bien de la chose que de nous-même, tantôt le pur Un, sans multiplicité, tantôt le *aussi* résolu en matières indépendantes les unes des autres; d'où cette conséquence que cette réflexion première devient l'objet de notre seconde réflexion et nous apparaît inhérente à la chose elle-même". Jean Hyppolite, *Genèse et structure de la Phénoménologie de l'Esprit de Hegel*, I, 113.114.

[27] B., p. 172. *Phän.*, p. 97.

[28] *Ibid.*

of perception seeks to save these moments [singleness and universality] from their contradiction, tries to keep them fixed by distinguishing between 'aspects', by using terms like 'also' and 'so far as', and seeks in like manner to lay hold on the truth by distinguishing the unessential element from an essential nature opposed thereto".[29] The subject tries to reconcile the antithetical elements by leaning for support on empty abstractions and evasive arguments. But this proves to be of no avail, for the perceptual process is determined by at least three axiomatic insights. In the first place, unity and multiplicity are radically opposed, and their reconciliation is not within the power of perception. This first remark calls for a second, namely: a thing becomes distinct only when distinguished from other things. And thirdly, the object's nature is not wholly independent of the subject's perspective.

We must try now to be more precise as to how the sophisticated subject apprehends the object and reconciles its antithetical aspects. Let us begin by saying that a thing can be posited as having a being of its own, as existing for itself, or as an unconditional negation of all otherness. It should be clear, too, that this kind of negation implies self-relatedness and specificity. However, a specific otherness presupposes objects specifically other than it. This is emphatically true, since the subject cannot apprehend the object as specific without relating it to the specific elements it excludes. Therefore, the negation of otherness is a negation of the object's own otherness. Now, if this be the case, further analysis of this relationship must lead to a new determination of universality. The unity of the thing is not only determined but constituted by its relation to other things, and its nature consists in this very relation. Thus, the thing is intrinsically itself through its opposition to other things; it is, as Hegel says, "the opposite of itself—for itself 'so far as' it is for another, and for another 'so far as' it is for itself".[30] It would, of course, be fair to say that this is not a genuine universality, but one affected with an opposition. Accordingly, to attempt to push this sophistical inquiry further would be to exceed the limits of perception or, more exactly, to seek to describe sensuous universality in terms of pure concepts. This, however, is not within the capacity of perception to accomplish; it is the task of understanding.

Since Hegel approaches the problem of consciousness from the generic viewpoint, it is safe to say that his method is very akin to impersonation. Although Hegel's intention is to describe perception in isolation, he is not

---

[29] B., p. 176. *Phän.*, p. 100.
[30] B., p. 175. *Phän.*, p. 99.

limiting his report to what is apprehended by perception alone. However we interpret Hegel we cannot go so far as to pretend that perception can disclose its own nature. It is characteristic of perception that it cannot even say what it is itself, or what its object is, without first appealing to thought and judgment. It is just as much a matter of conceptualization and judgment to know that an object exhibits unity and diversity, as it is to know that unity and diversity are antithetical categories. Hegel's rational distinctions plainly suggest that he has recourse to abstraction and judgment, and it is actually these abstractions and distinctions that make his notion of perception so difficult to grasp.

CHAPTER VI

THE UNDERSTANDING SUBJECT

We have accused Hegel of having injected into perception a cognitive act that pertains to thought and judgment. However, if we turn our attention now to the newly emerging pattern of consciousness, we will see that the injection of conceptualization constitutes an indispensable condition of effecting the transition from perception to understanding. Since clarity in this matter is essential to the proper apprehension of transition we must digress here to deal with it.

As was indicated in the preceding chapters, the subject of sense-certainty had for its object the unmediated and ineffable singular. With the insight that the primary act of taking cognizance ends in an impasse, the subject rose to perception and took for its object universality affected with single-ness. What has always been characteristic of perception as an intermediate stage in the coming-to-be of consciousness proper is that it has preserved the distinction between singleness and universality, now concentrating on singleness, now stressing the importance of universality, and finally attempt-ing sophistical reconciliation of the two. Although the issue is not quite so simple, it seems safe to say that from sense experience the perceiving subject inherited its attachment to singleness, while from the universalizing activity of the subject sprang its openness to universality. There is nothing strange, then, that the percipient fluctuates between the sensible and the rational, between pre-reflection and reflection. The difficulty here is that, since the percipient has not effectively reconciled the sensible and the ration-al, he cannot lay claim to complete intelligibility. And so, the cognitive pattern of perception such as Hegel depicts it calls for radical reconstitution. It hardly needs saying that the principal source of this reconstitution is the subject itself. Which is but another way of saying that the advance to the new position is necessitated by the universalizing action of the subject.

Since the subject is inseparable from its performances, the universalizing agency operative at the level of perception develops the subject, making demands that the element of singleness be dropped out altogether. Thus the subject embarks on mentally acute struggle with what it regards as an obstacle to real understanding and rationality. In other words, if subjectivity is to break the bonds of sensibility and be truly rational, the notion of unconditional universality must be introduced into the dialectical discourse. Still, if we consider the conditions which must be fulfilled in order that the subject begin a rational life, we must concede that it is not enough only to contemplate the idea of unconditional universality. The subject must find a general concept that is both distinct and transitional, non-sensuous and universal. According to Hegel, only the concept of force has these qualifications.

We may ask ourselves, first of all, whether the concept on which hinges the dialectic of understanding has any connections with the pre-Hegelian account of force. Hegel himself, of course, offers no clue to the historical roots of his notion, and the interpreters are left to their own surmises. Wilhelm Purpus suggests, for example, that Hegel's concept of force has a direct parentage in the philosophy of Leibniz.[1] This may be true enough when properly established, but the procedure of Purpus is somewhat preliminary. He begins his exposition with a long citation from *Hegel's Lectures on the History of Philosophy*, which is immediately followed by a series of quotations from two major Leibnizian sources : the *New Essays on Human Understanding* and the *New System of Nature*. Purpus assumes that these quotations, more than any rigorous analysis, can reveal the historical roots of Hegel's transitional concept. In the first passage, however, we find merely a general description of Leibniz's monadology. Perhaps the most interesting aspect of this passage lies in this that Hegel regards monads as universal entities, insisting that "universality is just simplicity in multiplicity, and therefore a simplicity which is at the same time change and motion of multiplicity".[2] Hegel then notes the connection between the idea of substance and force, but he does not give any very detailed considerations to this issue.

It can hardly be denied that there exist certain resemblances between Hegelianism and the thoughts of Leibniz. Indeed, Hegel may have brought these ideas into relation with his own phenomenological studies. However, even if one can show how the concept of force is derivable from the monadology of Leibniz, it does not follow that it was actually so derived.

In view of the transitional character of force it might be said that this

---

[1] *Zur Dialektik des Bewusstseins nach Hegel*, pp. 169-172.
[2] *Lectures on the History of Philosophy*, III, 334.

concept was probably inspired by Hegel's desire to find an explanatory category, in which the contradictory moments of perception are reconciled. This consummating relationship was long in coming, but incessant shifting of positions made it inevitable that an act of perception be looked upon as implying a distinction between what the thing is in itself and what it is for another. The perceiving subject alternately attributed to the mind the object's unity and diversity and alternately regarded the object as manifesting two opposed forms of existence, simply because the act of perceiving was bifurcated and shared between the object and consciousness. To say this, of course, is nothing more than to recognize that there is a distinction between being-for-self and being-for-another. However, by negating these one-sided notions, the subject realizes that they "essentially exist in a single unity". Or to put it in another way with Hegel : the negative result of perception "has inherently a positive significance" for the subject, for "it has established the unity of existence-for-self, and existence-for-another; in other words, absolute opposites are immediately posited as one and the same reality".[3] Thus, by stitching being-for-itself to being-for-another, Hegel has made an advance to the notion of *relation* as a condition of pure universality. "But to be in general for-self and to stand in relation to something else constitutes the very nature and meaning of that whose truth lies in being unconditionally universal".[4]

The notion of relation clarifies not only the condition of universality but also the movement of opposed elements, or, more correctly, their transition into one another. It is very important that this point should not be misunderstood. Relation by its very nature builds the bridge between unity and diversity. It constitutes the essence of the thing; so that, apart from the relation, the thing could not be understood and expressed. This suggestion gives hint as to the procedure employed by Hegel. Relation does not leave out the notion of movement, which is the activity by virtue of which a pure unity passes into diversity, and a diversity sinks back into unity. Therefore Hegel does not waste time assuring us that "the elements set up as independent pass directly over into their unity, and their unity directly into its explicit diversity, and the latter back once again into the reduction to unity. This process is what is called *Force*".[5] The necessity of self-relation to pass into relation-to-other is simply the necessity of force to manifest

---

[3] B., p. 181. *Phän.*, pp. 103-104. This is an important statement, though not really new : if there is to be a cognitional advance at all, there must be a *negative* performance of the subject.

[4] B., p. 182. *Phän.*, p. 104.

[5] B., p. 183. *Phän.*, p. 105.

itself. For force is the grasping into unity of a pattern of two aspects : one of the aspects is the *expression* of force, the second is force *proper*, that is, "force withdrawn from expressing itself and driven back into itself".[6] In other words, the concept of relation requires the concept of force as the intelligible factor synthesising the underlying active power and the external manifestations. Since force and its manifestations are inseparable, the initial concept of understanding expresses the object's unity in diversity or identity in difference.

Curiously enough, there is more than one concept having the property of embodying unity and diversity and in addition of explaining the peculiarities of the thing. Form, for example, is a concept by means of which a perceptible object may receive distinct intelligibility. On the other hand, form, perhaps more than force, is capable of explaining the principal difficulties inherent in the perceptual situation. And this is also in tune with the history of philosophy, for an impressive historical illustration is available to justify the chosen point of departure. Indeed, after Aristotle, every major philosopher had to turn his attention to form as a explanatory category peculiar to understanding. If, then, the task of understanding is to grasp things, its approach must be to penetrate their intelligibility by subsuming it under some universal concept. Thus, in order to understand things one must look for the underlying reality of which they are the sensible manifestations. But what is meant by saying that things are the sensible manifestations of the supersensible reality, if not that the reality which the sensible perfections manifest is some substantial form.

The appeal to form, however, is an appeal to a kind of conceptual evidence which has meaning only for the philosophic consciousness. The very fact that Hegel has chosen force instead of form would seem to imply that understanding must begin not from a distinctly philosophical notion, but from an artless and simple explanatory term. Hegel's purpose is not that we make some radical and unforeseen leap to a philosophical theory about things, but that progressively we grow into a generic career of understanding. Obviously, force is in accord with one's perceptual consciousness and congenial to primitive speculations about the causes of change and motion. Precisely, then, because the cause of change furnishes the primary intelligibility in the understanding of the thing, it is the concept of force which is called upon to act as a transitional concept. Though Hegel makes no effort to put the concept of force into an historical framework, it might be said that he has maneuvered himself into the ancient position of nature-philo-

[6] *Ibid.*

sophers. Understood in this way the notion of force is traceable to Anaxagoras and Empedocles, who envisaged the task of explaining physical phenomena and looked "for a force which is the cause of motion".[7] This, of course, does not involve disregarding or suppressing McTaggart's suggestion that the name of force was "taken from a conception used in empirical sciences".[8] The point is that we have here a sort of twofold reference : force is an explanatory term proper to the natural sciences of Hegel's time, but the cognitive status of the term can be apprehended only by going back to the very beginning of human thought. The initial argument of understanding, which first appears as a discussion of a purely dialectical order, rests ultimately on an observation of historical significance. What dominates the problem is the fact that the idea of force belongs to the infancy of rational understanding. Such a conclusion is most satisfactory in view of cognitive and historical exigencies of the *Phenomenology*.[9] To appreciate the importance of what is at stake we have only to remember Hegel's contention that history "is the process of becoming in terms of knowledge".[10] And if we insist on this point, it is only because we wish to stress the relation of the *Phenomenology* to history.

It is impossible to appreciate Hegel's notion of force at its true value without first determining its exact connotation. W. T. Stace, for example, insists that the term "force" is essentially metaphorical.[11] Thus, when Hegel says that the first concept of understanding is force, he does not really mean force. He simply means that the term force is used in place of another by way of suggesting a likeness between them. Though it is evident that force has many metaphorical meanings, it is not evident at all that Hegel uses it in any figurative sense. It is not necessary to press the Hegelian texts in order to find in the notion of force all that we might hope for. Rather, it is quite enough to understand them as Hegel himself did, not in the order of metaphor, but in that of direct and literal meaning. We are convinced, therefore, that when Hegel says "force" he means force and uses the term

---

[7] Wilhelm Windelband, *A History of Philosophy* (New York : Harper, 1958), I. 41.

[8] John M. E. McTaggart, *A Commentary on Hegel's Logic* (Cambridge : The University Press, 1910), p. 145.

[9] We agree with Georg Lukács that Hegel's *Phenomenology* is centered around two fundamental problems, namely : cognition and historicity. More than anyone else, perhaps, Lukács has stressed this in his book on Hegel's early work. Cf. *Der Junge Hegel* (Zürich-Wien : Europa Verlag, 1948), p. 568.

[10] B., p. 807. *Phän.*, p. 563.

[11] *The Philosophy of Hegel*, p. 206. Prof. Stace believes that this was also the view of McTaggart.

to connote a reality purely unitary as well as plural. What he asks of the notion of force is that it permit the subject to speak rationally of things without falling into pure perception. It is not likely that Hegel did anything more in this matter than set forth a general concept to be explored dialectically by the conscious subject in its rising from the inconsistencies of perception to the rational realization of self-consciousness. The importance of this, of course, lies in the subject's attempt to reconcile the assumed unity of the thing with its variety of aspects by subsuming them under the universal notion of force. Whether or not one agrees with Hegel's interpretation, one cannot fail but be impressed by the novelty of his solution to the problem of perception.

If we are to conform to the method that has guided the present work from its beginning, we must now examine in some detail the career of understanding. Let us start from Hegel's conclusion that "force driven back into itself *must* express itself; and secondly, in that expression it is still force existing within itself".[12] There is nothing paradoxical in a statement like this when we recall that force is strictly correlative with manifestation. There can be no force without manifestation, nor any manifestation without force. This first observation indicates that force, in its phenomenological structure, is not itself conceived of as something simple, but as bifurcated into distinct elements. Although understanding has left behind the dialectic of perception, the subject of rational cognition fails to remove the difficulty relating to perception. In other words, the understanding subject commits itself to conceptualization, only to end up proposing an explanatory category that consists of virtually distinct moments. Force duplicates itself : it represents union of the supersensible and the sensible, signifying that some unobservable reality expresses itself in certain sensuous manifestations. Therefore, a force which does not include any dualism is not a real force. Essential here is the relation between force as antecedent to its expressions and force as operative and exercised. Still, it is not sufficient to recognize the presence of these distinct aspects; Hegel demands a dialectical process, which is, here as elsewhere, the self-authenticated root of human cognition. That is why his emphasis on the dialectical tension within the concept of force is so insistent : force cannot reveal its nature except in "the process by which both moments get themselves fixed as independent and then cancel their independence again".[13] And such in Hegel's words is the general procedure of the subject committed to conceptualization and scientific explanation.

[12] B., p. 183. *Phän.*, p. 105.
[13] B., p. 184. *Phän.*, p. 106.

The task of the understanding subject is to explain sensible things by postulating an unmanifest force whose primary function consists in underpinning all sensuous manifestations. Starting from the experience of outward expressions, the subject immediately attempts to *understand* this experience. As soon, however, as the subject realizes that the inner nature of the thing must be explicated in terms of unobservable or "withdrawn force", the problem assumes a supersensible dimension. Now, it is possible to think what is not sensed, precisely because the subject has recourse to a purely conceptual mode of cognition. Accordingly, to say that the understanding subject seeks to postulate a withdrawn reality to explain the appearances offered us by perception is to say that the main problem confronting the subject consists in reconciling the sensible and the supersensible. The question, however, regarding the scientific explanation and reconciliation aims at a much more profound issue. Its orientation is toward the question of self-consciousness. Thus, when the subject wanders out of the dialectical wonderland of scientific explanation it had itself wrought, it is bemused by the discovery that "understanding's function of explaining furnishes in the first instance merely the description of what self-consciousness is".[14] Whatever may be the full detail of this process, it is enough for us to stress this one point : the understanding subject must by its own logic be driven to a position where it comes to recognize itself as the capacity for scientific conceptualization. In other words, to speak of self-consciousness is to speak of a mode of existence which the subject acquires when it becomes aware of its own explanatory "force". The process that lies ahead consists in submitting the concept of force to a series of analytical considerations, wherein it is viewed from contradictory aspects.

Since the concept of force establishes itself in and through consciousness, it seems that there can be no question of looking for the meaning of force outside and independently of consciousness. Thus to speak of force and its moments is to speak of conscious performance, whereby the subject confers upon it the existence and internal tension it has. Therefore, it is not surprising that, by inquiring phenomenologically into the dual structure of force, the subject comes up with the realization that "the distinction consequently exists only in thought".[15] This is, of course, an acceptable view, but one which overlooks the fact that "force is the unconditioned universal, which is in itself just what it is for something else, or which holds difference within itself — for difference is nothing else than existence-for-an-other".[16] From

---

[14] B., p. 210. *Phän.*, pp. 126-127.
[15] B., p. 183. *Phän.*, p. 105.
[16] *Ibid.*

this it is clear that, if force is truly an unconditioned universal, then it cannot be simply a notion obtained as a result of purely immanent conceptualization. Since force is in itself just what it is for another, the subject must withdraw from the position which sets up force as a reality constituted merely by thought. For force to be what it really is, its status must be understood as the independently real. In other words, force can function as force only when it is posited "as the substantial reality" without reference to consciousness. Therefore, the significance of the initial view is that it indicates the starting point of understanding and records an unsuccessful attempt to enclose force in thought. And it is precisely the unconditionally universal status of force which brings into clear light the abortive attempt to isolate force from its objective "realization".

With the insight that force has to be completely set free from thought, the subject eventually abandons the endeavor to look in consciousness for the source of dual characteristics, considering that force is "essentially self-contained" and its different moments, too, remain "subsisting each on its own account".[17] All of which brings us back to the same issue of opposition, but this time on the objective side.

Although by the act of insight force becomes reinstated as objective, the distinct aspects do not cease being distinct and opposed to each other. To put it differently : when force is understood as owing none of its characteristics to the subject, it is still grasped as bifurcated, the dualism being transferred from the subjective to the objective pole. Despite the difficulties of this abrupt transposition, it is clear that the principal discovery of the subject is thus plowed back into the object. And it is for this reason that the shift to the object is so important.

Taking as his point of departure the unitary character of force, Hegel insists that force is a whole. But if the unity of force is stressed, the different manifestations of it deteriorate into "mere forms, superficial vanishing 'moments' ".[18] This, of course, seems to leave open the possibility of cancelling the sensible aspect altogether, since to understand that it is a mere form is to know that it is really negligible. Accordingly, if one wishes to cancel the sensible, one must be ready to assume that the supersensible is directly intelligible. The direct appeal to supersensible force, however, is an appeal to a kind of reality which is inaccessible to the understanding subject — precisely because the act of understanding moves from perceptible data to their imperceptible cause. Therefore, taken independently

---

[17] B., p. 184. *Phän.*, p. 106.
[18] *Ibid.*

of its external manifestations, the supersensible source of force turns into a sort of entity without discernible properties and becomes as such totally unknowable. Because the sensible and the supersensible aspects of force can only "subsist within one unity", the subject must renounce the thesis that they are radically independent. This is doubly true, since the sensible aspect is fundamentally such as to require the supersensible for its explanation, and the supersensible aspect is fundamentally such as to appear in the sensible. Thus, the subject can reconcile these distinct aspects of force by elucidating their mutual interdependence. Instead, then, of bifurcating the concept of force, the subject's effort at reconciliation saves it from an untenable position. Indeed, the unmanifest force would have no being if it did not express itself in certain sensuous manifestations, and at the same time these manifestations would have no intelligibility if they had no basis in some non-phenomenal power.

From one point of view this can be looked upon as a conclusive discovery of the subject. But it is precisely the mutual interdependence of the sensible and the supersensible which is the unsolved problem. Admittedly, force as latent and force as operative constitute the notion of force. But this is not saying enough. The fact of interdependence as such does not explain how or why force should pass out of its latent state and become operative. As Hegel sees force, it is not completely intelligible except in terms of the notion of incitement. The reason for this is precisely that the force cannot emerge from its supersensible state unless some external agent solicits (*sollizitiert*) it. Of all the conditions required for an act of force to be possible, the first and most important is that it be provoked by some active agency. This is the central issue. Hegel's further analysis, laden with passages that are almost untranslatable, having no other aim than to put the issue into dialectical framework.

Hegel's notion of incitement seems especially construed to afford a transition from force to the play of forces, which "is what understanding has directly to do with".[19] Once it is seen that force is an expression of the passage from concealedness to unconcealedness, it is immediately evident that it has its ground in the soliciting action of another force. Such an assertion simply says that force can be awakened into activity only by another force. That aspect of force is very clear and it should not cause any ambiguity. However, if the preceding considerations tend to make us think of force as totally dependent upon another alien force, it is only because we see it as carrying no implication of reciprocal action. Now,

[19] B., p. 193. *Phän.*, p. 113.

Hegelianism is unquestionably more complicated. Therefore, if we are to understand it properly, we must also consider the view that a force which is incited into activity is the inciting agency for the other force which incited it, even though this means that we shall have afterwards to cancel our discovery by marshalling all the conceivable evidence against it.

Let us proceed then on the assumption that there are two operating forces, for "the notion of force becomes actual when resolved into two forces".[20] But to assume the existence of two forces, is to be face to face with one major issue : it is as completely impossible to reduce one of these forces to the other as it is to isolate them. The force to be one must suppress the distinction between the incited factor or the passive medium and the inciting factor or the active medium. This decision, however, entails many problems, the most important of which relates to the possibility of forfeiting the play of polar forces. This may seem insignificant, but the emergence of polarization is dialectically inevitable. The notion of both forces is the same notion, but since the negative attitude of the subject does not recognize anything lasting, it passes out of the unity into duality. "Instead of the opposition continuing to be entirely and essentially a mere moment, it appears to have escaped from the control of the unity and to have become, owing to this diremption, two quite independent forces".[21]

Having gone this far, the question arises whether these forces are radically independent. Hegel believes that they can function as forces only when apprehended as organically related, precisely because each has "to get its position purely through the other".[22] The act of incitement is the determination exercised by each force on the other, since the incited force implies the action of the inciting force, and the inciting force itself requires the action of the force it produces. The gist of the issue seems to be this : a provoked force depends for its being on the provoking force, and the provoking force acquires its position from the one it eventually provokes. Different forces are what they are only through their mutual contact with each other. What is more, the full reality of the force includes whatever it actually presupposes. Thus, for the sake of specifying a force as inciting, the subject of understanding must ascribe to it incited character. What is presented as inciting must be understood as incited, for it can be said that to act is constantly to be acted upon. The reason for this is that the individuality of the force lies in a special togetherness of activity and passivity bound

[20] B., p. 188. *Phän.*, p. 109.
[21] B., p. 186. *Phän.*, p. 107.
[22] B., p. 188. *Phän.*, p. 109.

to each other by reciprocal determination. Their nature consists in each being through the other and each ceasing to be what it really is through the other. In all this, however, the existential independence of force has been undermined, since its polar aspects have "no substances of their own which could support and maintain them".[23] To speak of force, then, is not to speak of a mode of substantial existence; rather it is to speak of the *concept* of force viewed under the aspect of universality.[24]

As we saw, the efforts of the understanding subject were intended as an apprehension "of the true being of things", but they succeeded only in establishing a "mediated relation" to the supersensible ground of force. In other words, since the inner being of things "does not exist immediately for consciousness", the subject can reach it only "through the intervening play of forces".[25] In one sense, then, the work of understanding is no other than an inferential act, whose premises are the imperceptible nature of things and the conceptualizing performance of the subject, and "its middle term the sphere of appearance",[26] the sphere of appearance signifying in this context the same as the play of forces. Since the work of the subject on this level is to consist for Hegel in apprehending the supersensible through the sensible, it can be looked upon as "the relation of understanding to the inner world through mediation".[27] Now, this sort of relation we can qualify as "negative", not in a pejorative sense, but in the sense that it is a mediating act. It is precisely the mediation of the play of forces which brings into clear focus the true significance of negativity. Considered in this way negativity is something more than a mere "vacuum that elicits notion".[28]

Once again, then, the importance of negativity is brought to the fore. It is to be noticed that the negativity was never intended by Hegel to be "the gap and the tension between the subject and the object".[29] It cannot

---

[23] B., p. 189. *Phän.*, p. 110.

[24] "The true nature of force thus remains merely the thought or idea of force; the moments in its realization, its substantial independence and its process, rush, without let or hindrance, together into one single undivided unity, a unity which is not force withdrawn into itself (for this is merely one of those moments), but is its notion *qua* notion". B., p. 189. *Phän.*, p. 110.

[25] B., p. 190. *Phän.*, p. 110.

[26] B., p. 191. *Phän.*, p. 111.

[27] B., p. 193. *Phän.*, p. 113.

[28] Helmut Rehder, "Of Structure and Symbol : The Significance of Hegel's *Phenomenology* for Literary Criticism", *A Hegel Symposium* (Austin : The University of Texas, 1962), p. 129.

[29] *Ibid.*

be reiterated too often that negativity is the distinguishing mark of the subject. As we have pointed out before, the subject derives its priority over the object from negativity. The subject is not merely a substantial bearer of consciousness; it is a negative being, who recognizes only one principle : to reject every particular viewpoint, and knows only one activity : to be constantly on the move. The subject destroys every conceivable position of consciousness, not for the sake of destruction, but for the sake of establishing a new mode of cognition. This becomes manifest when different moments turn "directly into their opposite, the 'one' changing immediately into the universal, and vice versa".[30] "But this very unrest is the self",[31] the self being too undetermined to be easily satisfied. Exemplifying the dynamic character of the subject, negativity serves as the discoverer of new conscious attitudes. This is precisely what Hegel insists upon — but with relentless and intricate analysis. Therefore, it is only when the performance of the subject is cast in the form of a negation that the question of its dialectical progress becomes relevant and necessary. This is particularly important, since only in the light of the subject's unrest can we understand that the phenomenological discourse is an instrument of negative analysis, leading to "a metaphysics of subjectivity".[32]

As regards further development of understanding, to which we must turn next, the action of the negative furnishes the additional characterization

---

[30] B., p. 190. *Phän.*, p. 111.

[31] B., p. 83. *Phän.*, p. 22.

To characterize more precisely the unrest of the subject we can add Iwan Iljin's illuminating remarks : "Das Subject ist das Prinzip der schaffenden Unruhe : es 'bewegt sich', 'bezieht sich auf sich' in negativer Weise, und "erzeugt' sich in dieser Re-flexion. Es ist 'das Insichlebende' und sein Leben ist sein 'eigenes Thun'; es vollzieht in sich die 'dialektische Bewegung', setzt in sich selbst Widersprüche und 'vertieft' sich dadurch 'in sich selbst'. *Die Philosophie Hegels als kontemplative Gotteslehre* (Bern : A. Francke, 1946), p. 186.

[32] "Therefore with Hegel too the final result is only a formal philosophy of essence, which cannot rise beyond essence to Being, and form its conceptions from within Being. But then, since essence does not receive its foundation from Being, it can receive it only from subjectivity, understood now in an absolute sense. Thus it remains a metaphysics of subjectivity". Emerich Coreth, "Dialectic of Performance and Concept", *Continuum*, 3 (1964), p. 449.

Still, this view of Hegelianism as "a formal philosophy of essence, which cannot rise beyond essence to Being", ignores the existential dimension of Hegel's thought. For Hegel, to hold something to exist is not simply an act of positing essences, but a rational performance of the subject which makes existence thought and thought existing. In being thought, reality becomes fully, completely, and perfectly real. Hegel by no means implies that reality is an invention or construction of the subject.

of what the subject discovers in the inner nature of things by the aid of the play of forces. One thing of great importance here is the attempt to conceptualize the sphere of appearance or the sensible. Although the supersensible and the sensible are bound to each other by mutual implications, the first depends for its possibility and content on the mediating agency of the second. Thus, if the supersensible is for consciousness "the nothingness of appearance, and positively the naked universal",[33] the reason is that "its very characteristic lies in being *beyond* consciousness".[34] This idea of inwardness, to speak in Hegel's words, "suits those who say that the inner being of things cannot be known".[35] Though he does not mention Kant directly, it is very clear that Kant is among those Hegel has in mind when he speaks of the possibility of considering what is not known. According to Hegel, however, there is no knowledge to be had of the inner world, not because scientific understanding is restricted to appearances, but "because in the void there is nothing known".[36] Still, in accordance with Hegel's positive and creative function of negativity, which he never retracts, this "simple and bare beyond" must necessarily receive further modification. What induces consequent correction of the "naked universal" is the discovery, made in the process of the negative performance of the subject, that the relation of conceptualizing intelligence to the inner being of things is "its own process, by which the inner world will be found to receive fullness of content".[37] It is of course to be expected that major terms of understanding should here as elsewhere prove so variable. And so, as Hegel contends, the subject is called upon to dispel its previous distinctions such as they appeared through the play of forces :

There is thus neither force nor inciting and being incited to action, nor the characteristic of being a stable medium and a unity reflected into self, there is neither a particular which is something on its own account, nor are there diverse opposites. What is found in this flux of thoroughgoing change is merely difference as universal difference, or difference into which the various opposites have been resolved. This difference as universal, consequently, is what constitutes the ultimate simple element in that play of forces, and is the resultant truth of that process. It is the *Law* of Force.[38]

Hegel introduces distinctions as though they were permanent insights,

---

[33] B., p. 191. *Phän.*, p. 112.
[34] B., p. 192. *Phän.*, p. 112.
[35] *Ibid.*
[36] *Ibid.*
[37] B., p. 193. *Phän.*, p. 113.
[38] B., pp. 194-195. *Phän.*, p. 114.

and then points out that they are reducible to identity. It is as if the work of the understanding subject were essentially futile. Such a performance of the subject may seem paradoxical, but, in fact, it should not cause any ambiguity, for Hegelian distinctions have no intelligibility except as inseparable correlatives. The details Hegel examines are subtle and tedious, some appearing quite arbitrary and others totally insignificant. Nevertheless the main issue treated is of permanent cognitive importance. Fundamental here is the transition from force to the law of force. The significant outcome of the difficulties which have thus emerged may be conceived as the correction or reconstruction of the notion of force. Therefore, when the force vanishes as the concept expressing the sensible aspect of things requiring for its basis some supersensible source, its place is taken by the law of force, a more universal category signifying a relatively new mode of explanation.

One cannot escape the conviction that the law of force is force envisaged from the viewpoint of stability.[39] But once the law is recognized as having characteristics similar to force, the question arises whether the passage from the one to the other yields any consequences or whether their difference is really essential. Quite obviously, there is a definite advantage to be gained from the law of force, for the stable (*beständig*) presentment of unstable appearance, which is here the central concept, is an indispensable means in relation to the activity of the subject engaged in scientific explanation. Another advantage which Hegel feels he has gained by this negative and reconciliatory procedure is that it permits him to retreat from the notion of the supersensible nature of things, without abandoning the subject's determination to understand appearances, which manifest themselves through the play of forces. In order, therefore, that the notion of force become an explanatory category, it was necessary to modify it by some principle governing the constancy of appearance. Thus the play of forces finds its corrective in the law of force. No wonder then that knowledge of appearance is said by Hegel to be realized by knowledge of the laws governing constancy of the play of forces. In other words, the significant result of the play of forces is the emergence of the subject's capacity to conceptualize "the absolute flux of the world of appearance" as obeying an invariant law. By stabilizing fluctuations in the order of phenomenal forces, the law of force provides the subject with an invariant model of the existing realm.

---

[39] "In other words, negation is an essential moment of the universal; and negation or mediation in what is universal is universal difference. This difference is expressed in the law, which is the stable presentment or picture of unstable appearance". B., p. 195. *Phän.*, pp. 114-115.

If this is so, then the law of force will become the foundation of all scientific-
ally valid cognition unless the notion of law, as every other notion, contains
within itself incorrigible difficulties. The only problem, then, is whether
the law of force can adequately perform its explanatory function.

Turning his attention to the law of force, Hegel points out that this concept
"is indeed the truth for understanding".[40] Hegel felt that, in discovering
the law of force, he had attained the nerve of understanding, though he
was well aware that the notion itself should undergo a radical change.

Having refused to accept anything but the presence of the simple conception of law, the subject cannot escape the suspicion that this datum is
not so univocal as initially understood. It is not surprising, then, that the
subject should find in it the defects of variance, relativity, plurality, and
distinction. First of all, the subject observes that the original conception
of law fails to express "the fullness of the world of appearance".[41] The
main reason for this is that the reconciliation of the supersensible and
appearance has not been achieved. Appearance retains and continues to
exhibit the element of difference which is inadequately expressed by the law.
In other words, there is a lack of correspondence between the law and the
realm of appearance which the law purports to explain. Indeed, no law can
be completely explanatory until it exhibits the specific determinateness that
belongs to particular appearances, but no universal law is ever concerned
with the particular forms of appearance. Therefore, the law must be relative
to the realm of appearance it pretends to conceptualize, so much so that
"under ever-varying circumstances the law has an ever-varying actual
existence".[42]

The explanatory function of the law is defective, precisely because of the
law's indeterminate character. On the other hand, is it obvious that law
conceived as determinate cannot by any means be a universal law. Insofar
as it is determined by specific conditions, it cannot be called universal,
but since it must be applicable to different cases, it cannot be a single law.
Rather, it must contain within itself "an indeterminate plurality of laws".[43]
These remarks are important since they explain Hegel's distinction between
a universal law and a determinate law. The principal defect of the general
law lies in its indeterminacy, whereas the defect of the specific law
consists in this that it contains a multiplicity of laws. That a determinate law

[40] B., p. 195. *Phän.*, p. 115.
[41] *Ibid.*
[42] B., p. 196. *Phän.*, p. 115.
[43] *Ibid.*

is not universal might very well be disputed, and the fact that there are many such laws does not preclude them from being universal. However, when these determinate laws are conceived as one law, they necessarily lose their identity and specific character. "The unification of all laws ... expresses no further content than just the bare concept of the law itself, a concept which is therein set down as existing".[44]

The outcome of all this confusing and ever-shifting analysis is relatively plain : the emergence of two opposed categories of explanation as equally defective. Either the possibility of explanation pertains to the determinative laws, in which case their multiplicity "contradicts the principle of understanding",[45] or else it belongs to a universal law, in which case the explanation becomes abstract and superficial. This contains in a nutshell the main difficulties of law as an instrument of scientific explanation. All of which would seem to indicate that the subject has reached a drastic dilemma. Though this is a real impasse, it is not until the negativity of the subject had been fully exercised, that the explanatory effort of understanding could begin to bear tautological results.

Up to this point the career of the subject might well be looked on as an explicitation of ambiguity that belongs either to law as such or its conception. It is rather striking that, having established the superficial character of the universal law, Hegel should submit it to further analysis. Still, if we remember that the vital nerve of understanding "is the inherently universal unity",[46] the logical priority must pertain to the universal law. In other words, since the movement from particularity to universality is the main trend of the initial stages of consciousness, the understanding subject must continue its movement towards universality. Taking, then, as the point of departure the universal law, the subject can turn its attention to the content of the law, especially to the inherent claim that it "gives expression to universal reality as such".[47] This is but another way of saying that in assigning to law an explanatory function, the subject "thereby declares all reality to be in its very nature conformed to law".[48] It takes but little effort to realize, however, that the subject simply mistakes the conception of the law for the law itself. It is in this sense that the problem is to be understood, and this much is clear. What is less easy to understand, however,

[44] *Ibid.*
[45] *Ibid.*
[46] *Ibid.*
[47] B., p. 196. *Phän.*, p. 116.
[48] B., p. 197. *Phän.*, p. 116.

is Hegel's contention that the conception of law turns against the law as such.[49] In one sense this does not imply more than a distinction between the determinate laws, which depend on different sensible contents to which they apply, and the conception of law whose meaning consists in absorbing differences, and in such a way that it at the same time excludes specificity.

The law is thereby present in a twofold form. In one case it is there as law in which the differences are expressed as independent moments; in the other it is in the form of a simple withdrawal into itself, which again can be called Force, but in the sense not of repressed force [spoken of above], but force in general or the concept of force, an abstraction which absorbs the distinctions involved in what attracts and is attracted.[50]

However, when this statement is tested by the negative standards of the subject, difference and identity are found to be bound to each other by mutual implication. Either the different moments of the law are indifferent to each other, or else the universal law is indifferent to the division into distinct moments. "The distinction is, then, in both cases no distinction of an inherent or essential kind".[51] If, however, we are to judge whether interdependence of difference and identity has any real significance, we cannot be content with pointing out the details of the dialectical process; we must try to grasp Hegel's cardinal intent. Now, what Hegel is attempting with this last dialectical position is not so much to establish the mutual dependence of difference and identity as to place a steppingstone to self-consciousness.

The reason why Hegel did not disclose his intention at this stage of understanding is no doubt the same as his radical refusal to rest phenomenological ideas upon specific presuppositions and to introduce them ahead of time. In Hegel's eyes, the possibility of establishing the self-consciousness of the subject is nullified unless understanding enters the blind alley of tautological explanation. Once the tautological process is recognized as bearing fruitless results, the step to the realization of self-consciousness is not a long one, for in the repetitious performance the subject finds itself "in direct communion with itself" (in unmittelbarem Selbstgespräche mit sich).[52]

Now, Hegel would not establish the transition from consciousness to self-consciousness by asserting the inner tendency of understanding to pass over into self-certainty; he would simply let the subject continue

[49] Ibid.
[50] B., pp. 197-198. Phän., pp. 116-117.
[51] B., p. 200. Phän., p. 118.
[52] B., p. 210. Phän., p. 127.

the activity of differentiation and unification. Thus, when the subject cancels the distinctions present in law, the unity of force is set up, leading to a new distinction of force and law. But once the law is recognized as having characteristics similar to force, it becomes evident that this new distinction is no real distinction. Let us accept therefore that ways of establishing distinctions turn into ways of establishing identity. It should be clear, too, that taken in conjunction with identity, distinctions appear as touched by unity, while taken in conjunction with distinctions, identity appears as specified by determination. Still, the importance of all this is not so much in creating and annulling distinctions as in the realization that the activity of the understanding subject is essentially tautological, for "it really says nothing at all, but merely repeats the same thing over again".[53] From here on, the *Phenomenology* appears essentially a grotesque explanation and the philosophical problem is to indicate its abortive character. It is hardly surprising, then, that the subject, when hard pressed to continue an activity so incorrigibly repetitious and seemingly arbitrary, becomes engaged in the description of a new supersensible world which at every point runs counter to the first supersensible world. Whatever may be the full detail of this drastic inversion, it is enough for us to remember this one point : the subject finds itself enmeshed in the net of its own operations which bear meaningless, if not ridiculous, results. Crucial here is that scientific understanding has reached a radical impasse. But here as elsewhere in the *Phenomenology*, the subject finds a way out. To reflect upon tautological performance, thus seeking anchorage in the act of thought, this is what the subject must now do, in order to escape from the impasse brought about by fruitless redescriptions. In Hegel's eyes, the recognition of tautology prepares the ground for a fresh advance, precisely because the subject thus seizes the opportunity of turning the attention on itself.

It is impossible to insist too much upon this truth because it determines the transition from consciousness proper to self-consciousness. According to Hegel, the subject engaged in the explanatory work seems to be occupied with a variety of independent objects, such as electricity, distance, velocity, attraction etc., but actually it is busied merely with itself. Until the subject recognizes these objects as constituting "the content of the moments of

---

[53] B., p. 201. *Phän.*, pp. 119-120. In this process, understanding progressively negates each successive attempt to grasp and to explain the objective world, thus arriving at the idea of the inverted world. Consequently, a certain disappointment sets in as an important preparation for a fresh advance. Cf. Joseph C. Flay, "Hegel's 'inverted world' ". *Review of Metaphysics*, XXIII (1970), 662-678.

the [explanatory] process",[54] it is precluded from becoming self-conscious. Prerequisite for self-consciousness dialectically marshalled is an introvert subject, its activity being the gradual process of self-examination. Introversion, as Hegel sees it, is a propensity of the subject for realizing the "reflectedness into self".[55] Now, what inspires the subject to practice self-examination and become introversive is the explanatory performance grown tautological. To say that an explanation presents itself with tautological character to consciousness is to say that it has been constituted as such by the subject. As soon as the possibility of tautological work is seen to depend on mind's activity, the subject proceeds to a new level of consciousness. It is for this reason that tautological activity is so important. In apprehending the repetitious nature of explanation, the subject becomes conscious of its capacity to explain. To be sure, consciousness of an explanatory effort grown fruitless is "indeed itself necessarily self-consciousness, reflectedness into self, consciousness of self in its otherness".[56] If, then, we assume with Hegel that an unsuccessful explanation renders the subject self-conscious, the problem of transition is solved. Thus, self-consciousness comes out of concealment and provides a basis for the reflective career of the subject.

Further light is thrown upon Hegel's procedure of effecting the transition from consciousness to self-consciousness when we consider the final attempt of the subject to distinguish what is hardly distinguishable. Thus, when the subject tries to differentiate itself from its own conscious performance, it cannot escape the conviction that this distinction has no validity. The subject thrusts itself away from its essential act, but this which is distinguished cannot be recognized as really distinct, because the conscious subject and its cognitive operation are apprehended as inseparable correlatives. This would seem to imply that the act of differentiation itself depends for its possibility on the self-identical nature of the subject. Therefore, no rational attempt at differentiation is possible unless the subject recognizes itself as the self-same being. And this is the same as saying that the subject to be able to distinguish and cancel its distinction must enjoy consciousness of being self-identical. With this as a starting point Hegel can then say that self-consciousness is "a distinguishing of what is undistinguished".[57] It is precisely here that the exact meaning of "consciousness of self in its

---

[54] B., p. 200. *Phän.*, p. 127.
[55] B., p. 211. *Phän.*, p. 182.
[56] *Ibid.*
[57] *Ibid.*

otherness" in Hegel's thought comes out. What he is affirming here is a penetrating insight, which discloses that the subject, being unable to differentiate itself from its own operation, unveils merely itself in the very act of differentiation. This also brings to light the fact that "consciousness of a thing" which characterizes all previous attitudes of consciousness finds its corrective in self-consciousness. What lends profound significance to this issue is the elevation of consciousness to the reflective mode of cognition. With self-consciousness as transparent awareness, subjectivity enters "into the native land of truth",[58] for "being 'in-itself' and being 'for an other' are here the same".[59]

At the end of this attempt to clarify Hegel's notion of subjectivity in the sphere of consciousness proper, we must note that the actual career of understanding is not altogether in accord with the conception of the subject as endowed with an unrestricted capacity for conceptualization and explaining. Although the development of the understanding subject is extremely intricate, dynamic, and dialectical, it is in fact limited to a few general concepts. Possibly it is right to attribute rigidity and fixity to the "faculty" of understanding, but it is neither possible nor desirable to limit it to the concept of force and its immediate correlatives. This fact is important enough to require our attention a little longer.

If we are to grasp the incompleteness of the understanding subject, we must see it in terms of the goal Hegel set for it in the *Preface*. It is here that we first get the impression that "understanding always takes a survey of the whole".[60] If the action of understanding is to establish a "survey of the whole" and a "table of contents" relating to abstract notions, then this would seem to imply that understanding is more than an analysis of force and laws. Judging from the numerous passages devoted to this problem, we may conclude that understanding is the agency of conceptualization. Therefore, we should recognize its presence in all abstract notions and ideas. For the abstract aspect of thought or the action of separating opposed characteristics is said by Hegel to be the "exercise of the force of understanding, the most astonishing and greatest of all powers, or rather the absolute power".[61] In holding this view he implies that understanding cannot be confined to a limited set of concepts: the operation of understanding consists in determining opposites as mutually exclusive and in

---

[58] B., p. 219. *Phän.*, p. 134.
[59] B., p. [218]. *Phän.*, p. [133].
[60] B., p. 112. *Phän.*, p. 45.
[61] B., p. 93. *Phän.*, p. 29.

raising them all "to the level of universality in general".[62] We might say that understanding follows the Aristotelian laws of logic, seeking precision and distinction in everything it encounters. Small wonder, then, that understanding leads to rigid and abstract notions, tending rather to promote than to eliminate the mutual independence of all our ideas.

It is rather remarkable that having spoken so much about understanding and its abstract conceptualization in the *Preface,* Hegel did not take the trouble to explain the conditions of the "schematizing process" or to propose a "table of contents" of universal concepts. However, it seems clear enough that such a table of contents is indispensable for further phenomenological development, for only when all mutually exclusive abstractions have been clearly established, will it be possible to grasp them as mutually complementary and interdependent.

Although it would be logically correct to ask for a complete elaboration of abstract concepts, we do not believe that its absence invalidates either the phenomenological procedure or its conclusions. The whole question is whether Hegel has succeeded in establishing the firm steppingstone to self-consciousness. Now, it seems that the real reason which mediates the passage from consciousness to self-consciousness is not this or that specific concept, this or that set of mutually exclusive abstractions, but the subject's propensity to move from the extroversive viewpoint to introversive viewpoint. The introversion of the subject is indeed the road leading to self-consciousness. This problem, however, is the objective of a new chapter.

---

[62] B., p. 94. *Phän.,* p. 30.

Part Three : The Self-Conscious Subject

CHAPTER VII

THE RISE OF THE SELF-CONSCIOUS SUBJECT

The impact of understanding and its explicitation by reflective consciousness can be found in some form or other in practically all philosophical systems which arose after Aristotle. Quite frequently, however, the contrast between consciousness and self-consciousness has been overlooked, so that these different forms of consciousness were simply taken to express two distinct aspects of the same act. The first philosopher to recognize their fusion and distinction was Hegel. And his intention was to show that self-consciousness grows dialectically out of consciousness and becomes a species of cognition in its own right.[1] For this reason alone Hegel's effort deserves the most serious attention.

The importance of self-consciousness can hardly be overestimated, for it exemplifies the decisive step in the self-realization of the knowing mind.[2] Judging from the numerous works devoted to Hegel's notion of self-consciousness, we may easily assume that it constitutes the principal clue to his philosophy of subjectivity and we cannot but wonder why self-conscious-

[1] Cf. Henry B. Smith, *The Transition from "Bewusstsein" to "Selbstbewusstsein" in Hegel's Phenomenology of Mind* (Pulaski, Va. : Press of B. D. Smith & Brothers, 1909). Although the purpose of this special study is to show how self-consciousness grows out of consciousness proper, the explanation of transition is merely a sort of paraphrase in English of the opening chapters of Hegel's *Phenomenology*.

[2] "La conscience de soi est immédiatement désir, et l'objet hors d'elle est seulement l'objet de son désir. La connaissance est ici identique à la vie, et le vivant qui désire ne considère pas la chose desirée comme étrangère par essence". Jean Hyppolite, *Études sur Marx et Hegel* (Paris : M. Rivière, 1955), p. [11].

Hyppolite, like Hegel himself, introduces the experience of desire too abruptly. Desire is one of the most important acts in the constitution of self-consciousness and at the same time one of the most difficult to relate to subjectivity. Without discussing it in greater detail at this point we might note that the self-conscious subject is in the state of desire simply because the unity of consciousness with itself is not yet fully realized and because the awareness of disunity invites and generates the "state of desire".

ness has taken on such an importance in the mind of the author and his commentators. At any rate, the doctrine of self-consciousness is worth stopping over long enough, if not completely to grasp its meaning and implications, at least to see its significance for the reality of subjectivity. As Hegel sees self-consciousness, it depends for its possibility on the coalescence of subject and object. Only thus can we understand Hegel's contention that self-certainty exemplifies the closest intimacy of the subject with the object in which the previous "opposition is removed, and oneness or identity with itself established".[3]

Whenever Hegel speaks of consciousness, he emphasizes two things : the dual structure of the conscious act and its immanence. No one, of course, can deny that every act of awareness involves the duality of subject and object, for consciousness is always consciousness of something. Now, to be conscious of something is to be conscious of an object. But as long as there is question of object, one usually adds that this object exists independently of the mind. As a result, it is no longer possible to assert that consciousness is pure interiority, absolutely with itself and wrapped up in itself. However, when one reads how Hegel describes consciousness, it becomes evident why he is accused of immanentism and radical idealism. For Hegel never maintains that all consciousness is consciousness of something which is not consciousness itself.

The meaning of this statement becomes somewhat clearer if we consider that Hegel's object is not an independent reality, for such a reality implies that the subject and its operations are left out of it. Even a casual examination of any act of consciousness will reveal that the subject is not able to think of an object without conscious performance. This is no more than to say that it is not possible independently of consciousness to make a meaningful affirmation regarding an object. Accordingly, the object can be said to presuppose a conscious relation, in the sense that it is impossible to know something while removing the cognitive act itself. In holding this view Hegel implies that the object is always considered from the standpoint of consciousness and this standpoint itself is constantly changing and shifting. Although it is indisputable that the object reveals itself only in and through the cognitive performance of the subject, it may well be doubted that to be aware of the object is to do away with its ontological independence. Thus, the crucial problem confronting Hegel is whether consciousness of object can be wedded to self-certainty without suppressing the ontological autonomy of the object itself.

[3] B., p. 220. *Phän.*, p. 135.

From the very beginning to the end of his philosophical career, Hegel insisted that everything about which a conscious predication is made is, by this very fact, an object. The object is always necessary to make possible its conscious affirmation. With this it is possible to say that the very nature of the cognitive act requires that the subject and the knowable datum remain distinct as well as united. Every cognitive act implies that the object enjoys a certain intimacy with the subject, for without this correlation consciousness would be precluded.

In knowledge, which Hegel calls sense-certainty, the duality of subject and object is incorrigibly radical. Making an object on this plane means isolating it from the subject, making it into something which is an object and nothing but an object. Therefore in sense-certitude the object least of all finds itself in the conscious subject. In his *Propädeutik*, written in Nurnberg, Hegel asserts that the exclusive object of sense-certainty is the *external* object.[4] But if this is so, in affirming the external object, the subject cannot but affirm the object's independence. In other words, the awareness of the object's externality is awareness of its "outer" mode of existence. However, since it is impossible to express and to specify an external object without relating it to consciousness, what the subject recognizes as external and independent is but a content of consciousness.

Perhaps the phenomenologist cannot escape making reality an object in the phenomenological sense of the word, just as the knower cannot escape making the datum known an immanent content of cognition. But the danger of phenomenological objectification is that it never is merely phenomenological, just as the danger of logical objectification is that it is never merely logical. Both of them carry ontological implications and presuppositions. Critical realism overcomes the objectifying scheme precisely by pointing out these ontological presuppositions. To say that an affirmation of objectivity is merely phenomenological is to say that really and objectively it is merely phenomenological. However, it is quite impossible to suppose that all affirmations are *merely* phenomenological.[5] Perhaps it is not enough to say that every phenomenological assertion implies objectivity — since that is merely a declaration of presupposition — somehow it must be shown that knowledge is a mode of existence, "a mode of placing oneself outside

---

[4] "Das einfache sinnliche Bewusstsein ist die unmittelbare Gewissheit von einem äusserlichen Gegenstande". *Sämtliche Werke*, Jubiläumsausgabe, ed. Glockner, Bd. III : *Philosophische Propädeutik, Gymnasialreden und Gutachten über den Philosophie-Unterricht*, (3rd ed., 1949), III, 103.

[5] Cf. Bernard Lonergan, "Metaphysics as Horizon", *Gregorianum*, 44 (1963) 309.

oneself and with the reality which is not consciousness itself".[6] It must be shown that an object is both a content of thought and a real reference point of affirmation and not necessarily such as to meet at all points the requirements of the subject.

In the eyes of Hegel, the dialectical process and its structure provide no basis for contrast and connection between phenomenological and metaphysical objectivity. According to him, the subject operative through consciousness is a being-with-objectivity. This statement, of course, can easily be misunderstood, for Hegel was never impressed by the view that consciousness is first separated from reality and then enters into contact with it by means of sensuous impressions. By phenomenological analysis is understood, not a study of some independent realm of existence, but an explicitation of the cognitive performance in terms of the uninterrupted sequence. Therefore Hegel would be willing to admit that all knowledge is subjective if his interpreter did not assume that in the explicitation of cognitive operation truth is surrendered to the arbitrary determination of the subject. An object is an object only because it has been apprehended by the subject. Still, even on the initial levels of consciousness Hegel's notion of objectivity is under a measure of immanence that is quite logical when one decides to remain within the reflexive sphere, but is to be removed when one is concerned with that which is not consciousness itself. If consciousness is said never to be consciousness of that which is not consciousness but always consciousness of that which constitutes consciousness, it is no longer possible to break through the immanence of the phenomenological performance and move onto the ontological plane of the object.

Be that as it may, sense-certainty helps to illustrate the radical but intolerable opposition between subject and object. Obviously, if the subject had completed its development in sensuous knowledge, there would be no need for perception and understanding that stamp the stages of cognitive progress with unity and universality. But though perception and understanding are indispensable steps and though they, too, collapse under the weight of the results obtained from them, it is not until the radical dualism had been eliminated, that the authentic certainty could begin to bear fruit. In order, however, that the certitude of things become a certitude of self, it was necessary to move from extroversion to introversion, that is, from consciousness ignoring itself in favor of its objects to consciousness that loses sight of external objects in favor of itself.

---

[6] William A. Luijpen, *Existential Phenomenology* (Pittsburgh : Duquesne University Press, 1960), p. 92.

Since it is necessary for consciousness to lose sight of itself in order that there be *objects* for it, it is also necessary for the same consciousness to grasp itself in order that there be *certainty* for it. Nothing is here so important as the shift to the subject. Now, two things, so it seems, have contributed to such a shift. The first is the activity of understanding growing conscious of its tautological explanation. The second factor that has contributed to the shift is the insight into the fact that understanding itself presupposes a conscious subject. These two references allow consciousness to outrun itself by recognizing the possibility of reflection and thus becoming self-conscious. In other words, the recognition that understanding and the understood are actually distinguished and identified by one and the same subject opens up the possibility of reflection. With this in mind we can focus our attention on the importance of self-certainty (*der Gewissheit seiner selbst*) and its fundamental features.

Gerhard Schmidt calls the introduction to the fourth chapter of the *Phenomenology* "the most difficult and the most fundamental part of the work".[7] It is true, of course, that in its original statement the section on self-certainty is difficult. Hegel's position is unusual; his terminology is neither familiar nor completely intelligible. His thought, as can be expected, develops in a dialectical order, but the dialectical structure is very complex and not easy to follow. It is also true that here more than elsewhere in the *Phenomenology* dialectical relations are more or less circular and abstract. But, then, a number of similar factors contribute to the obscurity of every other part of the work. And even if these formidable obstacles were removed, many passages of the work would still remain difficult because of the new philosophical ideas that they express.

Quite apart from the major difficulty it may cause the self-certainty is of interest and importance in its own right. And it has always been recognized that with self-certainty as transparent "reflexion into self", the subject emerges as the measure determinative of all objectivity and enters "into the native land of truth".[8] When we add to this Schmidt's assurance that at this level the concept of the subject is adequately equipped for expressing the objective pole of knowledge, we can say that the object is really what the subject conceives it to be. With this insight, the accent shifts from the distinction of subject and object regarded as external to each other to the distinction of subject and object conceived as immanent in the same conscious being. The very least that can be said is that the object ceases

---

[7] *Hegel in Nürnberg* (Tübingen : Max Niemeyer, 1960), p. 205.
[8] B., p. 219. *Phän.*, p. 134.

to be something radically "other"; it is not just any external thing, but an intimate entity within the same conscious reality. In Hegel's own words : "Self-consciousness is reflexion out of the bare being that belongs to the world of sense and perception, and is essentially the return out of otherness".[9]

Yet, there may be still some doubt as to just how significant all this is. But whether or not one accepts Schmidt's position that self-certainty constitutes the most important chapter in the career of the subject — and it is evidently not unanimous among the Hegelian scholars [10] — one cannot fail to appreciate its significance for subjectivity. For the characteristic feature of self-consciousness viewed as a distinct mode of knowledge lies in the subject's unquestionable primacy over the object. The importance of the chapter, then, is not so much in the agreement of the concept with the object as in the realization that the subject is the entity determinative of all that can rightfully claim objectivity.[11]

Still, it is not sufficient to recognize the importance of self-certainty, for Hegel demands a detailed unveiling of its content. Only in terms of dialectic can the subject's predominance over the object escape the danger of being conceived as an arbitrary construction. Furthermore, the spirit of the subject does not permit generalization, much less demand stagnation. Once conscious of itself, the subject can never again let itself be ignored; rather, it must move to a higher level of self-knowledge where subjectivity will appear in forms richer and more perfect. Now beyond the need to appeal to external objects, Hegel sees the subject faced with the heaviest pressures to explicitate its own conception of itself.[12] This is but another way of saying that the secret destiny of the subject is its complete self-realization, and this goal is to be persistently pursued.

---

[9] *Ibid.*

[10] A. Kojève, for example, believes that the most important chapter of the *Phenomenology* is "Independence and Dependence of Self-Consciousness : Lordship and Bondage". See his *Hegel : Eine Vergegenwärtigung seines Denkens* (Stuttgart : W. Kohlhammer, 1958), p. 45 ff.

[11] This comes down to an assertion that subjectivity is the principle of objectivity, precisely because self-certainty alone can guarantee the objective truth. As Wilhelmine Drescher puts it : "... Selbstbewusstsein allein die Wahrheit der Dingheit ist". *Die dialektische Bewegung des Geistes in Hegels Phänomenologie* (Speyer : Pilger, 1937), p. 74.

[12] By suppressing the opposition between subject and external object, Hegel sees the possibility of identifying consciousness and being. In being thought, the object reveals itself as a truly objective reality; it becomes real in the unqualified sense of the word. In achieving this decisive viewpoint Hegel finally resolved the major problem of the nature of objective subjectivity.

What is characteristic of self-certainty is that the subject is capable of self-differentiation : I am I (*Ich bin Ich*).[13] Quite evidently, the starting point of the new dialectic is essentially tautological, but it leads to what Hegel considers the very heart of self-certainty, namely the notion of desire and life. The process, however, is neither clear nor does it seem to be necessary. Hegel seems to have been unwilling or unable to write down a sustained intelligible account of what he believed to constitute the content of the transitory dialectic he attempted to describe. So the interpreter is obliged to reconstruct this by the contextual hints which complement the few general statements of a positive nature. Now, it seems clear enough that the tautological point of departure (I am I) is not a tautology of impasse. It arises on account of a conflict between consciousness of things and self-consciousness, between the subject's awareness of its objects and the subject's self-awareness. As we consider these two modes of consciousness that are inseverably related, we shall see Hegel's position on otherness or objectivity shift from independence and distinction to dependence and identity.

Let us begin by saying that for self-consciousness the other, exemplified by the predicate of the proposition "*Ich bin Ich*", is a distinct moment, but only as related to the unity of self-consciousness with itself. Without otherness nothing is known, but without consciousness of otherness self-awareness would be precluded. Pursuing this further, we shall realize that the other of consciousness must be regarded by the self-conscious subject as having an apparent independence. As we recall, otherness and independence were formerly conceived by consciousness as mutually implicative. Thus, one could say with perfect consistency that to be aware of the object as something other is to affirm its independence. However, the subject grown introvertive and reflective can easily grasp that independence presupposes dependence. But this is no more than to say that every object, precisely as object, depends on a reflective act of the subject. Whatever be the nature of the dependence involved, it is ultimately the "reflection into self" which constitutes the very objectivity of that which the subject considers. And this is the reason why the object's pretention to total independence must be abrogated once and for all. Precisely, then, because the independence of the object of consciousness is merely apparent, it "forms a distinction from self-consciousness that *per se* has no being. This opposition of its appearance and its truth finds its real essence, however, only in the truth — in the unity

---

[13] B., p. 219. *Phän.*, p. 134.

of self-consciousness with itself. This unity must become essential to self-consciousness, i.e. self-consciousness is the state of *Desire* in general".[14]

Though it is difficult to see how the notion of desire can so abruptly and straightforwardly be proposed, Hegel insists that all this has been determined by rigorous necessity. His best excuse for the hasty character of this transition lies perhaps in the consequent analysis of consciousness. There Hegel says that at this point of development self-consciousness has a twofold object : the first object has been inherited from consciousness of things, but remoulded by the negative operation of the subject, and the second object is consciousness itself. Now, we might say that this situation gives Hegel the opportunity to introduce the idea of desire, for self-consciousness may be said to have an urge to overcome the dualism just exhibited. Having described the object as involving duality, Hegel is quite consistent in assuming that the removal of this conflict is contingent upon some articulate desire. It becomes plain, as Hegel proceeds, that the unity of the subject is inseparable from desire, by which he means, not merely dynamic, but self-perfective operation. Through such self-perfective dynamism the subject exhibits its unappeasable nature, in order that this may appear with greater clarity and intensity : without such persistent desire there could be no further development towards true self-knowledge. In other words, only the desire can supply an answer to how the unity of the subject must be secured. We might say, therefore, that desire exists only to intensify the self-realization of the subject. What Hegel is also attempting with this new concept is to present the subject as a desiderative agency, effectively doing away with the immediate tautological position and progressively bringing the object into perfect harmony with itself. The subject's ability to desire indicates a search for gratification that prepares the way for the association of one individual subjectivity with another subjectivity. For it is only when the subject sees in the object nothing but another subject that complete gratification is attained.

The notion of desire as a novel experience is important enough to require our attention a little longer. Being the medium and condition for the subject's recognition of itself, the dialectic of desire reveals certain facts serviceable as contrivances to further development of subjectivity. For this reason it is particularly interesting to follow through the subject's struggle to solve inner conflicts that are generated by desire.

Hegel was deeply convinced that self-awareness is essentially an experience of desire. What is more, the very possibility of such an experience

---

[14] B., p. 220. *Phän.*, pp. 134-135.

depends on an alien and independent object. All this is very clear and presents little difficulty. But since the subject can acquire the certainty of its own self only by negating the independent object, we run into one of those difficulties which are constantly threatening the career of the truth-searching consciousness. It cannot be reiterated too often that the self-conscious subject is assured of itself through cancelling the other. For it is true that the subject really exists on its own account only by its negative relation to the object. "Convinced of the nothingness of this other, it definitely affirms this nothingness to be for itself the truth of this other ...".[15] Now, this is a significant discovery, for it guarantees the "true certainty". What is more, the acquisition of true certainty is a gratifying experience. The experience of gratification, however, does not contribute to the loss of the object's independence : gratification simply reintroduces it.[16] The point Hegel is trying to make is that the subject is "unable by its negative relation to the object to abolish it; because of that relation it rather produces it again, as well as the desire".[17] This, however, seems to leave open the possibility that any negation whatever can be effected by the object itself, especially when "it is inherently (an sich) something negative".[18] Indeed, the object, being an inseverable correlative of the subject, lends itself to mediation and negation. Since nothing else than negation renders cognition dialectical and since the subject alone is unable by its negative relation to the object to annul it, "the object must per se effect this negation of itself".[19] But this is the same as saying that the negativity of the subject is plowed back into the object, so that the nothingness of the object could come out of concealment. This seemingly absurd procedure has no other purpose than to render the distinction between object and consciousness untenable or

---

[15] B., p. 225. Phän., p. 139.

[16] Hegel's text does not support J. Loewenberg's contention that "it is the moment of gratification which effectively marks the loss of the object's alleged independence; ..." Op. cit., p. 80. Hegel's position is clearly different : "In this state of satisfaction, however, it has experience of the independence of its object. Desire and the certainty of its self obtained in the gratification of desire, are conditioned by the object; for the certainty exists through cancelling this other; in order that this cancelling may be effected, there must be this other. Self-consciousness is thus unable by its negative relation to the object to abolish it; because of that relation it rather produces it again, as well as the desire. The object desired is, in fact, something other than self-consciousness, the essence of desire; ..." B., p. 225. Phän., p. 139.

[17] Ibid.

[18] B., p. 226. Phän., p. 139.

[19] Ibid.

void.[20] The central problem here relates to the urgent necessity of establishing the object as commensurate with consciousness. In the struggle
between self-certainty and otherness, the self-conscious subject is called
upon to reinstate its own unity, and this task is accomplished when mere
objectivity vanishes in favor of consciousness. In Hegel's own words,
"when a self-consciousness is the object, the object is just as much ego as
object".[21] This is particularly important, since only in the light of this
problem can we anticipate the reduplication of consciousness and understand the subject's struggle with its own otherness. For to say that consciousness is commensurate with its object is to say that consciousness has an
object which implies its own otherness.

The self-certainty is such that all its acts reveal the same essence : the
relentless effort to reconcile the unity of the subject and the alleged autonomy
of the object. Now, the subject can only retain unity and attain gratification
when its object presents itself as something inherently negative. This means
that the unity and self-certainty of the subject are always conditioned by
negation. One the other hand, the essential nature of desire implies that the
subject can only find gratification in another and implicit in gratification
is the object's demand for independence. This is not merely a matter of
shifting emphasis, for the object desired must be something other than
self-consciousness. As can be expected, however, there occur important
changes in the structure of self-certainty which are brought about by radical
negation and mediation. The outcome of this self-edifying process is rather
striking : the subject identifies the object with consciousness and qualifies
it as otherness, for consciousness now is to itself its own object.

Further light is thrown upon Hegel's notion of desire if we consider it
in relation to life, which plays a particularly significant role in the subject's
rise to self-consciousness. If the dialectic of desire opens up the dimension
of another subject, the discussion of life leads to the vital sphere where
another essential mark of subjectivity is explicitly recognized. Although
life and desire are two different things, it is easy to accept the fact that life
is directly readable in the subject's desire and attempts to preserve its
own unity. In this sense desire is a concomitant of the perfection of life that
ensues from the identification of self-certainty with the self as living. To
be subject is to be capable of sensation, perception, understanding, and
self-certainty, but to be capable of all this is to stand consciously in reality

---

[20] "Since the object is in its very self negation, and in being so is at the same time
independent, it is Consciousness". *Ibid.*
[21] B., p. 227. *Phän.*, p. 140.

as living. For only a living being can adequately perform the functions of a self-conscious subject. Life, to put it differently, is the actualization of the self-conscious elements of being in their unity and diversity, in their continuity and articulation, in their identity and distinction. The identification of life and the subject had already been enunciated in the *Preface* [22] and tacitly assumed in the initial modes of consciousness, for every act of knowledge, be it a simple sensation or an instance of scientific understanding, is an act of a living subject. Though there are in the elementary modes of cognition direct allusions to the category of life, it was not until Hegel made dialectically clear to himself that "the object of immediate desire is something living"[23] that the concept of life is looked on as a constitutive element of subjectivity. Latent before, life comes out of prereflective experience and submits itself to the dialectical analysis. Now, the simplest way of summarizing what precedes is to say that the activity of self-consciousness and the perfection of life are mutually implicative, and the elucidation of this complex issue is perhaps the only way of gaining entrance into Hegel's notion of self-consciousness.

The substance of Hegel's dialectic of life can best be approached through a consideration of its circularity (*Kreislauf*), for what is really relevant is neither the setting up of individual living forms nor the continuous process of life, but the circuit of life, resolving its own development as a whole. Like force,[24] the simple and immediate unity of life differentiates itself into distinct moments, but since these moments are essentially interdependent, they are destined to "collapse into one another".[25] Life is inseparable from the very elements it integrates. Yet life refuses to be identical with them : it passes beyond them and moves towards "the universal unity, which holds all these moments sublated within it".[26] The process of life, which constitutes one distinct moment in the circuit of life, cut off from discrete individual forms becomes a mere abstraction and loses its alleged universality, for there is nothing specific to be subsumed under it. The main point here is that both of these moments — the general process of life and the particular forms of life — merge into a universal "reflected unity" which Hegel calls "genus". Together they serve to define what constitutive

---

[22] B., p. 80. *Phän.*, p. 20.
[23] B., p. 220. *Phän.*, p. 135.
[24] There evidently is no real similarity between force and life. The analogy lies simply in the dialectical categories of unity and multiplicity, of identity and distinction, of the universal and the individual.
[25] B., p. 224. *Phän.*, p. 138.
[26] *Ibid.*

elements enter into the real essence of life, how correct formulation of concrete universality is to be realized, and how the unity of life as genus is to be preserved. This new unity is called a "reflected unity", precisely because it is constituted in and through reflection. Reflected unity is nothing else than a rational synthesis of the universal flux of life and the particular forms of life. Hinging on the cognitive performance of the subject, the reflected unity can obviously exist only in the sphere of conscious thought. But as soon as the possibility of life as a reflected unity is seen to depend on conscious activity, the concept of life as genus is also seen to be the result of consciousness. For in the absence of consciousness, the view of life as genus would not be forthcoming. The gist of the matter seems to be simply this : the self-consciousness of the subject is the result of vital processes, but the realization of life as genus is the result of consciousness.

At this point of development we are faced with an interesting paradox of self-consciousness. It is plainly obvious that the aim of life is to break through the rind of the immediate and sensory, to emerge from the outsideness and otherness of the object, and to appear out of this externality transformed as self-consciousness. In the eyes of Hegel, a living thing exhibits a persistent direction towards the self insofar as it is a self-conscious being. In short, life is the process in which potentially self-conscious being becomes actually self-conscious being. All this is clear and causes little difficulty. But the problem is posed, as soon as one realizes that self-consciousness is something other than life or the "other life" for which life exists as genus. Now, the recognition of this fact involves for Hegel a true conflict, a conflict between the movement of life and consciousness as the "other life", for the notion of life as a "mode of being" is not identical in content and meaning with the notion of life as a "simple genus".[27] However, the notion of life as genus lifts the subject into the light of an insight. For it reveals that the immediate notion of life has been sublated and elevated to a higher and richer notion. Hegel implies that this higher notion — life as genus — can serve as a perfect mirror, in which the self-conscious subject can discern its own characteristics. Quite obviously, the generic conception of life is an expression of the union of different but inseparable aspects of life, and it is in the self-conscious subject that these distinguishable but inseparable factors are *de facto* unified.[28]

---

[27] Gerhard Schmidt interprets this conflict in a very radical way. He finds here a reduplication of consciousness as the result of the opposition between self-consciousness and life. He concludes his argument in the following manner : "So entzweit sich Selbstbewusstsein in ein Gegensatz des Selbstbewusstseins und des Lebens". *Op. cit.*, p. 206.

[28] Since "genus" exemplifies an "anundfürsichseiende" universality and at the same time excludes immediacy, the subject can easily recognize these features as its own.

The notion of life as genus throws an immense light on the nature and structure of self-conscious subjectivity and illuminates the details of its further development. For the subject, being the authentic source of the generic notion of life, is itself a genus, capable of remoulding itself in accordance with its desiderative attitude, which is really identical with negativity. It is not surprising, therefore, that the individual living form, which is the object of self-consciousness has canceled its independence in the process of life and ceased "along with its distinctive difference to be what it is. The object of self-consciousness, however, is still independent in this negativity of itself; and thus it is for itself genus, universal flux or continuity in the very distinctiveness of its own separate existence; it is a living self-consciousness".[29] This passage may be obscure, cryptic, and replete with ambiguities, but one thing in it is very clear : the living subject, being the center of perpetual negativity, can attain its fulfillment in a coequal object — another living and self-conscious subject.[30] But when the living and self-conscious subject finds its true object in another living and self-conscious subject, we have before us the notion of mind, but still in a sense not yet carefully differentiated from that of spirit. Since mind is the "native land" of the subject, we might say that from now on the career of the subject will be marked by transparency. Thus, the subject ceases to be merely desiring and living and steps into the social realm of the plurality of subjects, in order to discover what mind is. This complex problem, of course, demands a separate chapter.

[29] B., p. 226. *Phän.*, p. 140.
[30] B., p. 227. *Phän.*, p. 140.

CHAPTER VIII

FREEDOM AND DEPENDENCE OF THE
SELF-CONSCIOUS SUBJECT

The new mode of self-consciousness which we are about to consider is said by Hegel to deal with the mind, "which is the unity of the different self-related and self-existent self-consciousnesses".[1] To be sure, this is a genuinely distinct problem, but it is difficult to see how it grows out of the previous dialectic, for Hegel's text covering the transition is not very clear, nor is it free from ambiguity. Therefore, before proceeding to the new problem, we should briefly dwell upon the transition from the previous analysis to the dialectic to follow.

The preceding chapter hardly lends itself to a general statement. However, if we focus our attention on the desiderative aspect of consciousness, it seems clear enough that the independence of the other keeps the subject's desire persistent and operative. Now, since the certainty of the self is a concomitant of the subject's unity that ensues from the process of equating self-conscious thought with its object, there can be no self-certainty unless the independence of the object is canceled. But since the subject is unable to negate the otherness of the independent object, the object itself must annul its own otherness and independence. Hegel's procedure is certainly drastic, for an acceptable position implies that the other also be self-conscious subject, precisely because only a self-conscious subject can effectively negate otherness. This does not mean, of course, that the category of otherness vanishes from the dialectical arena, but only that it becomes identical in meaning with the other subject. Once this has been established, the other subject as the object of self-consciousness is brought to the fore. Consequently, the confrontation of one individual conscious subject with another conscious subject marks the starting point of the new dialectic.

Hegel begins his section on Mastership and Slavery with the following passage : "Self-consciousness exists in itself and for itself, in that, and by

---

[1] B., p. 227. *Phän.*, p. 140.

the fact that it exists for another self-consciousness; that is to say, it *is* only by being acknowledged or 'recognized'. The conception of this its unity in its duplication, of infinitude realizing itself in self-consciousness, has many sides to it and encloses within it elements of varied significance".[2] Evidently, no one will deny that the subject enjoying self-consciousness can recognize the presence of another subject. There is no philosophy which stops at the complexity of objects and is satisfied with an orderly description of them. Even solipsism recognizes the existence of another subject in its assertion that the other is not as fully subject for me as I am for myself.[3] In a certain sense, the other subject is sought for by no one more eagerly than by the solipsist. All this, of course, remains rather abstract and trite. One has only to look at Hegel's passage to become convinced that he has no intention to move on the level of common sense. His intention is to say something new : the constitution of one self-conscious subject entails a constitution of another self-conscious subject, distinct from and yet identical with the first. Hegel maintains, then, that the conscious subjects can become self-conscious realities only through mutual recognition of each other's subjectivity. Without this reciprocal recognition no subject can enjoy complete self-consciousness.

This speculation, which makes the mutual recognition the key to the reduplication of consciousness, is originally rooted in the fact that the action on the part of one subject is at once its own action and the action of the other subject as well. The nature of self-consciousness is such that it not only allows a distinction between subject and object — one that can be expressed in the correlative contrast and unity — but also such that one can even speak of a double process in the sense that the act of one subject is also the act of the other regardless of their differentiation. In other words, the cognitive activity of one conscious subject in relation to another subject can adequately be represented as the activity of one single subject. For implicit in the very activity of this single subject is the activity of another subject, since the performance on the part of the first subject has itself a "double significance of being at once its own action and the action of that other as well".[4] Whatever else this might be, it is an expression of Hegel's confidence in his dialectical method to solve the problem of inter-

---

[2] B., p. [229]. *Phän.*, p. [141].

[3] That the other person is not as completely subject for me as I am for myself does not condemn him to radical otherness and my subjectivity to hermetically sealed isolation. These doctrinal aspects of solipsism can have no philosophical validity if they are meaningful and verifiable only for one single subject.

[4] B., p. 230. *Phän.*, p. 142.

subjectivity without any appeal to the immediate encounter with the other subject.

The very least that can be assumed is that Hegel has recognized the social aspect of this problem from the very beginning. In his view, the most fruitful principle of intersubjectivity lies not without but within a social context. In such a context alone can a subject's authentic nature come out of concealment. To say this, of course, is the same as saying that conscious subjects are not constituted as self-conscious subjects except by being mutually recognized. Nothing is more characteristic of the Hegelian notion of self-consciousness than this adherence to mutual recognition. "They recognize themselves a mutually recognizing one another".[5] Each conscious subject functions as the mediating term to the other, through which each identifies itself with itself and finds its self-existence in the self-existence of the other. Therefore, a valid rehabilitation of self-consciousness cannot even begin without a plurality of subjects. Findlay suggests that the self-conscious subject "only knows itself for what it is, when it thus rises superior to the distinction of persons".[6] What Findlay says, however, merely anticipates what lies much further ahead and what subsequent process brings gradually to light. At the present stage of development, however, both selves must intersect and overlap, differentiate and unite; each must participate in an exchange and negation of its own determinateness. Therefore, concern with mutual recognition involves a transposition of the issue from the level of self-certainty to the level of self-consciousness. This implies that the act by which the first subject is recognized by the second and the act by which the latter is recognized by the first are bound to each other as the constitutive moments of self-consciousness. Separate selves can thus appear to themselves only insofar as they are actively relating themselves to each other. Thus, if the essential character of conscious subjectivity is mutual recognition rather than unilateral activity, the newly emerging ego must be seen as essentially *social* relation.[7]

But this is not the whole story. And it is perhaps unnecessary to insist that introductory section provides no more than the guiding principle of the new dialectic. For here we are made acquainted with the category of recognition requisite for the activity of self-consciousness that experiences

[5] B., p. 231. *Phän.*, p. 143.

[6] *Op. cit.*, p. 95.

[7] As N. Berdyaev points it out, the social category of Hegel is not a description of a factual human situation but "something deeper. It is the problem of the structure of consciousness". *Slavery and Freedom* (London : Geoffrey Bles, The Centenary Press, 1944), p. 60.

an intrinsic bifurcation. And it is by moving with bifurcation rather than against it that the subject has the best prospect of emerging as free agency. Although the concept of mutual recognition and the process of reduplication clearly coincide, not everything is said when this coincidence is affirmed. Accordingly, the concept of recognition, though indicating the necessity of a dialogue between separate selves, does not immediately reveal its specific character and consequently has neither intelligibility nor validity prior to its concrete application. Thus, if we are to understand the process in which each of the two conscious opponents tries to be recognized by the other as what it is for itself, we must work out the significant details of the entire cycle.

To facilitate the apprehension of this intricate cycle and to grasp the varied significance of emerging elements, one must revert to the point already made that self-consciousness is primarily simple existence for self and that it is desire. Since the self-conscious subject originally affirms itself in desire, and all desire tends to negate its object's otherness, it follows that the object can no longer be an object posited in its independence. The object exists *for* the subject. And thus we are brought back to the simple unity of the subject and to the focal point of consciousness. Now, as there is evidence for the necessity and satisfaction of desire, so also there is some evidence on its essential presupposition. To put it briefly, the desiderative consciousness presupposes another consciousness, for only the object that is also a subject can effectively annihilate otherness.

Exemplifying the negativity of the subject, the dialectic of desire serves as the agency effecting the multiplication of self-consciousness. Now, since the subject searches for its own nature in desire and since the immediate object of desire is life, one should look for the initial confrontation of one conscious subject with another conscious subject in the sphere of life. No doubt, life cannot be brushed aside, even though it exemplifies "independence without absolute negativity".[8] As we have seen, life presents itself as a vital basis of self-consciousness, and the subject cannot dispose of what is indispensable for its emergence. Appearing thus in their immediacy, the separate selves "are independent individual forms, modes of consciousness that have not risen above the bare level of life".[9] It is not surprising, therefore, that in the initial phase of their interplay both selves should recognize themselves simply as living beings. Now, each self is "certain of its own self, but not of the other, and hence its own certainty

---

[8] B., p. 233. *Phän.*, p. 145.
[9] B., p. 231. *Phän.*, p. 143.

of itself is still without truth".[10] Obviously, it is one thing to achieve and to enjoy the certainty of the self. But it is quite another for self-certainty to issue in truth, precisely because the other person is not completely subject for me as I am for myself.

As this is our main problem, it may not be amiss to repeat what has been said. Originally, each conscious subject is certain of its own self : it is *for* itself, and it sees itself for what it is. None the less, since the subject has not as yet overcome its duality, it must recognize itself completely in the other. Therefore, unless the subject grasps itself in the other for what it is in itself the attainment of authentic truth remains precluded. In other words, it is imperative that both selves recognize one another in the same manner as they recognize themselves. Inevitably, self-consciousness is both for itself and for another : for itself it appears in the shape of a conscious subject, but for another it appears as fused into one with life. This, of course, implies a real discrepancy and the attainment of truth is rendered ineffectual in view of the fact that the occurrence of recognition is ever conditioned by the other. Paradoxically enough, this situation is precisely what enables the subject to progress beyond mere self-certainty or merely subjective truth. We might say, therefore, that the awareness of the difficulty not only heightens the tension between self-consciousness and life but also provides ambivalent material for further analysis and progress. Accordingly, the new development has its beginning and inception in the tacit assumption that separate selves *can* succeed in bringing "their certainty of themselves, the certainty of being for themselves, to the level of objective truth".[11]

Let us try to catch this pursuit of objective truth in the act that implies contest and strife, dramatic effort and even violent exertion. Without this life-and-death struggle (*Kampf auf Leben und Tod*), as Hegel calls it, the conscious subject would remain in its routine of self-certainty and subjective knowledge. What breaks that stagnation and releases cognitive potentialities is the realization "that the essential nature of self-consciousness is not bare existence, is not the merely immediate form in which it at first makes its appearance, is not its mere absorption in the expanse of life".[12] All this, however, can be brought to objective fruition only through negation and radical struggle. Hegel was well aware that the course of the conscious subject would have been less dramatic and factual if he had chosen love, sympathy or even empathy in his exposition of mutual recognition. Yet to

[10] B., p. 232. *Phän.*, p. 143.
[11] B., p. 232. *Phän.*, p. 144.
[12] B., p. 233. *Phän.*, p. 144.

take the less dramatic course would have involved not only an immediate reconciliation of immature subjects but also an elimination of the problem of independence and dependence that grounds the dialectic of master and slave.

There is rather notable obscurity in the meaning of the phrase, life-and-death struggle. The precise nature of this act calls for attention. Quite obviously, the problem set by life-and-death struggle is not a problem of biological survival. Nor is it a study of aggressiveness of the primitive man. Rather, it is an attempt to examine self-consciousness involved in self-alienation, seeking to remove "the determinateness in which it (self-consciousness) is fixed".[13] Still, Hegel's attempt to explain the constitution of subjectivity in terms of distinct subjects engaged in mutual destruction lays him open to the charge of descending into the sphere of the contingent and factual. It is somewhat paradoxical that Hegel, who never acknowledged any factually fixed points of reference, should in this case depend on a notion derived from the realm of factual existents and occurrences. On the other hand, it is very doubtful that Hegel's treatment of the issue is so construed as to suit cognitive considerations as well as factual. At any rate, one can feel that the dialectical procedures have failed to free the notions of life and death from their factual quality. It seems, therefore, that the chief obscurity lies in the confusion that arises when one shifts from the domain of matters of fact to the properly conscious realm. One thing, however, is clear and beyond any doubt : between life and self-consciousness there is a necessary connection. The experience of this becomes increasingly intensified as the subject advances from primitive to more subtle and complex notion of interdependence. However, if there are to be self-conscious subjects, they must be completely independent; their existence must be "purely for themselves", and not the mere particularity that results from the process of life. In one sense, then, consciousness does not depend on life, for it is not life but thought that constitutes the subject as an absolute negativity. In another sense, however, consciousness does depend on life, for only a living subject can perform conscious acts.

The main lines of the Hegelian argument are grasped easily enough. Clearly, the fundamental act of consciousness lies in its negative performance. As was indicated before, the conscious subject is a dynamic reality whose activity consists in showing that higher contents of cognition emerge from negation of more primitive ones. But that is not all. If the phenomenological procedure is to be gradual, the negativity itself must assume different

---

[13] B., p. [229]. *Phän.*, p. [133].

forms or configurations. Thus, on the level of self-certainty, the negativity of the subject has expressed itself in the form of desire. But since consciousness reduplicates itself and since each opponent is a living subject, the negativity on both sides must manifest itself in the tendency of mutual destruction, for separate selves can prove themselves only if they stake their lives and at the same time aim at the death of each other. It may be noted, further, that the primary motive of this struggle is the reciprocal recognition.[14] But since such an activity of the subject implicates an effort to free itself from otherness, the struggle for recognition necessarily becomes a struggle for freedom. Thus, the occurrence of life-and-death struggle creates a fundamentally new problem. Still, in the beginning the subject must remain content to affirm freedom in a generic manner. What essentially is freedom, is to be determined by an appeal to subsequent development.

The same point may be put in another manner. Self-consciousness is essentially consciousness of independence, of freedom : the realization that the subject initiates all its determinations by itself or that it can reach valid conclusions out of its own resources. Similarly, to think is to act independently and to act independently is to be free. However, at first sight, this seems an impossibility within the concrete situation of the problem. For the problem arises inasmuch as consciousness implies life; and the solution has to be reached by the subject not merely as holding its self-affirmation above life, but also as recognizing that consciousness itself depends on life and that death is the negation of consciousness. Thus, if freedom is to be won, it is not to be won easily. "It is solely by risking life that freedom is obtained".[15] This means that the fundamental condition for the possiblity of genuine self-consciousness lies in the subject's decision to risk life.

This aspect of the matter deserves further attention. As Hegel himself puts it, "the individual who has not staked his life, may, no doubt, be recognized as a Person".[16] Every individual, therefore, whose existence is recogniz-

---

[14] It might, of course, be said that Hegel has slipped into an untenable position, since "for two subjects mutually to demand recognition presupposes that they have already achieved it." Robert R. Ehman, "Subjectivity and Solipsism", *The Review of Metaphysics*, 1-1966-10. But Hegelianism can explain this presupposition alleged against it by insisting that one can demand recognition from the other precisely because one has already achieved a recognition of oneself. This, evidently, is but a reiteration of the assertion that separate selves do not originally recognize one another in the same fashion as they recognize themselves.

[15] B., p. 233. *Phän.*, p. 144.

[16] *Ibid.*

ed by another individual, may aspire to authentic subjectivity. For each subject clearly knows that what the other does is indispensable for both. However, to say that the attainment of freedom has its basis in the recognition of the other is no more than to fulfill one of the generative conditions to which freedom owes its existence. Obviously, to attain complete freedom or true self-consciousness, the reduplicated self needs more than this. Therefore, unless both subjects recognize each other "as pure existence for itself or as absolute negation",[17] the process towards freedom cannot even begin. If we turn now to the conscious subject that anticipates freedom, it is plain that we have to do neither with the sensuous, nor the biological mode of existence. In a somewhat looser fashion, self-consciousness intent upon independence cannot be conceived as a mere absorption in the perfection of life. For here we are dealing with the constitution of subjectivity as an object for the self. And the crux of the matter lies in the subject's negative and dramatic attitude towards life.

As can be expected, the life-and-death struggle creates a complex situation. In the first place, to undergo this dramatic struggle is for separate selves to cancel the claim that consciousness had its locus in the alien element of vital existence. In Hegel's own words, "they cancel themselves and are sublated as terms or extremes seeking to have existence on their own account".[18] Secondly, this harsh process culminates in consciousness conceived as the "lifeless unity", for the division of consciousness "into extremes with opposite characteristics"[19] vanishes from the scene.

The lifeless unity is manifestly abstract expression by means of which Hegel indicates the point of departure of his dialectic of Master and Slave. This fact, of course, hardly comes as a surprise. For the notion of lifeless unity is replete with implications, and when a chance is given for them to come to light, the purgative reflection of the subject revises them and leads to an entirely new slant on the problem of life and self-consciousness. Consequently, the notion of lifeless unity itself is brushed aside, not because it is meaningless, but because its content arises through an abstract routine.[20] In short, the notion is vulnerable, precisely because it lends itself to an analysis that exhibits its spurious character. Now, since the dissolution of lifeless unity is latent in the very structure of that notion, it is not paradoxical that in this experience "there is posited a pure self-consciousness, and a

---

[17] *Ibid.*
[18] B., p. 233. *Phän.*, p. 145.
[19] B., p. 234. *Phän.*, p. 145.
[20] Cf. *ibid.*

consciousness which is not purely for itself, but for another".[21] Thus, the subject, in and through the experience of lifeless unity, becomes aware that both life and pure self-consciousness are the complementary factors in the mind's search for freedom. And in this fashion we are brought to grasp the constitutive elements of subjectivity engaged in self-alienation. Not only is there demanded a leap from the perfection of life, but also it is expected that life can be saved by renouncing immediate recognition. Not only is there demanded an independent mode of consciousness whose "essential nature is to be for itself", but also there must continue to exist a dependent consciousness whose "essence is life or existence for another".[22]

The Master and Slave dialectic is well known, and so there is no need to go over its somewhat intricate details.[23] Therefore, we will dwell on only those aspects which are essential for the constitution of subjectivity.

The dialectic of lordship and bondage is dominated by the idea of liberating consciousness from all heterogeneous and alien elements. The key point is to reach the stage of thinking self-consciousness, that is, consciousness which has no object other than itself. But to reach the level of thinking self-consciousness that matches the content of free subjectivity there is needed an effective manner of pulling the mind out of the estranged condition and of securing for it a conviction that it has no content other than itself, since it is only by becoming object to itself that the mind can realize its true autonomy. By itself, this is a very simple and univocal aim. Still, though the general purpose is quite clear, the achievement of freedom and the constitution of subjectivity as an object is an extremely difficult task. For it is not an easy matter to connect the attitude of pure self-consciousness with the attitude that negates consciousness. And it is not immediately apparent that such diverse attitudes can be combined into a single view. But far more significant than this recurrent conflict will be the task of closing the gap between the master who claims self-sufficiency and enjoys complete recognition and, on the other hand, the slave who experiences dependence, fear, and receives all the hardship. Let us add that this gap measures the subordination of the slave to the master and throws light on their unequal status, for "one is merely recognized, while the other only recognizes".[24] Such, then, are the guiding ideas of the section and they reveal rather con-

---

[21] B., p. 234. *Phän.*, p. 145.

[22] B., p. 234. *Phän.*, p. 146.

[23] It is interesting to note that the dialectic of master and slave owes its origin to the early theological thought of Hegel. Cf. Paul Asveld, *La pensée religieuse du jeune Hegel* (Louvain : Publications Universitaires de Louvain, 1951), pp. 148-152.

[24] B., p. 231. *Phän.*, p. 143.

vincingly the importance of the distinction between independent consciousness as a *pure* subjectivity and dependent consciousness as a subjectivity *for another*.

If we have succeeded in describing the constitutive modes of self-consciousness, there remains the question of the significance of their conjunction. Briefly, this may be indicated by recalling that the relation between the master and the slave is essentially dynamic and inventive. From this feature there follows its positive character, for it contains an invitation to the subject to explore the possibility of setting of the series of dialectical positions that would contribute to the real independence of self-consciousness. Evidently, the attitudes of mastership and slavery are not only distinct but also complementary. For the master begins from his independence with which the slave will end, and the slave begins from his dependence with which the master will end. Now, if the pursuit of the slave is thorough, then he is bound to attain a relatively independent consciousness of his own. Obviously, the slave has to take the necessary steps for that result to come to light, though his every step will be conditioned by his dependence on the master.

Originally, the master enjoys the recognition of the slave and feels completely independent. He has attained this position by holding his self-affirmation above his life. For if self-consciousness denotes independence, self-sufficiency, and self-determination, it is obvious that the subject must feel convinced of the unessential character of life and terminate its association with it. Only in the measure that consciousness experiences dependence, does life become problematic. The same point may be put in another manner. On the supposition of the duality of consciousness, it is easy enough to conclude that there is latent in it the element of otherness; and only the subject's negative attitude towards life puts an end, at least in principle, to this constant source of otherness and dependence. The consciousness of the master demands recognition and unconditional independence. Thus, in the eyes of the master, 'to be self-conscious' cannot mean 'to be living'. 'To be self-conscious' is just to be self-conscious. But when the master has effectively achieved this position that allows of no qualification, he realizes that he cannot proceed beyond it. Thus, the dynamic thrust of the master is replaced by sluggishness and then by deterioration. Master's position deteriorates, not by some external invasion, but by submitting to its own immanent necessities. The master understands, weighs evidence, and reflects, but when he so operates, his alleged independence gradually turns into dependence. Nor is the master totally unaware of the causes that restrict and modify his independence. He knows only too well that he depends upon those who acknowledge his lordship. It is the slave who makes him master and through the work of the same he is able to suppress all independent objects. Having interposed the slave between the thing and himself, the master "relates himself merely to the dependence of the thing, and enjoys it without qualification and without reserve. The aspect of its dependence he leaves to the bondsman, who labours upon it".[25] If, then, there is a master-subject who gets his recognition through the slave — whose identity consists in an unessential mode of knowledge — the doubt must arise concerning his claim to unconditional independence. From this uncertainty there follows its significance, for the master has to examine the compatibility between his original independence and the emerging dependence.

Now it is not difficult to grasp the relevance of these facts for our problem. Needless to say, the master has to shift his position with respect to his initial claim. After having followed the argumentation from within, he finds that its evidence is not in favor of his unconditional freedom. "It is not an independent, but rather a dependent consciousness that he (the master) has achieved".[26] Still, the master does not become a slave. Master remains a master because he has conquered the fear of death and envisaged the possibility of free subjectivity. And, even if his notion of subjectivity belongs to the realm of the possible, it expresses an ideal to which the subject must constantly revert. Thus, without any explicit repudiation of his lordship, the master must acknowledge that his independence includes dependence. To assert this, of course, is to assert that master's self-sufficiency is restricted, not in the external manner, but in the essential manner that follows from one-sided development of consciousness.

But just as mastership revealed its essential nature to be the reverse of what it intended to be, so slavery, too, must transform itself into the opposite of what it originally is. A general anticipation of this outcome is contained in the fact that the slave is "a consciousness repressed (*zurückgedrängtes*) within itself".[27] And since from the very beginning the slave is forced "to be dependent, to have his independence in the shape of thinghood",[28] we can expect that the conscious process shall be more complex in the slave than in the master. Being a consciousness dominated by the master, he is involved in a more difficult situation and he is open to more acute tensions and struggles. The slave lives and operates in the density

---

[25] B., p. 236. *Phän.*, p. 147.
[26] B., pp. 236-237. *Phän.*, p. 147.
[27] B., p. 237. *Phän.*, p. 148.
[28] B., p. 235. *Phän.*, p. 146.

of life. For him, therefore, things retain their own independence and he has to labor upon them. The slave is primarily and fundamentally a laborer. But that is his source of self-correcting development, of self-liberation. For labor contains an affirmation of dynamism, of directedness to independence, and of the attainment of richer consciousness. Through his hard work he imposes his own form on the object and thus becomes aware of his own negativity. In brief, the slave is depicted by Hegel not merely as the subordinate form of consciousness. On the contrary, his is the primary consciousness, and because it is more complex, it ranks higher in the realm of self-correcting process. And it is he who attains the mind of his own.

Hegel conceived slavery as heading beyond every positive achievement of the master. Unlike the latter, the slave operates, not in the light of a general and abstract notion of consciousness, but in accord with more concrete directives. For he is confronted with a world of labor in which he finds himself, to which he belongs, and in which he functions by accepting every hardship and suffering. As a slave cannot divest himself of his destiny, so he cannot escape from hard labor. Nor is there any escape from fear. But that is his salvation. To the slave, as Hegel himself puts it, "the fear of the lord is the beginning of wisdom".[29] Now, this human phenomenon performs for Hegel a triple function : it affords the necessary relation to the self-consciousness of the master, it gives rise to an experience of deep anxiety, which reveals self-existence from within, and it serves to anticipate the attainment of independence "in its own right and on its own account".[30] From this triple function of fear there follows its primary importance, for the experience of fear confers actuality upon self-existence or independence that otherwise is merely external, 'merely out there'.

Apart from its cognitive aspect, Hegel's notion of fear is an ontological concept, precisely because it expresses "the simple, ultimate nature of self-consciousness" itself.[31] It would seem adequate, therefore, to give a description of it in terms of anxiety, assuming that "fear as related to a definite object and anxiety as the awareness of finitude are two radically different concepts".[32] Likewise, since anxiety of the slave is not a mere psychological perturbation, there is no point in speaking of conquering or suppressing it. Because it denotes a conspicuous increment in self-knowledge, the immediate

---

[29] B., p. 238. *Phän.*, p. 148.
[30] B., p. 239. *Phän.*, p. 149.
[31] B., p. 237. *Phän.*, p. 148.
[32] Paul Tillich, *Systematic Theology* (Chicago : University of Chicago Press, 1951), I, 191.

problem is to determine its precise significance. Quite clearly, any significant increment in self-consciousness cannot be obtained by mere experience of anxiety, for "consciousness is not therein aware of being self-existent".[33] It is evidently not sufficient that self-existence be felt inwardly, if that does not also mean that self-existence comes to be recognized explicitly as one's own proper being. For the act of anxiety to begin to bear really significant results, there would be required not only a new type of activity but also a negative force. Thus, without the fulfillment of additional conditions, anxiety "remains inward and mute, and consciousness does not become objective for itself".[34] This restriction which Hegel has introduced is a recognition that the slave cannot have too much confidence that his anxiety has terminated in a "re-discovery of himself by himself".[35] The significance of anxiety, then is no more than relative because an experience of it merely hints at the slave's awareness of himself as factually and objectively self-existent.[36]

In order to understand how such an awareness of the slave is conceivable, it is necessary to grasp the meaning of labor. No one can deny, of course, that labor is the only form of activity accessible to the slave. This is far too obvious to be questioned. What is less obvious is the fact that labor possesses an assignable efficacy with respect to the constitution of subjectivity. Still, in the eyes of Hegel, hard work is precisely what enables the slave to move in the direction of independence. More than that, labor is not only an efficacious technique for finding essential conditions that reveal self-existence; it is itself an expression of negativity. Thus, what the notion of pure negation is to the master, labor is to the slave.

In this fashion we are brought to conceiving labor as involving two fundamental components : one component contains and expresses the formative and creative perfection of work, and it is positive inasmuch as it is molding and "fashioning the thing", the other component, however, is negative and consists in this that through labor the slave changes, modifies, and eventually cancels the independent form of the object. But there is a further implication. These two components are inseparable and complementary, for in forming the thing the slave becomes conscious of the value of his work and of its canceling potentialities. Labor, then, is not

---

[33] B., p. 238. *Phän.*, p. 148.

[34] B., p. 239. *Phan.*, pp. 149-150.

[35] B., p. 239. *Phän.*, p. 149.

[36] But if the significance of anxiety is no more than relative, still it truly is *positive*. And if it does not attain authentic self-existence or independence, still it contributes to the realization of self-existence or independence.

an ordinary effort to secure economic rights and better living conditions. Rather, it is a cognitive act, gradually revealing the latent negativity as the permanent ground of the self-sufficient being. Thus, the slave, as experiencing fear and hardship, as shaping things and exercising negativity, is carried by his very facticity to quite a different pattern of consciousness. For the awareness of his own proper negativity leads him to the discovery "of having and being a 'mind of his own' ".[37]

Though the self-correcting and self-liberating development of the slave gives rise to a feeling of free thought, still "the mind of his own" denotes no more than simple *stubbornness*. However much he may reassure himself of independence, still he suffers from the realization that his freedom "does not get beyond the attitude of bondage".[38] Slavery, then, exemplifies an incomplete subjectivity. It has the capacity to think for itself and to appreciate its growing sense of independence. It rises above a pure attitude of servitude. However, it fails to transform its negativity into a negativity *per se* and to rise above "a determinate mode of being".[39] Just as the master in taking cognizance of his dependence does not become a slave, so the slave does not become a master when unveiling negativity as the principal source of independence. True enough, the consciousness of the slave becomes an object to itself. And yet, it continues to regard the self-existence of the master as a real mode of consciousness. In other words, the servile subject fails to reconcile "the moment of itself as independent object, and the moment of this object as a mode of consciousness".[40] It is easy to see that these two moments are really identical. Since this distinction is a thought-constituted distinction, there results at once a new type of consciousness whose essence consists in unimpeded and unconstrained movement of thought. Such is the underlying necessity and from it springs the viewpoint that makes thinking or thought the sole criterion of freedom.

[37] B., p. 239. *Phän.*, p. 149.
[38] B., p. 240. *Phän.*, p. 150.
[39] *Ibid.*
[40] B., p. [242]. *Phän.*, p. [151].

CHAPTER IX

THE SELF-ESTRANGED SUBJECT

Remembering that dialectical method has only and exclusively the data of previous development with which to deal, we can understand that the point of departure of the new pattern of consciousness must be found within the field of antecedent knowledge. Further, since the cognitive experience of the slave has a striking priority over the master's, it is obvious that one should look for the key of this point of departure primarily in the actual achievements of the slave. For this reason it is necessary to focus the attention on the notion of stubbornness. As vague as this notion may be, it denotes a rudimentary self-assertion of the estranged subject. After all, the slave's stubbornness is his awareness of the importance of his own self, regardless of his actual dependence on the master. But this is precisely what characterizes the fundamental doctrine of stoicism : "Its principle is that consciousness is essentially that which thinks, is a thinking reality, and that anything is really essential for consciousness, or is true and good, only when consciousness in dealing with it adopts the attitude of a thinking being".[1]

On the general and common view, it is quite impossible for the slave to become a stoic because he remains conscious of his difficult predicament and the ensuing bondage. Still, slavery, as depicted by Hegel, exhibits a persistent effort to attain freedom, and thus it does not take long for it to topple over into an attitude of stoicism that describes the determinateness of the subject to withdraw from the world and to concentrate upon thought itself.

Original as it is, Hegel's transition has its shortcomings. It envisages the slave and the stoic as orientated towards thought's autonomy, and such a common ideal, originally introduced by the master, provides the necessary link between them. It offers as the characteristic feature of the stoic's con-

---

[1] B., p. 244. *Phän.*, p. 152.

sciousness the indifference to the world, and this propensity to ignore the vital conditions of existence can be conceived as marking the birth of formally rational freedom. But it does not explain why or how such indifference emerges in consciousness as the fundamental position; and it offers no clue to account for the fact that the value of life, of which consciousness in desire and labor was so explicitly aware, has no significant concern for the subject and the attitude of resignation is boosted into necessity. Paradoxically enough, there is a certain advantage in this transitional defect inasmuch as it enables Hegel to describe stoicism as a new mode of cognition that hinges on the refusal to question the self-sufficiency of thought.

By accepting the criterion that nothing is true or good unless it vindicates itself to thought, the stoic withdraws into his own mind. Consequently, to protect his rational freedom against all intrusion from without the stoic adopts an attitude of indifference and irony, dismissing as irrelevant the reality of life. Despite his endeavor to emancipate himself in thought from the determinateness of external reality, the independence of the stoic falls short of complete freedom. In the first place, complete freedom which alone motivates the conscious process of the subject cannot be realized except by tedious search for what the stoic has lost. Secondly, complete freedom denotes, not only freedom to think, but freedom to question, to criticize, to doubt, to disbelieve. As soon as this point in the stoic's thinking is reached, there is no longer any possibility of avoiding rigorous scepticism. Therefore, to consistently complete the stoic's position, it is necessary to move foreward to the position of his successor, the sceptic.

However, freedom's living reality can hardly be achieved by exercising universal doubt or unrestricted negation. Since sceptical consciousness is a dialectical resultant springing from stoicism, it must envisage the possibility of reconciling the realm which constituted the object of stoical irony and the critical thought as an exclusive norm of rational freedom. And yet, universal doubt cannot be exercised except at the risk of suppressing the doubting subject. In other words, if doubt is to be universal, the sceptical subject must include itself in the sphere of facts and events to be questioned. Inevitably, then, the activity of the sceptic is interrupted by a certain feeling of uneasiness. At any rate, the sceptic's failure to apply with uniformity his attitude of radical disbelief subjects his consciousness to self-alienation. In this fashion the critical thought of the sceptic is necessarily replaced by unhappiness. After all, unhappiness, to use the word metaphysically, is clearly an experience of self-alienation : it is an awareness of being the twofold consciousness of itself as self-correcting or self-liberating and as radically self-perplexing or self-destructive. Consequently, no authentic freedom is possible unless the subject can find an effective way of eliminating the duality that displays itself within the same self-consciousness. Such is the general plan of the subject's detour, and a more detailed account of its meaning now has to be attempted.

The historical stoicism is punctuated by persistent attempts to transform philosophy into a rational discipline which resents dualism and exalts freedom.[2] We know this not merely from the passages in Zeno, Cleanthes and Chrysippus, but above all from the arguments of Epictetus compiled and preserved by Arrian.[3] There is no doubt in Epictetus' mind that thought is something intrinsically important, for by performing the act of thinking man grasps his own identity and freedom. In other words, the self-identity may be attained only through the exercise of rationality, which constitutes the very essence of man, a point which Epictetus never tires of stressing, and which is stated with great clarity in the opening chapter of his *Discourses* : "What is this? The reasoning faculty : for this alone of the faculties we have received is created to comprehend even its own nature; that is to say, what it is and what it can do, and with what precious qualities it has come to us, and to comprehend all other faculties as well".[4]

Taking his cue from Epictetus, Hegel saw that nothing is so completely in the subject's power as thought itself : when thinking occurs, the freedom of the self becomes realized. Moreover, this amounts to saying that the free self does not emerge except in fusion with rationality. Indeed, the independence of the subject is so much fused into one with reasonableness that, when the subject posits its own freedom, it must utilize the same reasonableness. Therefore, to say that the stoic seeks anchorage for his independence in thought means that he understands himself as a certain belonging-to-himself on the ground of a reasonableness which is truly his own. Further, in thinking the subject enjoys freedom, because, to use Hegel's idiom, it is "not in an other".[5] All this is plainly in keeping with the dialectic of self-consciousness. Because the procedure in dealing with notions is a process within the same subject, it is clear that thinking should appear to the subject as its own essential reality. In brief, in thought the self

---

[2] Cf. D. W. Hamlyn, "Greek Philosophy after Aristotle", *A Critical History of Western Philosophy*, ed. D. J. O'Connor (London : The Free Press of Glencoe, 1964), pp. 67-72.

[3] "What say you, fellow? Chain me? My leg you will chain — yes, but my will — no, not even Zeus can conquer that". "Arrian's Discourses of Epictetus", *The Stoic and Epicurean Philosophers*, ed. Whitney J. Oates (New York : Random House, 1940), p. 225.

[4] *Ibid.*, p. 224.

[5] B., p. 243. *Phän.*, p. 152.

comes to recognize its independence, for consciousness, being object to itself, "becomes aware of being an element existing in itself".[6]

This fusion of freedom and reasonableness of the stoic constitutes his subjectivity. Freedom crowns the stoic with self-sufficiency, so that nothing can now impose itself on him as conditioning the experience of his autonomy. Nevertheless, the progress of stoical consciousness does not end at this point, seeing that it succeeds in grasping its own shortcomings. Surely, the affirmation of unconditional freedom is one thing, the adequacy of this claim is quite another. No doubt, the stoic did not come to realize immediately that in order to demonstrate the adequacy of his position it is necessary to take a meaningful and firm stand upon the criterion and content of thought. However, when asked for the criterion and content of thought, the stoic gets embarrassed and repeats the same thing over again : "the true and good are to consist in reasonableness".[7] With this as a starting point the stoic can then engage in a re-evaluation of his position.

It is obvious that being subject must be called being free, for it is freedom that constitutes genuine subjectivity. Yet the subjectivity which pertains to the stoic is essentially a subjectivity of abstract freedom. The reason for this is that the stoic is bound to the being of external things and the awareness of this predicament invites a continual challenge to his rationality. What is more, the stoic is compelled to acknowledge that he is not the foundation of "natural existence, and has, therefore, let this latter go and remain free".[8] True enough, if defined in isolation, the stoic does realize freedom. But if defined in relation to natural existence or life, he must regard this latter with apathy and retreat to the sphere of his own self. At any rate, the stoic is apt to discover that his freedom has significance only to the extent that it is exercised along with a conscious withdrawal from life.

But there is a further aspect to the matter which is quite genuine and meaningful. The stoic's withdrawal from natural existence is no more than a partial negation of otherness. For natural existence together with all those things which fall outside thought's control will continue to disturb the mind until suppressed by radical scepticism. Of all effective procedures and attitudes, as Hegel clearly implies, none can outrank the effectiveness of scepticism whose radical doubt swallows the element of externality.

---

[6] *Ibid.*

[7] B., p. 246. *Phän.*, p. 154.

[8] B., p. 245. *Phän.*, p. 153.

That real freedom is other than mere self-sufficiency of thought is capable of attaining represents the steppingstone to further development and subsequent transition. To abandon the attitude of indifference and resignation, thus recapturing the spirit of the master, this is what the subject must now do, in order to attain unconditional freedom through disintegrating performance. In other words, since the propensity of the subject is to move towards unrestricted autonomy and since the stoic's deliberate indifference towards life might lead to estrangement, the subject must perforce accept the doubt of the sceptic and dissolve the otherness of life once and for all. This is of course simply a corollary from Hegel's thesis that scepticism is the realization of that of which stoicism is only the abstract notion.[9] If so, the transition is latent in the fact that to aspire to unconditional freedom and to realize such freedom are two different things. Thus, the real crux of the issue lies in the stoic's inability to transform his aspirations into concrete reality. This being so, the transition to the sceptic becomes not only conceivable but compelling and inevitable. Consequently, forsaking the abstract notion of freedom, the self-conscious subject enters the realm of thorough negation, hoping that the exercise of doubt will effectively undermine the element of otherness, remove from it all independent reference and preclude alienation.

The emergence of scepticism is an expression of the subject's capacity to envisage everything as succumbing to doubt and universal negation. We can clarify this, as Hegel himself does in the section on scepticism, by considering "thinking which wholly annihilates the being of the world".[10] Scepticism, as a phenomenological resultant springing from the stoic's impotence to vindicate himself as the absolute negation of otherness, fully realizes that thought involves essentially the power of negation. No wonder then that sceptical consciousness expects to achieve complete freedom only by suppressing the existence of whatever seems to be dubitable. The position of scepticism is essentially negative; it is not designed to set up a rival view. For the sceptic considers as irrelevant the fact that in order to demonstrate the dubiousness of some view it is indispensable to take one's stand on some other point. This is typical of scepticism : it always moves from questioning to disbelief, from uncertainty to negation, from doubt to annihilation. However, having firmly decided to negate anything dubitable, and having just as boldly decided to seek assurance of his own freedom in the same act, the sceptic seems to be left with a growing suspi-

---

[9] B., p. 246. *Phän.*, p. 154.
[10] B., p. 246. *Phän.*, p. 155.

cion that universal doubt can hardly be exercised without exposing his
own existence to the danger of negation.

The sceptic prides himself on being a completely free subject for whom
negation is supreme. That is equivalent to defining subjectivity as that
reality which wages a radical war against the invasion of freedom by otherness.[11] Seeing that freedom depends upon the annihilative act which originates within his own mind, the subject feels justified in holding his freedom
as granted by and received from his own self. No doubt, the principle of
negation is a very clear thing, but to apply it with consistency is not so
simple. This is, of course, a matter of great importance, for it is evident
that what a polemical subject is committed to is the avoidance of inconsistency. No position, no argument, no claim can be rationally acceptable
or valid if it is inconsistent. Incumbent thus upon the sceptic is the task
of pursuing with consistency his decision to exercise radical negation.

Viewing himself as the source of his own freedom, the sceptic must
claim determinateness and identity for himself, in spite of the fact that
the act of negation has to do solely with what is determinate and individual. This is indeed the position of a self-conscious subject whose destructive act as sole ground of freedom may cause a series of insurmountable
difficulties. Naturally enough, the sceptical subject, though endowed with
the destructive capacity, is in his turn without power to control its implications and consequences. Thus, if the sceptic is to be consistent, he must
claim individual existence for himself and find his freedom "in the form
of elevation above all the whirling complexity and all the contingency of
mere existence".[12] But since the act of negation occupies itself with what
is individual, the sceptic is forced to alienate his identity and look for
the seat of freedom in non-identity, although, in so doing, he simply duplicates his consciousness. In short, universal negation cannot be exercised
except at the risk of exposing the doubting subject to the danger of self-
annihilation. Under such circumstances the intelligent thing to do is to
admit that consciousness has been enmeshed in the net of its own fortuitous
confusion (zufällige Verwirrung).[13]

From this general but suspicious insight there follow the directives,
first, of unveiling more clearly the inconsistencies wrought by unconditional
negation and, secondly, of trying to reconcile the negating subject and

[11] Hegel expresses this in his own way : "By means of this self-conscious negation,
self-consciousness procures for itself the certainty of its own freedom, brings about the
experience of that freedom, and thereby raises it into the truth". B., p. 248. Phän., p. 156.

[12] B., p. 249. Phän., p. 157.

[13] Ibid.

the subject negated, and to find a new guide-post to the self-correcting process.

The sceptic proclaims the nothingness of the object and of his cognitional function in relation to the object, and yet he experiences his own existence, metaphysical permanence and stability in the very act which accepts and affirms nothing. Surely, the sceptic fully realizes that such an act is really worthless even though he must admit that it lends him an existential support and tenure. On the other hand, the identification of the subject with the source of negativity places a restriction on what the subject can negate. Therefore, the sceptic must explain how he can draw the line between those things which are open to negation and those which are not. What is more, if the sceptic decides to negate, he must know the reasons for negating. In this manner, the struggle for freedom takes on the aspect of a struggle between unrestricted negation and being. It is impossible, however, to draw a line between those things which lend themselves to negation and those which do not, for universal negation cannot tolerate any restriction, and the only reply available to the sceptic is that his situation is both self-contradictory and hopeless.

Perhaps there is nothing strikingly original in this self-criticism of the sceptic; but there is something significantly original in the subject's experience of contradiction and hopelessness. Since there is no curb on negative activity, scepticism, when carried on to extreme lengths, inevitably brings in its train the negation of the sceptic himself to whom the destructive thought is essentially and existentially related, and this consequently terminates in a clear-cut alienation between the subject as a permanent source of negation and the changeable, fortuitous thought that is marked by the impotence to eliminate its own confusion. Last but not least, it is significant that all this necessarily involves an apprehension of the severe division within the one and the same self, so that the subject is revealed as essentially a double self-consciousness, as a split subjectivity.

The phase at which self-consciousness has arrived is said by Hegel to be one of "Unhappy Consciousness". It makes explicit the experience of tormenting dualism that has been latent in the sceptical consciousness. This is not to say, however, that scepticism was "held by Hegel to be infected with an inherent but unrecognized contradiction".[14] The premise that the sceptic did not recognize the inner contradiction militates against Hegel's text : "In Scepticism consciousness gets, in truth, to know itself as a consciousness containing contradiction within itself".[15] It is because Hegel

[14] J. N. Findlay, *op. cit.*, p. 98.
[15] B., p. 250. *Phän.*, p. 158.

was convinced of this that he is so concerned with convincing his reader that sceptical consciousness is "the aimless fickleness and instability of going to and fro, hither and thither, from one extreme of self-same self-consciousness, to the other contingent, confused and confusing consciousness".[16] It is precisely the awareness of this restless movement which brings into clear light the sceptic's feeling of hopelessness and his impotence to advance beyond the impending contradiction. Keeping doubt and the doubter apart, the sceptic experiences himself not as a divided self but as an individual who perforce assumes different attitudes towards negation and existence. Fundamental here is the contention that consciousness "does not itself bring these two thoughts of itself together",[17] that is, it does not see them as constituting its very essence. Small wonder, then, that the sceptic is precluded from grasping the ensuing drama of self-alienation which is necessarily accompanied by the feeling of misery and unhappiness. To speak of contradiction, therefore, is not to speak of the self-alienation; rather it is to speak of "a squabble among self-willed children, one of whom says A when the other says B, and again B, when the other says A, and who, through being in contradiction with themselves, procure the joy of remaining in contradiction with one another".[18]

If self-alienation meant only contradiction, it would hardly represent an advance over the sceptical consciousness and would not merit being considered as a distinct and terminal stage of the self-conscious subject. We may say, however, that there exists a latent self-alienation, immanent and exerting influence in the sceptic's consciousness. But it has to be made explicit, to be brought out into the open in clearly defined notions and experiences. Furthermore, there must be a reasonable latitude in the emergence of self-alienation. In the framework of the self-correcting process, this means that the self-alienation of the subject cannot occur until the self apprehends itself as a divided subject, and it cannot attain such an apprehension until the conflicting attitudes of the sceptical consciousness are seen as the constitutive "modes" of one and the same subjectivity.

Hegel was certainly not the first thinker to introduce the concept of alienation (*Entfremdung*). Long before him St. Augustine employed the term *alienatio* and explored its moral significance.[19] Nor was Hegel the first to insist

---

[16] B., p. 249. *Phän.*, p. 157.

[17] *Ibid.*

[18] B., p. 250. *Phän.*, p. 158.

[19] According to St. Augustine, man, being a rational and free creature, is his own master. Thus, he is required to understand and evaluate his natural impulses and urges objectively. He has to commit himself in voluntary decision and choice to one or another

that the development of subjectivity is dialectical rather than temporal, pursuing its course from self-affirmation to self-alienation. But he was certainly the first thinker to articulate a reinterpretation of self-consciousness in reference to self-realization. According to this view, self-alienation alone can bring self-consciousness to fruition and one should look for its possibility in a subject able to negate and perform the act of self-mediation. This does not mean, however, that "for Hegel alienation was the driving force of the dialectical development".[20] As we have pointed out before, the driving force of the dialectical process lies in the subject's negativity, whereas self-alienation ensues from the process that causes an inner schism within the self-conscious ego.[21] The distinction between self-alienation and negativity is not merely semantic. Self-alienation is a dialectical resultant arising from the awareness of bifurcation immanent in a single subject. In relation to self-alienation negativity is a primary concept, constantly operative and gradually unveiling the subjectivity in a variety of interrelated phenomenological forms. Not only is negativity a constant struggle against the invasion of subjectivity by determinism, dependence, otherness, and dualism; it is also a constant attempt to eliminate the intolerable and tormenting presence of inner bifurcation.

Another misunderstanding which must be avoided in determining the specific function of self-alienation is that of considering it as a sort of externalization (*Entäusserung*).[22] That the concept of externalization (*Entäusser-*

---

or to none. This self-committal in decision and choice, however, may take the form of abandoning oneself to the bodily urges and surrendering the will's power to act freely. That is precisely what St. Augustine calls "alienation" (*alienatio*) which leads man to slavery. Cf. *De Trinitate*, X. 5.7; XI. 5.9. *Retractiones*, II. 15.2.

[20] Louis Dupré, *The Philosophical Foundations of Marxism* (New York : Harcourt, Brace & World, 1966), p. 122. For Dupré, the entire phenomenological development of consciousness should be looked upon as involving the concept of alienation. There is, unfortunately, a certain negligence in the way he employs the term alienation : sometimes distinguishing thereby the inner estrangement within one and the same self; sometimes merely the otherness of consciousness. Cf. *op. cit.*, pp. 28, 34.

It should be noted here that Dupré's emphasis on the positive meaning of alienation is not misplaced. He points out that alienation is the "forward movement which makes man a self-creating process, rather than a static being". *Op. cit.*, p. 122. Whenever, then, there is alienation or estrangement there is an attempt at self-realization. For the most part this means becoming a more objectified and a more concrete subject.

[21] Cf. Hans Wenke, *Hegels Theorie des objektiven Geistes* (Halle : Max Niemeyer, 1927), p. 96.

[22] Gustav Emil Mueller claims that for Hegel *Entäusserung* means "estrangement" and *Entfremdung* — "alienation". He also says that estrangement can be corrected,

ung) does not belong to the phenomenological order is clear from the fact that the latter is neither spatial nor temporal.[23] The point, however, is that we see here a sort of analogy : what the notion of *Entäusserung* is to spatio-temporal process, the notion of *Entfremdung* is to phenomenological process. None the less, it remains that there is a sense in which self-alienation of the subject entails externalization, for the cleavage between a negating self and a negated self cannot be described as cleavage unless they be regarded as external to one another.[24] It is clear, too, that without ceasing to be external to each other, both modes of self-consciousness must be envisaged as belonging together, since the subject retains its singleness and self-sameness in the dual attitudes it assumes.

Still, it is not sufficient to recognize the presence of these two modes of consciousness enclosed within the same subject. For Hegel did not consider them as complementary aspects of the same subjectivity but as complete strangers. The unhappy subject sees itself as one and at the same time sees itself as constituted of two rival and distant subjects. Now, if subjectivity is thus divided, the conscious activity is divided too : the one self alienates itself from the other self and sets itself in opposition to it. But with the occurrence and the subsequent experience of such dualism, the subject comes to realize that its essence lies in the unification of the estranged selves. "It is itself the gazing of one self-consciousness into another, and itself is both, and the unity of both is also its own essence; but objectively and consciously it is not yet this essence itself — is not yet the unity of both".[25] Hegel's text bears witness that self-unification is really on the estranged subjects' mind. Although much can be made of the radical split between the two selves, implicit in the self-estranged consciousness is the intense desire for integrated subjectivity. Paradoxical as it may seem, the experience of dualism for the subject is clarification rather than confusion. And once we recognize

whereas alienation "is incurable". See his *Origins and Dimensions of Philosophy* (New York : Pageant Press, 1965), p. 380.

It is doubtful whether Hegel's text bears out this interpretation. In any case, it is somewhat misleading to translate the German *Entäusserung* by "estrangement", since the term in no way indicates a spatio-temporal element which is essential to the notion of *Entäusserung*. For a more accurate distinction, cf. Joseph Gauvin, "Entfremdung et Entäusserung dans la Phénoménologie de l'Esprit de Hegel", *Archives de Philosophie*, 25 (1962), 555-571.

[23] Cf. Jan van der Meulen, *Hegel : Die gebrochene Mitte* (Hamburg : Felix Meiner, 1958), pp. 297-298.

[24] Keeping this fact in mind, Jan van der Meulen coins a new term in German and names it "*entäussernde Entfremdung*". *Op. cit.*, p. 295.

[25] B., p. 251. *Phän.*, p. 159.

this, it is but a short step to see that the subject is heading not for annihilation but for rational self-affirmation. None of this, of course, is intelligible except in terms of the gradual development, for the subjectivity thus understood is but an anticipated subjectivity. Therefore, the subject must first address itself to a serious task of reconciling the permanent self and the restless self. Nor is the subject totally unaware that such reconciliation cannot be achieved by simply desiring to do so. Small wonder, then, that the subsequent phenomenological quest is bound to become a painstaking, slow, and long search for true unity, liberation, and happiness. By the same token, it is a relentless search for authentic subjectivity.

Remembering that Hegel's dialectic is essentially presuppositionless, we can rightly say that the process of reconciliation must begin with an immediate experience of the inner split. Accordingly, if a reconciliation is to be achieved at all, it must be sought in the continual revisions of position with respect to the immanent division. In other words, since the urgent problem confronting the subject consists in the achievement of self-unification, the estranged consciousness must submit itself to a series of dialectical positions which are to be judged by their own implications.

If, then, we assume with Hegel that the point of departure can be found in the immediate experience of self-alienation, it is obvious that the subject should consider the unchangeable self as essential and the changeable self as the unessential. This is no more than to say that the nature of the relation between the permanent subject and the restless subject is initially such that if essentiality constitutes the distinctive mark of the first, unessentiality constitutes necessarily that of the other. It is significant, too, that for the estranged subject this relation is not merely a mental relation; instead, it is a real event of consciousness. By distinguishing within itself between what is fundamental and what is incidental, however, the subject recognizes its restlessness and assumes the "aspect of changeable consciousness and is to itself the unessential".[26] This, of course, does not involve disregarding the unchangeable; instead, it involves viewing it as "foreign and extraneous" and at the same time regarding it as constituting the essence of the estranged subject. In other words, just as consciousness of the subject's unessentiality is at the same time a consciousness of its unchangeableness, so too the unchangeableness relates itself to the unessentiality of the subject as its "ultimate essence". In being essential and also unessential, the estranged subject ceases to be "an indifference of one to the other"; it remains, however, "divided and at variance within itself", for when the inner structure

---

[26] B., p. 252. *Phän.*, p. 159.

of the subject is focused upon, it must be viewed as a relation of essence to the unessential, and when the singleness is focused upon, the distinct aspects must be regarded as "equally essential", but without asserting their actual compatibility, since contradiction remains, precisely because mutually exclusive predicates are attributed to the same subject under the same aspect. Thus, dialectical tension continues to flourish regardless of the initial attempt to suppress it.

Still, the conflict between the unchangeable self and the restless self does not seem to entail an even contest. Looking upon the inner split and dual complexity, the estranged subject refuses to be identified with the changeable self and tends to elevate itself beyond it. This fact hardly comes as a surprise, for the reluctance to be associated with the changeable self is due to the subject's deep-rooted aspiration to attain true and pure subjectivity.

Hegel's treatment of this issue brings to light a new feature of self-alienation, for the whole procedure is especially designed to introduce the notion of singularity and particularity. Therefore, it is fair to maintain that Hegel is now directing the course of dialectic from the subject's attempt to achieve union with the unchangeable to the subject's awareness of itself as single, particular, and individual. Thus, when the subject makes the effort to elevate itself beyond the changeable, it realizes that it is the same changeable self which seeks union with the unchangeable one, and that the latter cannot be distinguished as such without relation to its opposite. That this should be so is not difficult to understand, from Hegel's point of view. The estranged subject owes its specific nature to the division into distinct selves, and distinct selves, being mutually related, acquire their own identity only by means of differentiation. Thus, the unchangeable self involves reference to the opposite self as a condition of its own identity, and, analogously, the subject is said to be changeable because it is distinguishable from the unchangeable. Now, if the unchangeable aspect of the subject seems more fundamental than its opposite, it can appear so only insofar as attention is focused upon the mind's aspiration toward a true subjectivity. Still, to say that the subject passes to the unchangeable implies saying that it remains attached to the changeable. In short, the attempt to transcend the changeable self or to isolate the unchangeable self is foredoomed to failure, for the distinct selves must be taken as inseverable constituents of the alienated subject.

If, however, the subject is to become an unconditional reality never to be satisfied with particular and specific determinations, it must devote considerable attention to just what restrictions and difficulties individuality is going to impose upon it. Thus, there emerges a problem of fundamental importance, namely, the interpenetration of unchangeableness and particularity. At the same time, such an inevitable problem indicates that we are back once more to the pressing issue of self-alienation. This is not, however, merely the return to the predominant task of closing the gap between the unchangeable self and the changeable; it is an advance in the sense that it is an insight into particularity as the embodiment of estranged subjectivity. Quite obviously, the notion of particularity is rich and intricate for it relates itself to the unchangeableness in a variety of ways and leads to a new slant on the problem of self-alienation.

With a discovery such as this, the subject observes first of all the interpenetration of the changeable and the unchangeable aspects of the self, seeing that both inhere within the same individual. In face of this extraordinary relation there arises the distinction between unity and diversity, and a new quest is anticipated concerning the middle term, linking the opposed aspects of subjectivity. At this point, however, we have only an inkling of what to expect, as the subject detects a threefold relationship between particularity and unchangeableness. Specific rendition of the middle term must await a final stage of self-consciousness that results from the gradual process of relating the particular to the unchangeable, the individual to the universal. Obviously, in the absence of a gradual unfolding of particularity, the subject can claim neither inner reconciliation nor complete freedom.

But there is a further aspect to the issue, and it has to do with Hegel's sudden shift to the religious realm. In one sense, such a procedure is quite understandable. To the extent that the subject's search for the unchangeable selfhood is similar to the religious' quest for the Absolute Being, it belongs precisely to the task of the *Phenomenology* that its work move in the spheres that exhibit illustration and concrete clarification. In another sense, however, this may suggest that the *Phenomenology* is either a dialectic of factual history, or that it is viable only in a framework of dated events.

According to Jean Wahl, whose meticulous work on Hegel's notion of unhappy consciousness appeared in 1929, the allusion throughout the present section of the *Phenomenology* is essentially to a religious experience.[27]

---

[27] *Le malheur de la conscience dans la philosophie de Hegel* (2nd ed.; Paris : Presses Universitaires de France, 1951), p. [10].

Like Jean Wahl, J. N. Findlay relates Hegel's notion of alienation to the double consciousness of medieval Christendom. J. N. Findlay, "Hegel", *A Critical History of Western Philosophy*, ed. D. J. O'Connor (London : The Free Press of Glencoe, 1964), pp. 328-329.

This tendency among Hegel's commentators to draw parallels between medieval

Although admitting that the experience of unhappy consciousness is not drawn from a definite historical period or one particular philosophy,[28] he feels that much of the intense profundity of Hegel's text is here due to the concealed presence of a Judaic-Christian framework.[29] However, despite Jean Wahl's insistence on religious experience as the object with which Hegel is concerned, it would be a mistake to interpret unhappy consciousness as a religious consciousness, for it is only on the pre-final stage of the *Phenomenology* that the subject emerges in a univocally religious form. The occurrence of religious consciousness is simply impossible on this plane, for it transcends in cognitive import the rational, spiritual, and moral forms of subjectivity. Hegel could see as little reason for supposing that the nature of estranged subjectivity can be discovered merely by describing the religious experience of the Middle Ages, as he could for proposing to depict the subject's attempt to escape from the predicament of self-alienation simply by pointing to the Christian's inquietude and his search for the Absolute Being.

Although it would be a misunderstanding to look upon the unhappy subject as primarily a mystical mind rather than as a secular consciousness, it should be clear by now that Hegel's allusion to religion is not insignificant. All of which makes one wonder if the estranged subject gives rise to the initial religious attitude or whether what is found in a dated religious experience is merely analogous to self-alienation. Hegel's reluctance to enlarge on this matter at greater length seems to imply that religion does not play a major role in self-alienation. Were this more explicitly developed it might eliminate some of the difficulties which render the estranged subject so ambiguous. There is, however, considerable significance in the fact that religion is totally absent from the subsequent stages of consciousness. Though we must avoid the temptation to oversimplify, we can say that Hegel's references to religion on this plane of the *Phenomenology* have no other purpose than to show that the subject's struggle for inner reconciliation is analogous to the quest of the religious for the Absolute. Still, even if we agree with W. Dilthey that Hegel's references to historical events are merely illustrations,[30] it should be obvious that the awareness of the

---

Christianity and the estranged subject is unsatisfactory, since the latter has not yet reached the level of religious consciousness.

[28] *Le malheur de la conscience dans la philosophie de Hegel*, p. 19.

[29] *Ibid.*, p. [119] ff.

[30] "Sie [*Phänomenologie*] ist mehr als alle seine späteren Werke, weil ihr Problem eine Theorie ist, die sich gar nicht in das Geschäft des Universalhistorikers einmischt, die nicht

affinity of self-alienation and religiousness contributes to the growth of the subject. For once the unhappy ego recognizes that he has experiences similar to those of the religious, he awakens to a deeper knowledge of his true position.

Having said this much of the analogy and relationship between religion and self-alienation, it might be appropriate to spell out in some detail the lines along which Hegel sought to elaborate this analogy and prepare the stage for rational subjectivity. In brief, our primary concern is the systematic genesis of estrangement. In order to be precise about the structure of the dialectic to follow, three dynamic patterns of experience must be distinguished : devotion, self-enjoyment, and renunciation. A development so conceived progressively reveals the career of the estranged subject, and in so doing, it gradually reshapes the subject into a rational agent.

What must be mentioned first is Hegel's deep conviction that the progress of self-consciousness toward reconciliation and unification is the progress of subjectivity toward rationality. But since the subject cannot appeal to anything except its own relational structure, it moves toward that goal by simply attempting to construe the relation between individuality and unchangeableness as conjunctive. That is to say, only if the wall of separation between the particular and the universal is effectively removed, can subjectivity be authentically rational. Now, one way to assure unity and to eliminate the tension between the opposed aspects of the estranged subject is to assume the attitude of devotion, the attitude of zealous adherence to pure consciousness. Quite evidently, in all this Hegel is explicitating something that has always been present in the divided subjectivity, namely, the irrevocable attachment to the unchangeable. To speak of devotion, however, is to speak of what is essentially emotive, and to speak of what is essentially emotive is to speak of a yearning whose object is bound to appear as something external, alien, unapproachable, and vanishing.

A further point to be taken into consideration here is that devotion, having grown out of a latent attachment to the unchangeable, is marked by deficiency and precluded from recognizing its object in terms of intelligible concepts. A unification that remains on the level of devotion is little more than an emotionalism. Yet such an act is a dialectical necessity.

---

prätendiert, den Sinn der Geschichte erschöpft zu wollen. Historische Züge sind da nur Illustrationen für seeliche Verfassung, Übergänge einer Stufe in die andere drücken innere Notwendigkeiten psychischer Art aus, kein faktisches, einmaliges Geschehen als solches". Herman Nohl, ed., "Fragmente aus Wilhelm Diltheys Hegelwerk", *Hegel-Studien*, I, 134.

In it a link between the particular and the unchangeable has been secured, but, as we indicated before, it is found to be an inadequate link, since the object conceived as the unattainable beyond conceptually eludes the subject. True enough, there is a sort of adorative thinking discernible in the attitude of devotion, but it is a thinking wholly "musical" (*ein musikalisches Denken*).[31] We might say, therefore, that devotion, admittedly adorative, involves no reconciliation but rather emotive response. It exemplifies the subject's abortive attempt to achieve self-unification and emotionalism permeated with bitterness and diremption is its inescapable concomitant.

That such an emotive response should be neither an identification of the subject with the essentially real nor a grasping of the object as particular may well seem the fundamental thing to explain,[32] but Hegel insists that the real issue confronting the subject here is "the *grave* of its (own) life".[33] It is not at all strange, however, that Hegel should address himself to the description of the "tomb of consciousness," since this event marks the dissolution and termination of the attitude of devotion.

Seeing that the object of feeling cannot appear in conceptual form, the subject realizes that by devotion as such one will not be relieved of self-alienation. Accordingly, by the very fact that the unchangeable has vanished, the subject should give up looking for the unchangeable as particular and stop pursuing the unapproachable ideal of devotion, unless there is some other way of discovering particularity in its true form. The estranged subject's dilemma is thus unavoidable : either the subject ignores the conceptual requirements for identifying the object of devotion, in which case the subject becomes stagnant and persistently holds on to what has already vanished, or else, the unhappy consciousness takes cognizance of these requirements, but being unable to fulfill them immediately, continues to feel its object, and in that case, it falls back upon itself, securing thus the immanent certainty of its particular existence. Indeed, to the extent that "in itself this feeling is *self-feeling*",[34] the consciousness of self-feeling includes also that of itself. This, however, is but another way of saying that to experience the object of one's own feeling is to grasp oneself as that object. The factual truth of what is said here is simply this : unable to objectivize the unchangeable, the subject rediscovers merely itself in the very process of

---

[21] B., p. 257. *Phän.*, p. 163.

[32] "Thus, just as, on one side, when striving to find itself in the essentially real, it only lays hold of its own divided state of existence, so, too, on the other side, it cannot grasp that other [the essence] as particular or as concrete". B., p. 258. *Phän.*, p. 164.

[33] *Ibid.*

[34] B., p. 259. *Phän.*, p. 165.

objectivizing it. Shaken by the awesome experience of the vanishing ideal, the subject retreats into itself and awakens to a deeper understanding of self-alienation. Paradoxically, then, the attitude of devotion has the effect of clarifying rather than obfuscating the prospects of cognitional growth.

What must be mentioned next is Hegel's explicit claim that "the withdrawal of the emotional life into itself",[35] basically as a confirmation of the subject's own certainty, marks the transcendence of devout feelings and an emergence of a new perspective. Taking as his point of departure the conviction that a bridging of the gap between the ideal and the actual should be accessible to the subject, Hegel has been forced to maintain that devotion must by its own immanent logic and results be driven to a higher position, in which the unchangeable should be reinstated as transformed. Once this is granted, the only alternative left is to nurture the performance of the subject, in order "to attain, in work and enjoyment, the feeling of its own independence"[36] and supremacy. For that, however, it needs only stable adherence to the dialectical principle which demands that aspects internally conflicting should achieve harmony. Thus, the emotional "ideas" that plagued and puzzled the subject before are left behind, since the "return into self" means growth of a subject better equipped to understand the "actual reality" through its own performances. Hence Hegel's conviction of desire, work, and enjoyment as exemplifying a higher stage in the process of self-alienation intent upon meaningful reconciliation.

The subject, thrown upon its actual operations, must first of all re-examine the disappearance of the unchangeable. Now, one can very well say that there are several reasons why such a re-examination should be attempted. First, the notion of the unchangeable must not be abandoned but reinstated because the distinction between what an objective reality is in itself and what it is for the subject has not been retracted, and at the present moment that "reality is taken to be the form and shape of the unchangeable".[37] Since the unchangeable and reality appear as identical and since the subject's performance is to be fruitful, the unchangeable itself must be allowed to shed some light on its own nature.

Secondly, the unchangeable is an unutterable thing if regarded as an object of devotion. Accordingly, isolated from the actual and the particular, the unchangeable is but an ideal void of intelligible content. As conceptually unqualified the unchangeable resembles in vagueness and remoteness

---

[35] *Ibid.*
[36] B., p. 260. *Phän.*, p. 165.
[37] *Ibid.*

the unintelligible, the unapproachable, and the ineffable. Still, even in a non-conceptual view the unchangeable has the advantage over them, for it "has in itself preserved particularity".[38] What is more, the actual being, on which desire and cognitional efforts are directed, is, from the point of view of the estranged subject, an instance, mode, and "embodiment of the unchangeable".[39]

It is in this sense that the appearance of the unchangeable in the form of particularity must be understood. Nothing is here so important as the effort to preserve, transfigure, and elevate the notion of the unchangeable. It is clear, of course, that the transfiguration described here is not a transfiguration accomplished by the subject as particular; it is the inevitable self-modification of the unchangeable itself. Seeing that the subject manages to re-examine the unchangeable and cancel its unapproachability, "this must come about through the unchangeable itself when it disposes of its own form and shape and delivers this up for consciousness to enjoy".[40] The unchangeable, instead of retreating further and further into the beyond, descends to the level of particularity, bringing itself thus closer to the estranged subject. Accordingly, the unchangeable is no longer something in itself void and ineffable; rather it exhibits a recognizable meaning and implants the universal form in the concrete individual whose "particularity as a whole has the significance of *all* actuality".[41]

Despite the fact that the notion of the unchangeable gradually descends to the level of particularity to imbue the subject with universal form, the anticipated event of reconciliation is not even in sight. One would think that, having arrived at the notion of the "unchangeable appearing in the form of particularity", the subject could feel assured that its singleness has been reconciled with the universal. Indeed, one can easily make a meaningful synthesis of the unchangeable and the particular by simply asserting their actual unification, but to do this would be to skip a process whereby the particular rises to the level of unchangeableness. For Hegel, the appearance of the unchangeable in the form of particularity is one thing, the constitution of the particular in the form of unchangeableness quite another. Therefore, if the unchangeable as universal sinks to the plane of particularity, the particular is impelled to meet such performance with a transposed action. Only by counterbalancing the movement of the other extreme, can the particular

---

[38] *Ibid.*
[39] *Ibid.*
[40] B., p. 260. *Phän.*, pp. 165-166.
[41] B., p. 260. *Phän.*, p. 165.

achieve desirable synthesis. If Hegel is to be consistent, then he must allow the "internally shattered" subject to discover the truth that it is itself "this particular fact in the unchangeable".[42] Not arbitrary, therefore, at this stage, is the decision that the subject as particular should be permitted to complete its dialectical course.

In order that the relation between the particular and the universal become a relation established by the individual subject as such and in order that their unity be brought to light as a consciously mediated result, it was necessary for Hegel to begin from a concept that characterizes the shattered subjectivity. Now, *activity* is precisely such a concept with the aid of which a particular subject can extricate itself from its relative and calamitous position. All this would certainly encourage the uninitiated, giving the impression that the process so unequivocally charted guarantees a smooth sailing. However, the eventual development is abstruse and replete with intricacies.

First of all, if the proposed process is to be dialectically possible, the subject conceived as active and willing must have its negative counterpart — the passive reality. Now, since both extremes are "firmly established in themselves", the subject must qualify them as "withdrawn into the unchangeable".[43] It is not difficult to perceive that this statement lays bare the relatedness and compatibility of both extremes. Yet, the task which the subject has is their mutual transfiguration or *Aufhebung*, and this means that both extremes must be looked at as not only mutually related but as opposed. Here as elsewhere in the *Phenomenology*, the very purpose of the play requires that both terms, being virtually vulnerable, be brought into mutual interaction without which the further progress would be precluded. In their dialectical transactions, however, only "the extreme of passive reality is sublated by the active extreme".[44] The passive reality, being through and through passive, is obviously not equipped to transfigure the active extreme, and the only way out seems to be to let the latter sublate itself. Hegel gladly accepts this alternative, but, as a result, the subject suffers a new division and alienation and "repels itself from itself".

But there is a further aspect to the matter. Since the active force is able to disintegrate the actual reality, the subject has no choice but to qualify this destructive agency as a manifestation of an essential and independent power. Now, since the distinction between what an essence is in itself and

---

[42] B., p. 253. *Phän.*, p. 160.
[43] B., pp. 260-261. *Phän.*, p. 166.
[44] B., p. 261. *Phän.*, p. 166.

what it is for the subject is still valid, the independent or inherent power must as a matter of course be ascribed to the "other". And so, the active extreme can be looked upon as the reaffirmation of the beyond, proving self-activity to be entirely frivolous and fruitless. As a result, the subject alienates itself from the unchangeable, represented here as universal might, and denies itself the capacity of being actual and active in its own right.

Though it is difficult to see how a situation such as this can lend itself to further development, Hegel insists "that the unchangeable consciousness condemns its specific shape and form, and abandons it entirely, while, on the other hand, the individual consciousness 'gives thanks' ".[45] Here once again we run into one of those difficulties which from time to time reoccur in Hegel's *Phenomenology* and which threaten to make its procedures exceptionally obscure or arbitrary. Besides, Hegel himself would be the last to claim that we have here the emergence of a novel conception of self-alienation, differing noticeably from the conception that involves inner division and opposition of universal and particular.[46] For this reason it is particularly frustrating to follow through Hegel's punctilious exposition which culminates in an old posture. Little shrewdness is needed to see that the subject merely reverts to self-division and once again "recognizes the other extreme as its true reality".[47] Apart from this repetitive element, however, by examining the hidden implications of the dialectic, we may anticipate that the subject is going to get a lot, because it is asking for a great deal. After all, when Hegel has decided "to repeat the cleavage into the opposed consciousness of the unchangeable and the consciousness of a contrasted opposite in the shape of willing, performing, enjoying",[48] he meant by that to clarify two things : first, that the appearance of the unchangeable in the form of particularity does not suffice to engender reconciliation, for the particular, true to its nature, must discover a self-mediating approach to the unchangeable, and, secondly, that the two extremes "in which both parts give themselves up the one to the other" must be permitted to expose their latent alienation before some reconciliatory agency within the subject could be posited. Indeed, no mediating link is discoverable unless the opposed

---

[45] *Ibid.*

[46] "... By these two moments, in which both parts give themselves up the one to the other, there certainly arises in consciousness a sense of its *own* unity with the unchangeable. But, at the same time, this unity is affected with division, is again broken within itself, and out of this unity there once more comes the opposition of universal and particular". B., p. 261. *Phän.*, p. 167.

[47] B., p. 262. *Phän.*, p. 167.

[48] *Ibid.*

traits of subjectivity are shown as inseverably related and presupposing some rational mediator within the same consciousness. And so, the further development can be looked upon as the search for self-mediation, showing self-consciousness to be essentially rational and directing its destructive power against its own particularity. In other words, the triumph of estranged subjectivity consists in the capacity to connect the opposed aspects of consciousness by means of the middle term that obeys the laws of an inferential procedure (*Schluss*).

This third attitude of self-consciousness, which serves to effect the transition to the genuinely rational sphere, deserves close attention, for here the subject abruptly assumes new significance and status. Starting with the act of mediate relation, the subject discovers behind such activity the real agency generating it. This is not to suggest, however, that the subject did not or could not perform any mediating act before. On the contrary, being the essential part of the negative process, mediation has always been on the phenomenological scene and played the most vital role in each and every preceding dialectic. But what the subject could not understand before was that it is itself the rational mediator and that consciousness can be defined as the principal determinative of all reality. By thus exploring the conception of mediation, Hegel has made it possible to posit reason as an authentic absolute.

Progress in reconciliation, then, involves more than the exoteric transformation of the particular into the universal; it means the emergence of the rational medium which presents both extremes to one another and promises to relieve subjectivity of its self-alienation. Now this fact possesses its clarity and significance, but its proper apprehension calls for a relatively detailed description of the function of the middle term which exhibits a variety of overtones.

As we have pointed out before, the bond connecting the unchangeable and the unessential is regarded here as having its basis in the conscious mediator. For this mediator, both the feeling of unhappiness and the pitiable performance that ensues from the wretched individual, are the points of contact with the unchangeable. In the mediator, then, the unessential consciousness sees a liberator, a reconciliatory agent who enjoys a "direct communication with the unchangeable".[49] If so, this may be said to justify Hegel's view that in the mediator the unessential subjectivity gets freed from its petty activity and decision, from the enjoyment and the results of its labor. However, to say that the subject renounces all its activities

---

[49] B., p. 265. *Phän.*, p. 169.

and enjoyment, implies saying that it also disclaims its power of independent self-existence. In short, the self-abnegation is possible only at the cost of stripping the unessential subjectivity of its Ego and of converting it into a thing, into a mere objective presence.[50] This *gegenständliches Sein*, as Hegel calls it, is a concomitant of the self-renunciation that follows from the effort of eliminating the "concrete particular in the functions of animal life" as basis of the subject's unhappiness. Now, all this seems to be a serious consequence, for in abandoning its individual distinctiveness, the subject ceases to be a self-conscious being.

Despite all the uncertainty and complexity involved in describing subjectivity from this standpoint, one thing stands out clearly : the eclipse of self-consciousness is a necessary event, whose purpose is ultimately to remove all deceptions and inconsistencies, which conceal from the subject the true essence of particularity. Recognition by the estranged subject of these self-imposed deceptions and illusory claims has the effect of intensifying its search for rational mediation. To put it in another way, the unessential or the particular is simply not susceptible of growth and progress except to the extent that it is the correlative of the unchangeable or the universal, so that a fruitful activity on the part of the particular subject necessarily implies a correlative activity of the unchangeable subject. Thus, the attempted cancellation of the particular must be understood as affected through the operation of the unchangeable. Here, as elsewhere in the *Phenomenology*, the method of this thorough-going procedure is grounded in negativity, and to the extent that phenomenological process hinges on reconciliation, it belongs precisely to the subject's nature that it should invoke the act of self-mediation. It is precisely mediation that transcends opposition and onesidedness. Seeing itself as a mediator, the subject proclaims to the unchangeable consciousness that the isolated particular has renounced itself, and to the particular consciousness that the universal is no longer a mere beyond, but is one with it. The message of the mediator is simply this : the polar opposites are required to constitute a genuine unity, and this unity reveals itself to be reason. In other words, by uniting the diverse traits of self-consciousness and by recognizing itself as the substantial principle of mediation, the subject discovers within itself a rational power and gains certitude that such a power, in its organic particularity, is identical with all reality.

The rational subject is the self-conscious subject aware of its mediating power that rescues subjectivity from self-alienation and validates its unity.

---

[50] B., p. 266. *Phän.*, p. 170.

What is more, for the rational subject that notion of unity signifies the unity of the rational and the real. Initially, however, the equation of the rational and the real is conceived by the subject as a vague epitome. Thus, starting with a rudimentary assertion of equation, the subject seeks rigorous confirmation that the rational is the same as the real. This is in fact the basic task of the integrated subject, and it will be explained somewhat more clearly in what follows.

Part Four : The Rational Subject

CHAPTER X

THE ACTIVITY OF THE RATIONAL SUBJECT

For Hegel, the turn to rational subjectivity is a return to the origin of idealistic thought, because reason's unwavering certainty of being all reality expresses the fundamental principle of idealism. In a lengthy note on identity of the rational and the real that opens the new chapter Hegel associates reason's self-assurance of being all truth with the factual position of German idealists. He turns to this issue to make clear his distinction between the initial claim of reason and the complete truth of reason, a distinction presumably not recognized by Kant, Fichte, and Schelling.

As a first step in establishing his starting point, Hegel examines the question of the object-subject as object which is posited to exclude the existence of any other reality whatsoever. Much of the material utilized in this analysis is simply a review of what has already been demonstrated. What is novel in the treatment of consciousness as object for itself is an attempt to situate his position in relation to Kant and Fichte. Keeping this in mind, Hegel shows that the initial claim of reason is infested with difficulties when isolated from the dialectical process that aims at synthesis. One cannot wonder, then, that every deficient version of idealism is abrupt and lacks foundation, for it refuses to follow the dialectical course that leads up to mature consciousness, and by which it is justified. What is more, the career of reason cannot get its solution prior to the comprehension of the inorganic, organic, and human nature in terms of rational images. In brief, nothing less but the whole gamut of rational activities, including reason as legislator and judge, can validate the identity of the rational and the real. Therefore, the claim that reason is the principle of all reality is a formal and abstract assertion that, because it is formal and abstract, must leave inexpressed an indefinite number of insights that constitute "reason in truth" and that can never emerge in full-fledged form either through Kantian categories or Fichte's *Anstoss*.

Once it is recognized that mature self-consciousness takes reality to

mean what is really its own, the stage is set for the central project of reason :
that of "objectivizing" the rational subjectivity, wherein Hegel sees the
possibility of closing the gap between the subjective and the objective,
the rational and the real. In other words, the dialectic of reason poses the
problem of the subject's intent to conquer "otherness" once and for all.
And with this crucial issue Hegel's philosophy of subjectivity reaches its
climax.

Up to the present the self-conscious subject "sought to save and keep
itself for itself at the expense of the world or its own actuality, both of which
appeared to it to involve the denial of its own essential nature".[1] As a
result, the subject maneuvered itself into a situation involving choice between equally unsatisfactory alternatives : either the subject affirms its
own independence and freedom, in which case it must retain a negative
attitude towards the objectivity of the world, or else it must posit the world
as independent, in which case its own independence becomes groundless.
As we will recall, the subject accepted the first alternative : it asserted
its own independence and chose to jeopardize the actuality of the world.
But with emergence of rationality, the subsistence of the world appears
in a different light, for the subject, being certain of its own objectivity
and freed from the immanentistic perspective, can regard the world as subsistence no longer involving the denial of the subjective mode of existence.
Even if we prescind from the problem of whether this objective world
really exists independently of thought, we can safely say that the subject's
negative attitude towards otherness has now turned into a positive attitude.
However we interpret this mutual intimacy of subject and object, it is
neither a strictly realistic openness to the world nor is it a sort of idealistic
constitution of objectivity. Let us examine this with caution and perseverance.

As Hegel sees reason, it is destined to become equally the essence of the
subject and of things. However, the subject cannot possibly constitute
itself as rational by simply descending into the depths of consciousness,
nor can it discover reason in the nature of things by probing and analyzing
the manifold diversity of the world. For an authentic "objectivization" of
rationality something more radical is demanded — and this something
more radical is for Hegel the transfiguration of "thought into an existent
thought, or being into a thought-constituted being".[2] From the common-
sense point of view this can be looked upon as the cognitive movement

---

[1] B., p. 273. *Phän.*, p. 176.
[2] B., p. 283. *Phän.*, p. 185.

from consciousness to reality and from reality to consciousness. According to Hegel, however, it is primarily the subject's attempt to indicate its own objectivity as condition for the rational self-realization and objective knowledge of the world. If the subject is at all aware of being self-conscious it is conscious of itself not only as subject but as object as well. Small wonder, then, that the subject "should look at and see itself as concrete reality, and find itself present in objectively embodied form"[3] in order to discover the "world as its own new and real world".[4]

To the subject to find itself "in objectively embodied form" is for it to initiate the act of conscious and selective observation (*Beobachtung*). Though it is difficult to see how the meanings of such apparently distinct realities can be identified, Hegel believes that the observing subject may, without relinquishing its self-consciousness, impersonate the "concrete sensuously-present" mode of existence. Be that as it may, the problem here is to show that the subject has its own objectivity. The subject must lose itself "in the shape of a 'thing',", and this is precisely what enables it to capture the meaning of thinghood. Thus, the experience that gives the recognizable character of objectivity also gives the subject a communication with sensuous things. If one conceives of rational subjectivity as an awareness of the subject's own concrete thinghood, then one can describe it as a fruitful return to things of the world. Now, this is important. Since the subject must initially take its own "reality in the sense of immediacy of being"[5] whose activity consists in observation, then it can claim to be desirous to discover not itself, but, on the contrary, the intrinsic being of things as such.

But there is a further aspect to the matter, and it has to do with the shortsightedness of the subject. Thus, being conscious of performing an act of deliberate observation, the subject turns to things with the assumption that it is considering them as sensuous objects opposed to its own rational nature. When the subject approaches things in this way, however, it faces the difficult task of finding in them its own rational expression. Fortunately, the very purpose of the act of rational observation is to eliminate the myopic condition of the subject. Since the initial rational activity consists in thoughtful observation and since the meanings of things can reveal themselves only in the form of concepts, then to know things is not to examine their sensibility of which the subject is conscious, but rather to transform their sen-

---

[3] B., p. 282. *Phän.*, p. 184.
[4] B., p. 273. *Phän.*, p. 176.
[5] B., p. 282. *Phän.*, p. 184.

suous character into conceptions. Now, since "things have truth merely as conceptions",[6] then the essence of things and the essence of the subject must be viewed as one and the same.

For Hegel, there is an inseverable connection between the contention that things are intelligible and the contention that the subject is a knower. The mere fact that things can be subsumed under rational concepts is for Hegel a sufficiently clear indication that they possess the same nature as subjectivity. This is but another way of saying that the subject can know things simply because they reflect the subject's own reality. In this sense, things are consciously observed as conforming to the subject's rational nature. If so, the knower and the known are identical in principle, even in their first rational encounter, when the subject assumes the role of a deliberate observer.

Apart from such cognitional conformity, the introduction of conceptualization has the effect of refusing to consider rationality as an immediate object of rational consciousness. Although the conceptualizing subject really operates as rational, its object is not rationality as such. Being totally preoccupied with things, the observing subject loses itself in cognitive activity, without knowing that it does so only to achieve its own rational completion. This means that rationality is an entity of a kind such that its nature cannot be determined prior to its exercise. All this simply implies that awareness of what rationality itself is lies not at the beginning but at the end of a conscious and deliberate observation.

In the paragraph with which he concludes *Observation as a Process of Reason* Hegel speaks of the "various moments" of the "observational phase of reason" and suggests that in a field so vast and intricate as nature it is necessary to make a somewhat general but programmatic division. Obviously, being prepared to assume the role of the rational observer, the subject should not be allowed to sail an uncharted sea of nature. Assuming that prerequisites for deliberate observation of nature are prior delimitations of the field, Hegel brings the chart of the subject's odyssey to a level comparable to the one that has been proposed by physics, biology, and psychology respectively. Thus, the tacit assumption of rational subjectivity is that distinctions among inorganic, organic, and mental levels of nature need not be secured by gradual dialectical differentiation. Although this type of procedure misses the phenomenal unfolding of nature, Hegel believes that the borrowed division is readily justifiable in view of the

[6] B., p. 283. *Phän.*, p. 195.

fact that the subject acting as rational observer is acting as an attentive selector.[7]

As Hegel sees observation, it is not merely an act of reason but also an expression of its selectivity. To observe is to distinguish the universal and to disregard the sensuous particular; to recognize the essential as essential and the insignificant as insignificant; to grasp the relevant and to neglect the trivial. In short, observation goes hand in hand with the selectivity of reason, for "its whole concern is not simply a matter of perceiving".[8] Advancing this view, Hegel notes that there are only a few vague analogies in perception for the observational and selective activity of reason.[9] What Hegel is denying here is that the subject's observational attitude towards nature should be one of passive and perceptual attentiveness, waiting upon the sensuous utterances of nature and perpetually moving through its various "stages into the endless particularization of the chaos of plants and animals, kind of rocks, or of metals, forms of earth, etc., etc".[10] But what he is asserting are two things at once : first, that the observing subject must find means of compelling nature to yield intelligibility, devising distinctions between the essential and the unessential, the necessary and the unnecessary under which things will no longer remain silent with regard to the identity of the rational and the real; and, secondly, that the subject must eliminate the unavoidable suspicion and hesitation as to whether what is essential for consciousness is equally essential for things themselves, that is to say, the subject must find a way of determining whether or not there is exact correspondence or conformity of nature to conceptual "signs" (*Merkmale*) derived through the observational procedures.

Still, this methodological position is not something that precedes observational activity of reason but something that ensues upon it, or at least emerges simultaneously with it.

Be that as it may, more fundamental than the question of methodological procedure is the question of its presupposition. This presupposition reveals itself when Hegel introduces a distinction between the "system of marks"

---

[7] "When the unreflective consciousness speaks of observation and experience as being the fountain of truth, the phrase may possibly sound as if the whole business were a matter of tasting, smelling, feeling, hearing, and seeing. It forgets, in its zeal for tasting, smelling, etc., to say that, in point of fact, it has really and rationally determined for itself already the object thus sensuously apprehended, ..." B., p. [284]. *Phän.*, p. 185.

[8] *Ibid.*

[9] It is difficult to take seriously the suggestion of J. Loewenberg that "the consciousness to which we are bidden to return is chiefly that of perception". *Op. cit.*, p. 121.

[10] B., p. 285. *Phän.*, p. 186.

devised by reason and the "system of nature" itself, insisting that the first "must conform" to the latter.[11] Now, since the conformity of the conceptual order and nature is grounded in the "very principle and meaning of reason", Hegel is convinced that the validity of this presupposition is uncontestable, and that every attempt to suppress it would merely testify to the presence of rationality to which alone the subject owes fidelity. Therefore, if Hegel is to be consistent, he must intentionally confine the subject's inquiry of nature to that which provides supporting evidence for the postulated axiom.

All this suggests that the central contention of the rational observer is that the conscious mind, following its own deductive procedure, can reconstruct the whole of the natural realm from certain basic axioms. The assumption is that nature is orderly and uniform, and is constructed along the same rational lines as those of the conscious mind. Seeing that what pertains to reason, must also pertain to nature, the subject is assured of finding itself in things by means of the observational operation. Now, once this "instinctive" principle of reason has been introduced, the investigation of the relation of self-consciousness and nature is expected to yield objectively valid results. Indeed, when the categorical demands of reason's postulate have been displayed, it seems that beyond these there is nothing to understand and nothing to seek.

If so, the subject's proposed procedure, because of its presumptive elements, seems to prejudge the outcome. However, the renewed extrospective attitude of rational consciousness militates against the preconceived identification of the subject and object. In addition, any meaningful understanding of observation as an act of reason resists it as well. Evidently, in the hands of rational subjectivity the conformity of thought and nature becomes an instinctive description of nature, and one can be certain of the rational demand but not of what will be actually observed. Besides, the rational agent, being conscious of its mediating capacity, knows only too well that the terms of the subject-object relationship are intelligible and valid only through each other. Thus, the subject can stand firmly in doubt and hesitation as regards its instinctively constituted postulate. A proposed correspondence of thought and nature might really mean the constituting of what is observed, but such a constitution would be purely immanentistic if it did not include reference to what is observed. Now, reaching out to a realm of nature, rather than immanence, is the distinguishing mark of the observing subject. But this points to a continued and effective separation of the subject of observation from its object. If we are to understand their

[11] B., p. 286. *Phän.*, p. 187.

relation through observational activity, we face the problem that confronts the self-transcending subject : "What enables things to be *known*?"[12] But the experience that raises this problem has never endorsed reason's presupposition; rather, it has endorsed the subject's deep-seated propensity of transcendence, of reaching out to a world.

The rational subject has at first simply overestimated its own image in the object observed, and it must not hesitate to go on to assume complete possession of the rationality instinctively assured to it. When consciousness responds to the activity of observation and loses itself in it, the subject situates the issue more emphatically than ever in the dimension of reaching out to a world. A complementary result is that the observing subject readily escapes in part its own presupposition, because it seeks to explore the relation of thought and nature without appealing to anything outside observational activity. And this simply suggests that an act of observation will give reverent ear to the nature of both the observed and the observer.

Since there is an "inexhaustible supply of material for observation"[13] and since there can be no limit to descriptive and classificatory operation, the subject must assume the attitude of self-correcting explanation and begin to understand things by means of scientific laws.[14] This is not to suggest, however, that the subject reverts to the level of understanding as such. If in the career of understanding the problems of the passive picturing of the object were uppermost, here where the primary concern is over the nature of the subject, the problem of things' rationality and intelligibility dominates. Consequently, the observational activity is a gradual sharpening of rational grasp, a relentless effort to show that laws alone can bear out the subject's requirements for universality and necessity. But if we put the question here in terms appropriate to instinctive reason, we would ask : How can an observing subject elicit a universal and necessary law from the contingent events of inorganic nature? To be sure, for the subject universal law is viable only in an experiential framework, which means that experience alone can confirm the law with its essential characteristics.[15]

---

[12] B., p. 285. *Phän.*, p. 186.

[13] *Ibid.*

[14] The text mentions three stages of the observational process : description, classification, and explanation. Since description almost immediately gives rise to classification and since the transitional forms of nature integrate what reason intends to distinguish, and separate what reason intends to unite, the subject must perforce pass from a classificatory to an explanatory stage of observation.

[15] "To the consciousness observing, the truth of the law is given in 'experience', in the way that sense existence is object for consciousness; ..." B., p. 289. *Phän.*, p. 189.

That is to say, all particular objects of sense experience should supply evidence of the specific law to enable the very fact of this law to be ascertained. Still, the subject is fully aware that the assertion of a specific law does not involve an experiment with all sensible objects. It merely implies that an experimentation has been tried with a sufficiently large number of objects, and from cases actually observed the subject can by analogy draw an inference about the rest with the highest probability. Such a procedure, however, lacks the universality to make the law really necessary, though it furnishes a sort of generalization which at least rises above the particular instances as such.

We can indeed say loosely that the law of gravitation, for example, enjoys universal validity, since "the assertion that stones, when raised from the ground and let go, fall, does not at all require us to make the experiment with all stones".[16] It means merely that all stones hitherto observed have exhibited certain behavioral uniformity; and this is only a compendious way of saying "This stone has fallen, and that stone has fallen", and so on till the list is sufficiently extensive to permit analogical reasoning, an inference from the falling bodies actually observed to other bodies. If it means no more than this, it is a generalization endowed with greater or lesser probability. Consequently, the proposed law may be described as general; but the failure to apply it to bodies beyond the present range of observation is enough to refute its claim to be unconditionally universal and necessary. Like every other law, the law of gravitation could be a strictly universal law if we could elevate the probable to the level of truth, but, for Hegel, "be the probability as great as it may it is nothing as against truth".[17] Quite obviously, the attempt to elevate probability to the level of truth is unmistakably precluded as long as the analysis of inorganic nature is confined to the observation of contingent instances. If so, the subject runs the risk of not knowing completely what is present in experience.

Hegel concedes that there is no decisive argument that can prevent the subject from lowering the truth of the law to the level of probability. But he also concedes that there is no decisive judgment that could suppress reason's demands for universality and necessity. Though he sharply curtails the role and significance of truth in probability, Hegel refuses to allow a complete opposition between generalization and universality. And though generalization falls short of universality, it supplies an answer

[16] B., p. 290. *Phän.*, p. 190.
[17] *Ibid.*

to why the notion of law initially and immediately appears in an imperfect form.[18] Be that as it may, law resists being resolved into the general statements which express sheer probability, not simply because it is "in its very nature a notion", but also because it presents itself "in the sphere of appearance" as objective and real. What is beyond dispute is that reason clings to the notion of universal and necessary law, and if the subject gives it an empirical tone, this could be taken to mean that the law must pass the test of the positive experiment. However, the previous failure of the subject to deal adequately with contingent data opens up the opportunity to introduce laboratory procedures, in order to determine "pure conditions of the law". Perhaps this is not so surprising as it seems, for experiment, being dependent upon artificial conditions, offers a stable structure upon which the subject can focus and enables one to convert the contingent into the necessary. What is more, in the capacity of these experimental procedures to solicit reason beyond actually observable data lies the secret of their being essentially non-empirical.

Law is pre-eminently an expression of reason, though it is not completely indifferent to actual and contingent events. Thus, for an adequate appreciation of the conception of law the subject must hold together both the order of appearance and genetically more fundamental demands of reason. A question can arise, of course, over whether Hegel is meaning quite the same thing when he speaks of law as rational and when he speaks of it as experimentally verifiable. This is not simply a technical matter which it is a waste of time to examine. On the contrary, it raises a basic issue of nature's reducibility to laws. If Hegel really thinks that he can start from observational sphere and infer from this to necessary law, then he is falling into a vicious circle, for it is impossible to deduce necessity from empirical data, however much experimentation has altered the circumstances surrounding them. This terminology, however, should not lead us into the error of thinking that on Hegel's view scientific experimentation is the same thing as deduction. The crux of the matter seems to be this : What is grasped as empirical must eventually be seen as rational, since the artificial conditions of experiment free the subject from dependence on any sensuous datum and hence from the determinate inorganic realm. "As the outcome and truth of this experimentation we find *pure law*, which is freed from sensuous

---

[18] "It is when reason does not find necessity in them [laws] that it resorts to making this distinction, and lowers the truth of the matter to the level of probability, in order to bring out the imperfect way in which truth is presented to the consciousness that as yet has no insight into the pure notion; for universality is before it merely in the form of simple immediate universality". B., p., p. 290. *Phän.*, pp. 190-191.

elements; we see it as a concept, which, while present in sense, operates there independently and unrestrained, while enveloped in sense, is detached from it and is a concept bare and simple".[19] But with this the concept of the law strains against the contingent sensuous order with the same impact with which the system of marks contrived by reason contrasts with the system of inorganic nature itself. Consequently, if conceiving experiment as rational permits it the constitution of universal law and unveiling of nature's intelligibility that it seems to imply, it still does not reconcile the conceptual and the natural, nor does it account for the identity of the rational and the real. And once this discrepant pattern has been disclosed, the investigation of the relation of consciousness and inorganic nature is declared to be terminated.

Even if one accepts Hegel's conclusion, one may still hold that it is abstract and totally useless with regard to further development. How can the subject pass from the notion of pure law that describes the inorganic realm to organic nature and its manifold forms? Still, to question this is not to deny that it is possible to find a concept requisite for the transition to as yet unexplored levels of nature. This is obviously a difficult issue, but we need not make it more difficult than it is. Hegel's treatment of inorganic nature may be sketchy and his solutions inadequate, but if we accept his view of observation as itself a multiform activity of reason, which changes in character with the objects observed, we begin to realize that one type of observational procedure, when completed, should give way to another type of observation. Hegel at once makes it clear that there is no question of grafting further analysis on the pure notion of law. On the contrary, we have to consider the methodological potentialities of the observational activity. Only because of this insight into the variable character of the observational performance is Hegel able to say of organic nature that it must be the object of the subsequent analysis.

Whatever be the initial difficulties of the observing subject, the distinction between the non-living and the living is obvious and commonly accepted. If this is so, there must be characteristics given to the subject by reason at the service of observation. Because certain things are manifestly dynamic and their determinate features can hardly be detached from the organic whole, these characteristics must appear as equally important and "under the control of the single unity".[20] Still, this conception of the organism is as yet vague and in need of clarification. It is to the task of clarification and

[19] B., p. 293. *Phän.*, p. 193.
[20] *Ibid.*

phenomenological elucidation that the observing subject must now address itself.

The organic mode of existence is admittedly a "fluid condition", and its adaptedness to the environment does not fully account for biological differentiation, since it cannot be thought that an organism is purposive only because it responds to environment. The really essential point which should not be obscured is that in the last resort Hegel disclaims a necessary connection between the environment and the organism. Therefore, what the observational subject has to avoid is the substitution of the teleological relation for the purpose.[21] To do this is to undermine the organism's real specificity, for a living entity is not really organic in virtue of being responsive to the conditions of the environment : it is essentially organic only if it acts for the sake of purpose. Understood in this way, the concept of purpose is a more adequate category of explanation than the concept of the environment. In this respect, the subject's insight into the meaning of purpose is on the same footing as the subject's insight into the essence of the organism.

What is interesting is Hegel's view that the observing subject instinctively sees itself in the notion of purpose, but it is powerless to transform this vision into a full "prise de conscience". The instinctive reason operative in observation "does not know itself in what it finds",[22] for it loses sight of itself in favor of a purposive organism that demands a distinction between what it is and what it seeks. For though the notion of purpose is seen as constituting the inner being of the organism, the same organism, being active, is also seen as seeking to achieve some final end. But if the consistency of both terms is hardly debatable, still the boundaries between what the organism is and what it seeks can be shown to be no boundaries at all. If so, the dialectical constitution of purpose converges with that of self-consciousness and its basic elements.

This sounds as if it might identify purposive action and rational performance, and in a sense it does. Undoubtedly, the subject can link these two issues — purpose and rational consciousness — as realities that are similar in that they involve the act of differentiation, but "without any distinction being thereby established",[23] and also insofar as they are indispensable for the constitution of subjectivity. Needless to say, the notion of purpose is expected to emerge dialectically, and this is precisely what makes it

---

[21] "If the relation, above alluded to, of organic existence to the elemental conditions of nature does not express its true being, the notion of Purpose, on the other hand, does contain it". B., p. 296. *Phän.*, p. 195.

[22] *Ibid.*

[23] B., p. 297. *Phän.*, p. 196.

conform to the requirements of the rational subject. If so, the purposive structure of the organism can serve as an external analogue in which the instinctive reason may recognize its own nature. Still, the subject does not find a perfect image of itself in the notion of purpose and its fusion with reason is marked by ambiguity. This ambiguity is not an incidental misconception; rather it arises from the fact that the organic realm does not allow itself to be transformed into univocal conceptions of purpose or law. It is for this reason that purpose becomes a stumbling block and "is put on one side as against consciousness, and in the latter finds its opposite".[24] Now, whenever consciousness has to do with something with which it does not constitute a dialectically mediated unit, something whose mode of existence is like that of an external object, the subject may not identify that "something" with its own rational nature, although this merely widens the gap between the subject's intention and its actual existence.

Ultimately, the subject's decision to take up this distance is based on the faulty intelligibility of the organic sphere and the inevitable process of differentiation. Nevertheless, the subject, so it seems, undertakes again what has been envisaged as a blundering and stultifying project. Thus, the subject chooses to remain dupe of its stumbling and fruitless efforts until it becomes absolutely clear that no identity of the rational and the real can develop upon the shifting and treacherous field of organic nature. But no other course is possible on the assumption that the meaning of purpose is that of a genesis and that it cannot be pursued without dialectics.

Let us point out first that it is the organism itself which is the purpose. The outward action of the organism, however, constitutes a new notion of purpose without suppressing the original one. It goes without saying that this is an expression of the distinction between the inner purposiveness and the terminus of the organismal self-realization. With this distinction we are in the midst of the Hegelian philosophy of nature. From this distinction, which is of crucial importance, springs Hegel's claim that the purpose lies apart from the organic entity presenting itself as a purpose. Now in the measure that one grasps the objective and independent character of the new notion of purpose, one possesses the base from which one can proceed to the claim that purpose falls "not within the observing consciousness, but within another intelligence".[25] Regardless of how deeply the subject penetrates the newly constituted notion of purpose it always finds there the reference to another reason (*Verstand*). Strange as it may seem, this new

---

[24] *Ibid.*
[25] B., p. 298. *Phän.*, p. 196.

perspective really threatens the observing consciousness, and, as a result, the problem of subject's integrity, identity, and unity becomes acute.

Fortunately, what is characteristic about the distinctions and relationships at this level is their dialectical orientation toward a mutual dependence. Although the instinctive reason is powerless to abolish a previously established distinction between the concept of purpose and self-maintenance, this reason does understand that the inner activity of the organism can mediate between its initial and its final stage, equating thus the dynamic being with what results from its operation. Consequently, organic structure and organic function fuse, for the observable constitution of the living being and its purpose, "concealed within the action of the thing", are seen as mutually implicative and interdependent.

In this way the subject realizes that mediating activity marks an advance in the observational process of nature and increases its experience of rational relationships. It must be admitted, however, that the subject encounters an inevitable obstacle when it turns its attention to "the inner operating activity lying between its first and last stage".[26] To this inner operating activity itself universal categories are strictly alien, and to introduce the latter into the former is to confuse the concrete organism and nature at large. All activity involves necessarily a singular living unity; in activity an organism does not reveal itself as something distinctly universal. Rather, every action springs from a particular living entity. Therefore, being an expression of the concrete living unit, the mediating activity does not depict the organic nature as such. In other words, being a manifestation of the singular living being, action ceases to be a function of the organic at large. The mediating act that reason ascribes to the organic whole is, therefore, always an achievement of the singular, not of the universal. But as long as the possibility of action is held to depend on the particular organism as such, the contrast between action and universality remains irreconcilable. Thus, with the observation that an action is the exclusive function of the singular organic unit, the subject must suppress the intent to speak of the organic universally. All this makes it easy to see why at this level "thought sinks to the level of mere ideal presentation",[27] indicating that the organic manifests itself as a relation of two static reference points : the inner and the outer.

One would expect that the application of this distinction would make the organism fall straight away into two parts, the observable side and the concealed side. This is, as a matter of fact, what actually happens, although

26 B., p. 299. *Phän.*, p. 197.
27 B., p. 300. *Phän.*, p. 199.

Hegel, as an external critic and spectator, warns us that "the organic being is, in undivided oneness and as a whole, the fundamental fact, it is the content of inner and outer, and is the same for both".[28] But being precluded from grasping what is so obvious to the phenomenologist, the observing subject has to accept the emerging distinction and be prepared to struggle with the difficulties latent in it. Hegel, of course, refused to endow the observing subject with a more mature knowledge of the organism primarily because the omission of the distinction between the inner and the outer would not have permitted him the necessary latitude to examine the correlation of the organism's threefold system with its threefold function. Perhaps Hegel was too careless to prevent the discussion from being pushed off into the merely fashionable, for it can be shown that the Hegelian solution of the problem takes its rise from biological considerations of his contemporaries.

Given the observational entity called organism, which expresses a mediated linkage of inner purpose and external action, all the rational subject has to do is to appropriate and then explicitate the old adage that the outer is an expression of the inner. Still, it is inevitable that rational consciousness should now have to face some rather difficult issues, for the whole conception of opposition of the two terms is shrouded in ambiguity. First, does the idea of the inner result from the expression and formulation of organic activity? Is it correct to say that a living being acts in accordance with its inner nature, and consequently that one can infer this concealed nature from the way it acts? Secondly, if the inner is not observable, how can a merely observing reason posit its existence prior to any deductive procedure? If inferential processes are foreign to the observing subject, then to import the first into the latter is to push the observing consciousness beyond its proper field. With this also arises the question concerning the connection with the classical approach : Is the justification for the distinction of the inner and the outer simply the principle of causality expressed in the traditional formula, "Operation follows being" (*operatio sequitur esse*)?

One thing must be emphasized immediately and stated as clearly as possible, if we want to understand and interpret the doctrine of the organism in Hegel's own spirit. For Hegel, "the inner is an object, or is affirmed as being, and as present for observation to deal with".[29] Hegel is arguing that the concept of the inner is necessarily involved in the observational process; that it is this idea which alone gives distinctive reference and clarity to the notion of self-purpose; and that this new concept is impossible apart from

---

[28] B., p. 301. *Phän.*, p. 199.
[29] *Ibid.*

"a being whose end is its own self". Since the notion of self-purpose has been a constant reference point throughout the entire career of the observing consciousness, Hegel feels that the subject may safely describe it in terms of the inner. Hence, to say that reason identifies the meaning of the inner is not to say that it identifies it by means of deduction. The inner is a notion that stresses the substantival reality of self-purpose, and for Hegel this terminates the dispute over its observational character. Although Hegel does not say that the inner is the soul, as does his translator Mr. Baillie,[30] he clearly alludes to a simple substantial principle whose justification is rather realistic and logical in character.

It is obvious how much that is questionable still remains in all this and, at the same time, how little is accomplished for the problem concerning the anticipated identity of the rational and the real. For it cannot be satisfactory when the observing subject, in face of of the vague notion of inner self-purpose, toys with the idea that it is possible and desirable to arrive at the organic properties of sensibility, irritability, and reproduction by means of an inferential act. It can be granted that "sensibility expresses in general the simple notion of organic reflexion into itself", that irritability is "the capacity to exercise the function of reacting simultaneously with self-reflexion", and that reproduction "is the operation of this entire self-reflected organism",[31] but it is very doubtful that the organic properties here described are not accessible to observation but deducible from the notion of the inner self-purpose. So remarkable a conclusion can hardly ever have been grounded on evidence so slight.

The entire argument that Hegel carries out, the threefold division of the organic functions into sensibility, irritability, and reproduction and their embodiment in the nervous, muscular, and intestinal systems, has a character of simple, direct correlation. If so, it does not lead the subject into a new dialectical career but is rather only an external means of connecting organic functions with their corresponding systems. What is more, there is no real novelty in Hegel's treatment with regard to organic functions and systems, for all of his distinctions and phrases came directly from his contemporaries; and the weakness of his argument from the modern point of view is that he accepted the nineteenth century scientific theories and hypotheses as

[30] The original text of Hegel runs as follows : "Die organische Substanz als *innere* ist die *einfache* in seiner Teilung ebenso allgemeine Flüssigkeit bleibt und daher in seinem *Sein* als das *Tun* oder die Bewegung der *verschwindenden* Wirklichkeit erscheint; ..." *Phän.*, pp. 199-200. Baillie's translation of the above passage is incorrect and misleading, to say the least. Cf. B., pp. 301-302.

[31] B., p. 302. *Phän.*, p. 200.

sound, valid, and final. Thus he missed, or scanted, some very fundamental questions which might have had decisive bearing upon the strictly philosophical concept of the organic being.

J. Loewenberg, or rather one of his interlocutors, says of Hegel that he "condemns all science, and not just biology, because the method employed is not dialectical".[32] This is an exaggeration, but Hegel actually gives some grounds for such a conclusion. For example, reading such a statement as this : "The actual expression of the whole, and the externalization of its moments, are really found only as a process and a movement, running throughout the various parts of the embodied organism; and in this process what is extracted as an individual system and fixed so, appears essentially as a fluid moment. So that the reality which anatomy finds cannot be taken for its real being, but only that reality as a process, a process in which alone even the anatomical parts have a significance",[33] one might at first think that this was a negative assertion, a disdainful repudiation of anatomy. But one has only to examine the context from which the statement was taken to be convinced that Hegel is merely reproaching positive scientific methods for not being equipped to penetrate the essential core of reality. His evaluation of scientific procedures and methods is a matter of considering them from a standpoint completely alien to them as scientific.[34] Besides, there is no need to attribute to Hegel a view incompatible with all we know of his philosophical position. Nowhere does Hegel contend for a negative view of the positive sciences. Rather, he insists upon a rigid and radical difference, a difference of philosophy and particular sciences. His problem is not the problem of repudiation or dethronement of empirical science, but rather his concern is to show that the methods and discoveries of the positive scientist concerning the phenomena, functions, and internal structures of the organism have no direct bearing upon the concept of vital process the philosopher has in mind.

The problem of the organism is further aggravated as soon as the subject moves from the correlation of organic functions and structures to the framing of laws peculiar to organic life. Needless to say, the latter does not refer to the decision to resume the abortive attempt of the understanding subject but rather pertains to the function of rationally awakened conscious-

---

[32] *Op. cit.*, p. 134.

[33] B., pp. 309-310. *Phän.*, p. 206.

[34] Cf. J. N. Findlay, *op. cit.*, p. 354. Let us add that Hegel never sensed any kind of antagonism between science and philosophy. Even in his *Introduction to the History of Philosophy* he made the claim that Bacon — together with Boehme and Descartes — was the first initiator of modern philosophy. See Q. Lauer, *Hegel's Idea of Philosophy*, p. 135.

ness whose intent is to unveil its rational image in the organic sphere. But certainly, this undertaking is also significant in the sense that the subject has not yet suppressed its intention of formulating meaningful propositions with regard to the inner and the outer. The fulfillment of this task, however, places the subject in front of a complex procedure that consists in determining the necessary connection between various organic properties, taking account of their being in one respect an inner element of definite organic unit and in another respect a fluid universal category, running through and pervading all parts of the organism.

The precise nature of the proposed methodical procedure may be vague and ambiguous. Nonetheless, one thing is clear. The idea of framing organic laws fascinates the subject, and since the search for such laws assumes this importance, there is a possibility of an immediate effort to take place. Now, having firmly declined to appeal to anything but the testimony of organic properties of sensibility, irritability, and reproduction, the subject is left with the conviction that laws peculiar to organic existence can only be discovered by scrutinizing all conceivable relations among so called organic properties and nothing more. If this means anything, it means that an organic law is conceived here by the subject as a relation of organic functions to one another. That the concept of relation forces the subject to retain an "indifferent independence" of sensibility, irritability, and reproduction and to ignore the fact that the essential nature of what is organic lies in having its vital properties as "permeating processes", and not in giving an abstract description of some stagnant opposition, causes Hegel no problem at all. To be sure, all this, as an attempt to initiate the dialectic of organic categories, is readily intentional and indeed desirable, if we admit or anticipate that the idea of a law in the case of organic existence is really destined to slip from our grasp and that the "thought of laws of this sort proves to have no truth at all".[35]

Thus, the phenomenological framing or deduction of laws turns on the fact that all organic properties have an oppositional significance, or that "each aspect would not be able to be equally named in place of the other".[36] Accordingly, the assertion that every organic function is in one respect a part of definite organic embodiment and in another respect a universal category which pervades and conditions all organic structures is equivalent to the assertion that each has a double relevance and meaning. In these statements Hegel recognizes explicitly that every organic property, function,

---

[35] B., p. 304. *Phän.*, p. 201.
[36] B., p. 310. *Phän.*, p. 207.

and moment has a character of distinction, differentiation, and specificity. Now this view is entirely in keeping with the procedure of framing the law. In order to assure oneself of that, one need only glance at the intrinsic requirements of the law, seeing that at the bottom of the latter lies just this that all the properties of the organism should be conceived in a determinate opposition, which provides the only secure basis for a dialectical search of organic relations. Thus the principle of opposition and differentiation is an indispensable condition of that argument which the subject so relentlessly pursues. But in virtue of this condition and requirement that the concept of the law places before the observing consciousness, the latter becomes aware of an enormous difficulty and inescapable failure. For in being kept opposed and distinct, the organic properties lose their true organic significance and become stagnant, inorganic factors, which can only serve to reduce the living being to the non-living. That the functions of sensibility, irritability, and reproduction obtain their original significance, their specifically organic meaning, only through their mutual interpenetration, and not through indifferent independence or distinctiveness — this is demonstrated by the fact that the authentic essence of organic moments as such consists in nothing other than fusing them together as permeating acts.

Here we stand at a point where an interesting paradox in Hegel's way of investigating the organic sphere comes to light. What he considers as the fruitful approach to organic nature is obviously the subject's resolute effort to discover rational laws in a dialectical analysis of sensibility, irritability, and reproduction. To see the significance of this we must remember that the chief purpose of the subject is the unveiling of the rational in the organic realm. But the observational process, its method and the ensuing distinctions are not the appropriate means for the accomplishment of this task, to say the least. Nor is this endeavor serviceable to prove the identity of the rational and the real. But if it is not possible to realize these important objectives, the entire dialectical phase of the organism seems to be wasted effort. If so, the subject should vehemently reject the whole dialectical course whereby the qualitative properties pass over into the quantitative factors and turn to the observation of the human nature, which, being the seat of rational subjectivity, promises to be the proper place for the reconciliation of the rational and the real.

But before the subject resolutely decides to abandon this type of observation, an attempt must be made to inquire into the necessitating motives of this decision and to prepare the path for another type of observation and for logical transition. Guided by this concern, the subject chooses to

expose the preposterous results of the observational consciousness, concentrating on the possible distortion which is brought about by the immanent
logic of straightforward correlation. And so, the entire weight of the argument rests on the fact that the qualitative properties of the organism become
distorted into something sensuous and even mechanical. In the fortunate
turn which Hegel gives the observational activity, the dialectic comes to
emphasize the irreducibility of the organic being. Taking, then, as its point
of departure the authenticity of the organic nature, the rational consciousness can turn its attention to the mediating capacity of the organic being
which contributes to make it precisely the kind of being it is, to the negativity
of the organism in which is found a principle of free relation to the inorganic
order, as also to the specifically organic categories, such as the individual
singleness of the organism, the organic universal or the genus, and the determinate universal or the species, all of which are recognized as belonging
exclusively to the living. All this, of course, supplies the solid foundation
for the radical departure from the inorganic. And with the gradual conquest
of this departure from the inorganic to the vital sphere, the latent question
about the relation of the individually singular organism to universal categories of life is bound to come to the fore and become increasingly conspicuous and acute.

The result is a remarkably rational representation of life — a know-
ledgeable system, a syllogistic structure (*Schluss*), as Hegel calls it,[37] where
one term is the universal life precisely as universal or genus, which disperses
itself into species or determinate universality, the other term is the universal
individual or life as a single totality whose singularity finds expression in
the singular individual. The intelligibility of this structure is deepened by
the subject's recognition that the middle term is constituted by both extremes, the first providing the category of the species and the other the form
of a singular individual. With this the barrier of mere singleness and abstract universality is finally broken. Such an elucidation, however, has not
pared away the subject's capacity for further complications. Because the
central issue here is the middle term, the subject is constantly critical of
what this term really implies. That reason, then, motivates the subject's
decision to check the constituents of the mediating term against the "two
extremes of inner universality and universal individuality".[38]

The subject draws most of the evidence for the projected comparison from
a consideration of previously established distinctions among the organic

---

[37] B., p. 324. *Phän.*, p. 218.
[38] B., p. 326. *Phän.*, p. 219.

categories. It seems obvious, therefore, that the middle term, preserving within itself only the species or determinate universality and the shape of a particular individual, cannot even assume to be the expression of pure universality or to become a "self-systematizing development". In a sense, this statement is merely preparatory, for it requires to be checked against the other universal categories. Despite the fact that between the determinate universality or species and the inner universality or genus there seems to be a prominent affinity, and that the single individual seems to fit into the category of universal individual, the possibility of identifing the two-categories in each set cannot even be described as remote or plausible, for they remain incomparable and broken up into clear-cut factors. In brief, the chasm between organic categories remains inexpugnably wide and deep. The subject can only swing back and forth between the terms present in each set and issue a qualifying statement to the effect that "the genus disperses into species in terms of the universal characteristic of number, or again it may adopt as its principle of division particular characteristics of its existence like figure, colour, etc. While quietly prosecuting this aim, the genus meets with violence at the hands of the universal individual, the earth, which in the rôle of universal negativity establishes the distinctions as they exist within itself, — the nature of which, owing to the substance they belong to, is different from the nature of those of the genus, — and makes good these distinctions as against the process of generic systematization".[39]

What this difficult passage precisely means Hegel did not explain further. One can only surmise that it refers to the fact that the entire organic process involves no rational organization and mediation. The emergence of concrete individuality demands an active participation of mediation, but no factual emergence as such manifests this mediating act. Therefore, seeing that the universality found in the organic mode of existence falls directly into the extreme of concrete individuality, without any self-initiated act of mediation and realizing that the organic whole is not present in the particular individual, the subject necessarily grasps its object simply as a crude and vague meaning (das Meinen). In the light of such a conclusion, however, one cannot raise the question whether the observational activity could get any further than to make quasi-meaningful remarks and propositions or to indicate rather conspicuous relations with regard to life in general and its categories. Now, if we agree with Hegel that "in the embodied organic existence observation can only meet with reason in the sense of life in general",[40] we can

---

[39] B., p. 325. Phän., p. 219.
[40] B., p. 326. Phän., p. 219.

safely say that with this insignificant achievement the subject has completed its work on the organic level and is prepared to initiate a new type of observation. It is rather clear that this completion is precisely the transition to the observation of human nature. And since the emergence of the notion of *das Meinen* draws attention to the realm of self-consciousness, the activity of observation sees this as the possibility to turn upon itself and to examine the laws of thought. Thus we stand here before a completely new task and thus before an extremely complex issue.

CHAPTER XI

THE SELF-EXAMINATION OF THE RATIONAL SUBJECT

The self-examination of consciousness, beginning with the analysis of thought and its laws, is the foremost trench to which the subject advances to defend the thesis that the rational and the real are the same. It is here, therefore, not in the observation of inorganic and organic nature, that one can succeed in locating Hegel's definitive defence of the rationalistic principle.

Turning from the organic nature to self-consciousness, the subject rises above the merely living and finds itself in a new observational field. Of course, the cognitive activity of the subject would be utterly inadequate if it did not recognize the immanent character of its new object. Thus, narrowing the range of observation to the data of consciousness itself, the subject has to denounce its outward approach and seek to conduct its efforts to an introspective analysis. At the same time, because thought has a subjective dimension, there arises the necessity of viewing the new object primarily as the original seat and locus of subjectivity.

Hegel's introductory section of the new chapter [1] covers the self-interrogation of thought in its pure state and in its relation to external reality. This time, fortunately, he abandons the quasi-scientific distinctions which created much confusion and led to a numbing ordeal in the preceding chapter. Here he picks up two prominent and relevant categories, the logical and the psychological, seeking to show that the latter grows out of the first without causing the scandal of an arbitrary reduction. But as if no longer trusting them to carry the dialectical process to fruition, he adds a complementary section in which the subject appeals to the speculative ideas proposed by Johann Kaspar Lavater in his *Physiognomische Fragmente* and

---

[1] Actually, this is section *b* of the previous chapter, entitled "*Observation as a Process of Reason*". Since the present portion of the *Phenomenology* examines a novel subject-matter, we refer to it as a new chapter.

also to Franz Joseph Gall's theory of phrenology. And so, the self-examination of the rational subject can be looked upon as a critique of formal logic, empirical psychology, and of the pseudo-scientific theories of physiognomy and phrenology. Still, this criticism should not be understood in the pejorative sense, for Hegel is neither degrading logic to psychology, nor is he proposing to abolish the pseudo-science of physiognomy and phrenology. It must be remembered, too, that at the present level of the phenomenological development the subject, being essentially *observational, instinctive,* and *abstract* — and all three qualifying adjectives have to be emphasized — is unprepared to examine the validity of all those doctrines and theories which are, in principle, beyond its apprehension.

For Hegel, the prospect of reconciling thought and being implies this : to be subject is by all means to be object. A subjective reality is an objective reality, at least from one side. The subject, instead of simply being self, must become relationship to self as concrete object. In other words, the authentic subjectivity has to begin its gradual self-realization by assuming the mode of being that is proper to a thing. To conquer the ignorance of self which characterizes reason when it thinks itself to be distinct from the being of a thing, such is the ambitious goal of self-realization. If so, we can anticipate that logical, psychological, physiognomic, and phrenological considerations will enable the subject to appropriate the objectivity of a concrete thing, establishing thus the identity of thought and being. And this project, for want of a better name, may be called the dialectical self-objectivization of reason.

Early in the first section, the rational subject witnesses enough problems concerning thought to warrant an expedient procedure to select the most urgent and the most immediate issue. For as soon as self-conscious subject turns in on thought it finds there a complex cluster of cognitional experiences and acts which contain and reveal awareness. Now, guided by the deeply-rooted intention to subsume the observable cognitional experiences under the category of law, the subject wastes no time in selecting the most appropriate problem for detailed analysis. Thus the introductory section, which is rather concise, seeks to conduct the rational subject to the consideration of the laws of thought. Needless to say, the subject commits itself irrevocably to this task alone, seeing that the essential feature of thought is to move in accordance with the fundamental principles of logic. All this, obviously, restricts the entire argument and its outcome, for, as William Earle has observed, "nothing *particular* follows from the 'laws of thought' or from logic in itself".[2] Be that as it may, the decision to examine the

[2] William Earle, *Objectivity : An Essay in Phenomenological Ontology* (Chicago : Quadrangle Books, 1968), p. 83.

laws of thought pushes the subject in one definitive direction, and when this occurs, both abstract and formal propositions are inevitable.

If we accept the laws of thought as the point of departure of the present dialectic, all following doctrines must be derived from it or related to it. This general remark already allows us to conceive the possibility of a continual progression from logical to psychological principles of thought. Proceeding as a rational and real agent, the subject is naturally tempted to think here of *true* and *real* laws. But this expectation is immediately disappointed. For to say that these laws are the laws of thought is to say that they are laws of thinking and not of reality. To clarify the issue, the subject must examine the universality of the claim to veracity implied in the laws of thought. Unfortunately, "they [the laws of thought] do not claim to be entire truth, but still formal truth".[3] And this should be accepted as the character and the specific peculiarity of each and every law. What is most decisive here is the affinity between the formal character of thought and the abstract hallmark of the law. Thus, seen in a purely formal way, the law reveals itself as an "empty abstraction" (*leere Abstraktion*).

Fortunately, this is an ephemeral conviction which vanishes as soon as the subject calls attention to the universality of thought and its unconditional character. What is inherently universal must be viewed as signifying the whole and nothing less. The universal cannot itself be conditioned with respect to truth; nor can it be a formal abstraction with respect to the existence of things. Thought carries in itself the character of the absolute and the unconditioned. Put in his own words, Hegel is saying that thought cannot be abstract or self-sufficient, for it "immediately contains being and therein all reality". Hence, the laws of thought "are absolute notions, and are in one and the same sense the essential principles of form as well as of things".[4] Surely, they are the essential principles of form in the sense that the negative function of thought is capable of dividing itself into its pure moments. All of which comes to one thing : It is precisely only negative action which enables the subject to distinguish and to think. However, the second part of the above proposition is more intricate. The laws of thought are the essential principles of things in the sense in which the word "thing" designates all being, except the sensuous. Still, the question as to whether logical laws are ontological is without significance. What is at stake, as Hegel sees the problem, is not the straight affirmation of external reality and its inherently logical nature, but the totality of the thinking

---

[3] B., p. [329]. *Phän.*, p. 222.
[4] B., p. 330. *Phän.*, p. 222.

process which alone can determine the complete value of these laws. But this task belongs to the speculative reason and, consequently, to what Hegel calls "speculative philosophy". Confining himself to phenomenology, Hegel was wise and prudent enough not to risk himself beyond the phenomenal level and beyond the abstract reason. Thus, before allowing the subject to continue its dialectical itinerary, Hegel makes a personal remark to the effect that he leaves a more detailed analysis of logical laws to a later date.[5]

The observing subject as such is concerned only with "fixed characteristics" of thought; or, rather, in abstracting laws from the indivisible unity of consciousness, in which they exist as vanishing moments, it treats these laws as if they were static, frozen, separate, and "detached necessities". The observational act disregards the unity of thought and its genetic constitution, and neglect of this is, obviously, the reason why abstract considerations have converted the thinking process into a rigid structure, in which "thought with its laws remains standing separately on one side, and that, on the other side, it obtains another objective being in what is now the object observed, viz. that acting consciousness, which exists for itself in such a way as to cancel otherness and find its reality in this direct awareness of itself as the negative".[6]

From this moment on, the subject becomes inextricably involved in the active consciousness because the latter, snatching the power of negation, emerges as the only agency determinative of subsequent development. The awareness of itself as the negative is the reason why the active consciousness ascribes priority to itself and refuses to continue the search for logical laws, since it depends for its self-realization on the diverse modes of its own reality presented to it in a form of otherness; and recognition of this dependence is, basically, the reason why logic develops into psychology. In short, since the acting consciousness with its inner life becomes an "objec-

---

[5] It seems safe to say that Hegel's *Science of Logic* is basically no more than a detailed exposition, with a broader content and a punctilious analysis, of the problematics set forth in the present section of the *Phenomenology*. Cf. Friedrich Bülow, *Hegel : Volk, Staat, Geschichte* (Stuttgart : Kröners Taschenbuch, 1942), p. 15. Accordingly, one may look upon the *Phenomenology* as a sort of logic whose purpose is the identification of all thought processes with the manifestation of reality in its totality. To say this, however, does not mean to identify the *Phenomenology* and the *Science of Logic*. In the *Phenomenology*, all cognitional acts and processes partake in the formation or constitution of the subject. In the *Science of Logic*, all cognitional performances are essentially notional, since they are the acts of the mature subject.

[6] B., p. 331. *Phän.*, p. 223.

tive being" and thus comes to the fore, the further search for formal laws is precluded and the activity of the subject must be shifted to other grounds.

What is emphatically dialectical in all this is that psychological investigations of the mind grow out of logical analysis. And we may ask with Hegel's commentators whether such a transition is unjustified and unjustifiable. Obviously, there is much truth in the assertion that logical and psychological aspects of thought are closely interrelated, although, factually and historically, logic and psychology appeared as separate and independent disciplines. Still, the idea of a rigorous transition implies that psychology is the fulfillment of formal logic, since the latter promises to attain what the first has failed to achieve. And yet, we do not have to suspect here a basic failure on Hegel's part to subordinate logic to psychology, in the sense that the first loses itself completely in the second. It seems safe to say that there is little justification in the contention that whenever the formal logician becomes engaged in the search for the laws of logic and then makes an effort to find their locus in the mind, he turns into a psychologist. We want to avoid drawing such and similar conclusions, the more so since Hegel never really claimed that what the logician is trying to find no one but the psychologist can discover. Nowhere else than at this point was he more prudent and scrupulous to prevent the question of transition from being misunderstood and misinterpreted. It is precisely for this reason that he decided to interrupt the dialectic of logic and hinted at the logic's immense future in the realm of the speculative philosophy.

Still, the dialectical connection between logic and psychology remains inexpugnable, although one may regret that Hegel himself was unable to use a clearer terminology in describing their mutual relationship. Since this question is rather important, it would seem necessary to say a few words concerning Hegel's position.

First of all, let us remember that logical laws alone, however richly furnished with intelligibility and however closely related to thought, do not establish contact with psychology and its principles; only the rationally oriented act of observation, assuming that the unified thought remains on one side and that, on the other side, there emerges the active consciousness with its specifically mental states and acts, provides this contact. Now, the relation between these two aspects of thought is such that the second enjoys primary status. The reason for this is that the active consciousness ascribes to itself the negative function and intends to be explicitly cognizant of itself. Since primacy of one aspect of consciousness over the other is a recurrent and ordinary fact in the *Phenomenology*, the transition from logic to psychology can be looked upon as an almost predictable shift in subject matter. Thus, the content of the psychological law is in no way grounded in the notion of logical law. Seen in this light, empirical psychology can be regarded as *parallel* to formal logic.

Just as logical analysis can be considered the search or even the critique of fixed laws of thought and yet retain an undisputed significance for the growing rational subject, so the observational psychology that is defined as the "collection of laws in virtue of which the mind takes up different forms of its reality given and presented to it in a condition of otherness"[7] here emerges as of relevant significance for the examination of the inner life. Although it is debatable that Hegel's definition of psychology is etymologically precise, historically relevant, and methodologically sound, it definitely suits the position of the acting consciousness which regards itself "as being wherein mind is reality and as such object to itself".[8] Now, to say that the "mind is reality and as such object to itself" implies saying that it seeks to become fully conscious of its own mental attitudes and operations. But when the mind speaks of its various attitudes, it cannot stop short at the description of their properties, characteristics, and mutual relations, but proceed to laws. Thus, like formal logic, observational psychology is faced with the problem of the law, which must be stretched to cover the entire sphere of the mental life. The only question, then, is whether the universally valid psychological laws can be discovered and defined.

To speak quite plainly, the subject can find the key to the explanation of the mental life in the very constituents of the law, which at the same time may be conceived as the correlative principles or conditions of rational self-examination. The attempt to locate the categories of explanation is justified by the observational method which seeks to contrast different observational elements and then to determine their mutual relation and dependence. Now, since the conscious individual is unquestionably given in every mental attitude and cognitive experience, all that is needed is that this individual should be recognized as the fundamental category of psychological explanation. The other condition of explanation arises when the conscious subject, by a sort of naively realistic glance, takes cognizance of the concrete environment with its habits, customs, ways of thinking etc.[9]

Still, since the individual subject conceived in this way has no other specification than that of being an acting consciousness, it is as yet a reality

---

[7] *Ibid.*

[8] B., p. 332. *Phän.*, pp. 223-224.

[9] With this, of course, the subject renounces the attitude of introspection and turns to extraversion.

awaiting further specification. To be sure, entering and facing the field of external circumstances, the subject regards itself as a "single individual mind" which is engaged in self-elucidation. Here, then, the subject possesses a thoroughly concrete character. However, when the subject refers to environment and is driven back to the notion of concrete individuality, it does not make itself unconditionally dependent upon the principle of the individual nor does it subordinate itself to circumstances. This suggestion is both positive and valuable, for it implicitly hints at the negativity of the subject and draws attention to the nature of self-knowledge whose foundation lies in the "universal element of mind" or in the "self-moving universality". It appears, then, that in dealing with its own inner life, the subject must be seen under the twofold aspect which it wants to retain throughout the entire process of self-interrogation. But certainly, such description alone would be enough to cast doubt on whether there is anything specifically novel in this recurrent correlation of individuality and universality. Nor is it sufficient to say that both poles of subjectivity are bound to each other by some sort of natural affinity. We can expect, however, that this two-fold characterization of the subject will receive its full sense and intelligibility through its relation to environmental influences.

The first point is that the subject's encounter with various circumstances and different mental attitudes has the effect of disrupting mind's unity and obscuring its singularity. According to Hegel, when the acting consciousness fixes its gaze on the external constituent of the psychological law, with the intent of capturing in the environmental conditions the image of its own nature, it "discovers all sorts of faculties, inclinations, and passions" deployed before the mind. This discovery, of course, forces the subject to behave "negatively towards itself as single individual mind",[10] for the manifest reason that the multiplicity of heterogeneous mental faculties and states militates against the subject's individuality as one unified whole. Still, in this sense the negative act performed by the subject does not designate a radical suppression of the unity of self-consciousness but is rather a narrow-minded understanding that depicts the mind as "a kind of bag" (Sack).[11] The basis upon which the subject makes this assertion is obviously trivial, since in spite of the fact that various mental faculties and inclinations are actually seen as restless processes (unruhige Bewegungen), they are posited to occur in the mind as if in a container. Apparently one reason which motivated Hegel to come up with such a conclusion was that

[10] B., p. 332. Phän., p. 224.
[11] Ibid.

he felt the need to expose the inaptness of the observational method to go beyond the facultative and passionate manifestations of the mind.

Hegel's second point is that the subject, seeking to know its own peculiar activity in opposition to external conditions and assumed attitudes, has to act negatively towards itself as the universal being, since the enlargement of universality at the expense of the individual cannot be tolerated. For it is clear that in depicting various universal faculties and passions, the mind necessarily "keeps to the universal aspect" and thus loses sight of itself as individual. It should be clear, too, that this restrictive procedure must be viewed as corrective of the farfetched intention inherent in the observational reason to seek the laws of human being instead of the human individual. Fundamental here is the view that the universal dimension of mind implicates an individual human being whose essence presumably is what it is in virtue of his surroundings.

The remainder of the present section consists in an explanation of how the environmental conditions are to act as a determinator of the individual. Changing the term "determination" into "influence", Hegel makes use of ideas that are relevant to the subject and consistent with the notion of the law. Thus, if the individual subject is to be studied methodically, psychology itself must become a rigorous discipline of the environmental influences. We may, then, say that the acting subject adopts as a hypothesis the view that its individuating characteristics must be due to the external causes. In a sense, this is the preconceived plan of observational psychology, by which one supposes that something in the mind as existing and adopted is always due to customs, situations, habits, religion, and so on. And it is this contention that makes the subject proceed to seek for the "psychological necessities" in the most diverse modes of external influence.

We will probably succeed in finding an explanation for all this if we fasten upon the very character of the relation between the concrete individual and the given environment. What must be mentioned first is that the individual and the environmental conditions are neither univocally nor deterministically related. Although the subject can assume the attitude of passivity and without any resistance "assimilate" the given circumstances, this does not in the least imply that the same kind of attitude will occur in all instances. It is, indeed, true that the individual subject, being primarily rational and negative, can jump abruptly from the passive attitude to the negative attitude, with the intention of "transforming and transmuting" the given circumstances. "On that account *what* is to have an influence on individuality, and what *sort* of influence it is to have — which, properly speaking, mean the same thing — depend entirely on individuality itself :

to say that by such and such an influence this individuality has become this specifically determinate individuality means nothing else than saying it has been this all along".[12] Here the subject remains entirely in itself and, at the same time, is, in principle, lifted beyond its milieu. What is more, being a free individual, the subject can adopt the position of complete indifference, neither permitting circumstances to exert a deterministic influence, nor reacting negatively to them. The recognition of this fact actually strengthens the ever present suspicion that the idea of psychological necessity is an empty contention, "so empty that there is the absolute possibility that what is said to have this influence could equally well not to have had it".[13] Thus observation, which is bound solely to the concept of influence, fails with the problem of the psychological law.

Up to this point the self-examination of the subject has been concerned with the relation of mind to external reality or environment. Having failed to establish a genuinely invariable connection between those two poles, the subject naturally arrives at the point of transition. Now, if there is to be a *dialectical* transition — and the word dialectical must be underlined — from the psychological self-interrogation to the subsequent self-examination, there must be a distinct point of departure. It is quite natural to assume that the key to this point of departure should be sought in the final conclusion of the antecedent dialectic and nowhere else. Indeed, there is perhaps no better way of discovering the new starting point than by examining the very outcome of the previous process. This is indisputable, but in order to explain it, one must remember the following. The fact that the subject has failed with the problem of psychological laws is certainly not the final positive result of the preceding dialectic. Nothing could be more pathetic perhaps than the assumption that Hegel has found the point of departure in the subject's deplorable failure to come up with psychological laws. Actually, the critical turn of the whole previous argument lies in the recognition of the self as individual. Hegel himself points this out clearly in the penultimate statement of the section :

Individuality itself is the cycle of its own action, in which it has presented and established itself as reality, and is simply and solely a unity of what is given and what is constructed — a unity whose aspects do not fall apart, as in the idea of psychological law, into a world given *per se* and an individuality existing for itself.[14]

---

[12] B., p. 334. *Phän.*, p. 225.
[13] B., p. 335. *Phän.*, pp. 226-227.
[14] B., p. 336. *Phän.*, p. 227.

Once appearing on the scene in the form of a true individual, the rational subject cannot let itself be ignored and neglected. It is not surprising, then, that seeing itself in this mode of existence, the subject should recognize itself as the principal term of the subsequent self-examination. Yet, the subject cannot begin to examine itself except in terms of the relation whose constituent elements are found in the individual precisely as individual. If so, the problem of transition is just this — how can the concrete individual establish a relational structure, which could be called upon to function as an efficient vehicle for the self-revelation of rational subjectivity. To speak quite plainly, the individual subject, taken as an indivisible unit, is not to be considered as offering a completely satisfactory starting point. One would expect, however, that the application of the observational method would make the indivisible individual fall straight away into two aspects : the inner-mental side and the outer-bodily side. This is, as a matter of fact, what actually occurs. Since the subject at this phenomenological level stands, as it were, in the middle of its being as individual, as concrete, and as psychophysical, it should consider itself under the conditions of and in relation to its own physical embodiment. To be sure, this recognition is a very significant achievement, and the expectation that the body will reflect the appearing of true individuality characterizes it as a symptom of transition to the next section of the *Phenomenology*.

The new section is remarkably lengthy and dense, and we may take this to reflect not only Hegel's outstanding command of physiognomical and phrenological themes but also the fact that about the end of the eighteenth century these themes gained unusual prominence in the public and academic circles. In the pages that follow, however, we shall not aim at locating him among the historical positions of Lavater and Gall but shall center upon the theme of subjectivity in its relation to the body.

There are various senses in which we can say that the bodily movements or actions *express* the individual subject. First, any observable manifestation of the body, be it of the "mouth that speaks" (*der sprechende Mund*) or the "hand that works" (*die arbeitende Hand*), will have a meaningful message, reflecting and revealing the essential marks of mind's constitution. When such a type of expression occurs, it may be interpreted as the objectivization of the inner itself, since through language and labor the individual subject itself breaks out in its manifestations and comes into the external world. But in all of this, the inner becomes not only exhibited, it is itself transmitted and manifested. If so, the mind is no longer an invisible center from which various meanings, intentions, and deeds radiate : it becomes embodied in perceptible forms. We may say then of the outer expression that it is absolutely identical with the inner.

But we cannot yet have done with this primary meaning of expression, for there is a further insight into the relational structure of the inner and the outer. Obviously, the inner is a distinct pole, and it can function meaningfully as the inner only when it renounces coinciding with what is expressed by the outer. Thus, such a view as that the inner itself has been exactly disclosed by the outer receives less credence. A fundamental objection that could be raised against it is that the precise mirroring of the invisible by the visible contravenes our understanding of the relational structure, and we can no longer maintain that there is a distinction between the inner and the outer, between the invisible depth of subjectivity and its perceptible surface. To say that the depth actually floats on the surface implies saying that the distinction between them cracks under its own weight. This consequence, Hegel admits, results from the subject's relentless effort to express the inner and to express it too much (*zu sehr*). Whatever may be the decisive reason for the subject's difficulty, it is plausible to assume that, by permitting the outer to usurp the place of the inner, Hegel has allowed the subject to make an unjustified use of the concept of expression which is in itself justified. And this unjustified use of expression has removed one of the essential conditions on which the subject's distinction rests and without which that distinction must collapse.

Secondly, if we consider the way bodily manifestations are externalized and cut off from the concrete individual, they renounce coinciding with the inner and set it at a proper distance. There are, however, many grave difficulties in expressing the immanent marks and qualities of the mind. To say this is nothing more than to recognize that there is such a thing as freedom. Being a free agent, the subject can consciously restrain itself and deliberately refuse to incarnate the immanent traits into the outer expressions. Since in speech and action many a man, for one or another reason, has no intention of expressing what really and truly constitutes their inwardness, when they do modify one of their expressions, it is because they are trying to conceal rather than reveal the inner.

There is, however, a much more intricate difficulty. It emerges from that quite familiar effort of a person who is making an effort to find the right word for his thought and to perform the right act for his decision, but is "too incompetent to give himself the outer aspect he really wanted",[15] and to give his words and actions such stability and univocity that his verbal behavior and his deeds could not become misconceived and/or misinterpreted by others. Now, since both the deliberate decision and deplorable incom-

---

[15] B., p. 341. *Phän.*, p. 230.

petence remain concealed, the observable expressions become simultaneously quite different for the subject and for others.

In the light of these obstacles, one is forced to admit that the inwardness of the individual does not reveal itself but remains shrouded in ambiguity (*Zweideutigkeit*). "On account of this ambiguity, we must look about for the inner as it still is within the individual himself, but in a visible or external form".[16] The precise point of this assertion may be doubtful. Nonetheless, one thing is clear. Once this inevitable ambiguity occurs it can never be overcome. Still, it can be understood by the subject as a warning not to look for the inner characteristics of the individual in those expressions which are bound to convey a double and opposed significance. It is in this sense only that ambiguity can function as a steppingstone to further self-examination. It will hardly be denied that the ambiguous event itself does not say anything explicit and positive with regard to establishing a novel line of dialectical analysis. This must be left to the rational consciousness itself. That consciousness, however, must endeavor to keep the idea of the expression well in view, and it must search for new manifestations which reflect the inner of the individual subject more adequately than the spoken word or the accomplished deed, without repeating what it has already said.

Beyond speech and action, however, there is a new way for the rational subject to envision the inner — a facial expression that seems to involve a direct relation to the mind. The appropriateness of the connection between the mind and the face emerges even more clearly when the subject recognizes that the facial expression has the advantage over word and action in attaining its externalization without producing a specific result, for face is neither an organ nor action. However, we have to speak with considerably great caution about this as constituting a noticeable advance in the course of the dialectic of physiognomy. On the whole, the analysis of the connection between the mind and the face is broadly the same as in the case of language and action. What we have before us is, obviously, a dense and subtle argument; and the specific mark of that argument lies in the fact that the phenomenological investigation of the facial expression is not possible apart from the word or the deed. And this is but another way of saying that the problem regarding facial expressions cannot be introduced except at the risk of reintroducing speech and action. "We look at a man's face and see whether he is earnest with what he says or does".[17] Although

[16] *Ibid.*
[17] B., p. 345. *Phän.*, p. 233.

the facial feature is expected to provide the subject with a reliable criterion, it can have no recognizable validity to perform that function if it itself sinks to the level of "mere existence", which is unquestionably "contingent for the self-conscious individual". But obviously, that which is radically contingent for the rational subject cannot provide it with a satisfactory mode of ingress into the essence of the inner. And this is said to follow because the face is not the innermost individual but a sign. And as soon as one has made clear that the face is "merely a sign indifferent to what is signified",[18] one can proceed to insist that there is no necessary link connecting the inner and the outer.

Perhaps the most fundamental fact in all this is that the significance of facial expressions depends on man's intentions and motives, and these are not susceptible to an observational inspection. To say this, however, is to say that the inwardness of the individual should be sought in the will, in the very locus of human intentions and decisions. Now, whatever the will may be said to connote, it is not identical with the face and its peculiar configurations, for these may easily conceal the true disposition of the individual. For the observing subject, then, the meaning of the will seems to be shrouded in mystery and ambivalence. From one point of view the will can be looked upon as the "individuality's existence within itself". But so long as the will remains just that, it is obvious that the intention, which has its genesis in mind, and the performed act could not be seen as correlatives. According to Hegel, however, the will pertains to the "meaning" regarding the deed and therefore to the deed itself. Now, since volition issues in doing and since the first connotes the true inner and the latter indicates the external aspect, the subject regards its own existence within itself as the essential reality and the performed act as an unessential externalization.

But such differentiation raises a further difficulty with regard to the physical form in which the individual is embodied. Obviously, the subject is not unaware of the significance of its own concrete embodiment, which appears as the visible invisibility of the inner. Thus here the inner and the outer are diametrically opposed to each other and only the outer is divided into two elements : the physical embodiment and the deed. The physical embodiment is, without any doubt, a concrete outer expression, and this consists, as it appears from the context, in a merely sensuous presentment of the invisible. To be sure, the deed is also an expression of the inner; but it is a quite inferior externalization, a purely incidental occurrence.

[18] B., pp. 345-346. *Phän.*, p. 233.

It can hardly be denied that the position in question is an extraordinary one. Still, the differentiation, as it stands, is a very dubious achievement, and its "presumptive" assertions characterize it as a symptom of physiognomic conjecture. Such procedure allows only one explanation : that the emerging distinction between the true outer expression and the unessential externalization is requisite for focusing attention on the physical embodiment rather than deed. Accordingly, this is quite in keeping with the principal hypothesis of physiognomy that the concrete presence of the mind in the physical embodiment is sufficient ground for the scientific attempt — if one cares to call it "scientific" — to disclose the inwardness of the individual.

When the subject's attention becomes diverted from the deed, there exists no alternative save to advance to the position that the individual can be grasped by relating a given sensuous fact to a supposed (*gemeintes*) inner. Reliance upon physiognomy to reveal the individual rests on the assumption that the inner aspect is something determinate which can be grasped as possessing a distinctive content. But the theory of physiognomy could never have become so attractive and promising unless there were evidence, or what appears like evidence, to justify it. If so, the subject must ask why the physiognomist should insist that the reality of a man is his face. This inquisitive attitude is essential, and places the subject in a critical position which enables it to guide its further development. Evidently, the actual question with which the subject has to deal here is the physiognomist's expectation to discover the so-called "physiognomical laws". For the physiognomist, the law is a necessary relation that holds between the inwardness of individuality and the bodily expression. Apparently, whether such a law is at all possible has to be decided from the very nature of the diverse aspects, which one seeks to relate and compare.

First of all, the physiognomist places in the bodily expressions far more than they deserve : he charges them with a variety of attributes which they do not possess. For instance, the physiognomist is unaware of the fact that every facial configuration or any other bodily expression is an "indifferent accident", an incidental occurrence. The physiognomist does not realize, too, that both the physical embodiment of the mind and the individual's inwardness itself are inexpressible (*unaussprechlich*). Thus, the physiognomist's account of the embodiment of subjectivity is totally barren. No wonder, then, that there seems to be more reluctance to establish universally valid laws in the physiognomical section of the *Phenomenology* than there was in the psychological section, and this unconcealed reluctance can be looked upon as an attempt to indicate the pseudo-scientific character of the physiognomical pursuits.

To go through the physiognomical phase is a hard and absorbing activity, which lasts as long as the subject does not engage itself in critical considerations. In effect, these critical considerations are accepted by the subject as offering a convincing refutation of physiognomy. What is more, their cumulative effect is to suggest that the two opposed aspects upon which the physiognomical conjecture was proceeding are to be canceled. Now, once these aspects have been seen as implying dialectical cancellation, and once it has appeared that they should vanish into a category that expresses the "true being of man", the subject can pause for a cautious deliberation. The subject is justified in asking whether the category needed for the anticipated cancellation and reconciliation is to be sought for among the concepts of the previous analysis — in which case the choice is limited to volition and action; or whether the search should be conducted with the presumption that there is no concept left which did not yet appear before the observational reason — in which case the subject should introduce a new concept capable of cancelling the passive physical embodiment and the inexpressibleness of the individual. It is doubtful, however, that the subject ever wavered in making the decision, for it abruptly selects the first alternative, being convinced that the physiognomical approach has unjustifiably diverted its attention from the deed. As we will recall, the deed has been degraded to an unessential externalization. But this is an utter absurdity. The truth is that only the deed can convey man's genuine being. The individual human being is what his deed is, regardless of what he may think with respect to the act he has just performed.[19] Even if it be a fact that a pretended intention underlies man's deed, the objectivization (*die Gegenständlichkeit*) by itself cannot change the nature of that deed.

Only one issue more needs to be touched upon, and it concerns the anticipated cancellation. Not only is the deed the adequate expression of the individual, it is a reality capable of performing the required act of cancellation. This is doubly true, because the deed, exemplifying a positive activity of the individual, does away not only with the presumed passive physical expression but also with the inexpressibleness of what the subject is in itself. And this, if it means anything, appears to mean that instead of the physiognomical law, the rational subject has discovered the deed as its

---

[19] "In the same way, on the other hand, when his performance and his inner possibility, capacity, or intention are opposed, the former *alone* is to be regarded as his true reality, even if he deceives himself on the point and, after he has turned from his action into himself, means to be something else in his 'inner mind' than what he is in the act. Individuality, which commits itself to the objective element, when it passes over into a deed no doubt puts itself to the risk of being altered and perverted". B., p. 350. *Phän.*, p. 237.

most fruitful conclusion derived from the endless conjectures of physiognomy. And with this insight, the dialectic must come to a stop.

Still, the self-conscious subject continues to be restless. Having thus corrected and overcome the presumptuousness of physiognomy, the subject must move on to a phase in which the self-conscious subjectivity can be observed standing towards its "actuality that is definitely fixed and purely existent".[20] Of course, one could insist that Hegel has demonstrated — when an outstanding commentator, such as J. Loewenberg,[21] helps him out a little in his reasoning — that the transition from physiognomy to phrenology is neither abrupt nor arbitrary. True enough, the subject's penetrating and critical analysis, based upon the presumptive premises of physiognomy, does, indeed, establish something relevant and significant. However, the disclosed fact that the "individuality is real in the deed" has no bearing whatever upon the new point of departure and has nothing to do with the transition to phrenology. It seems safe to say that Hegel has simply slipped over from "physical embodiment" in the sense of the outer that is dynamic, variable, and active to "physical embodiment" in the sense of something fixed, permanent, and stable. We know that Hegelian transitions in the *Phenomenology* differ in necessity, sophistication, abruptness etc. The view that Hegel did not derive the point of departure of the phrenological dialectic from the terminal insight of the preceding process but abruptly declared that there is still left a further aspect in which the individuality expresses its rational nature in a fixed and solid physical actuality, seems to be evident. The opening statement of the phrenological section bears witness to the fact that Hegel has decided upon a direct, unsophisticated transition. Here are his words :

If we look now at the range of relations as a whole in which self-conscious individuality can be observed standing towards its outer aspect, there will be one left which has still to come before observation as an object.[22]

And so, Hegel allows the subject to jump from the consideration of the physical embodiment of the mind in its variable aspect to the consideration of the physical embodiment of the mind in its concrete, solid, and fixed aspect. Insofar as the subject transforms the physiognomist's argument and discloses the significance of the deed, the subject's insight remains absolutely irrelevant to the new theme. Thus, instead of preparing the

---

[20] B., p. 351. *Phän.*, p. 238.
[21] *Op. cit.*, pp. 145-146.
[22] B., p. 351. *Phän.*, pp. 237-238.

way for the novel type of observation, the insight achieved remains isolated and sterile.

The continual concern with the concrete objectivization of mind's inwardness can be seen in many a passage in the physiognomical section of the *Phenomenology*. This issue had finally to move into the forefront of the subject's interest out of its originally common sense position with the noticeable shift from the ambivalent linguistic and facial expressions to the phrenologist's pretention to locate the mind in the structure of the skull-bone. Although the shape of the skull provides a conceivable mode of ingress into the inner, the chances of the phrenologist's success are from the very beginning extremely slight. Having refused to abandon the observational attitude and the claim that the individual's mind is open to inspection, but seeing that such an inspection is liable to a complete failure if it is conducted and interpreted in terms of variable expressions and signs, the subject finds itself in a difficult position.

The notion of the skull-bone may be legitimately introduced into a discussion when the subject has seen that there is ample evidence that it is, indeed, the fixed outer as opposed to the merely changing outer. The organs, language, and face proved to be incapable of being taken as trustworthy expressions of the inner, precisely because of their variability and ambivalence. Thus, only in terms of stability and fixedness can the attempt to relate mind and the skull-bone escape the danger of being interpreted as an ambiguous generalization.

Taken in its objective mode of existence, the skull is not an organ of activity, for it is not consciousness acting in a special way. Nor does it exhibit any symbolic significance, proclaiming that it stands for something else than what it is at first perceptual contact. But what has always been peculiar of the observable characteristics of the skull is that they register the simplest facticity. The skull-bone by itself is such a neutral object and such a naive thing (*der Schädelknochen ist ein so gleichgültiges, unbefangenes Ding*) "that there is nothing else to be seen in it or to be thought about it directly as it is, except simply the fact of its being a skull".[23] However, this notion of the skull's facticity, vague as it is, does remind one of the brain as an intermediate link between the self-conscious individuality and the skull. It is in the skull, then, that the specific functions of the brain would have to find their external reality revealed, "a reality which is none the less in the individual himself".[24] Thus, on one side the subject will find a number

---

[23] B., p. 359. *Phän.*, p. 244.
[24] B., p. 355. *Phän.*, p. 241.

of structural characteristics of the skull and on the other a number of cerebral functions or a number of mental properties, the variety and differentiation of which will depend on the subject's introspective capacity. It is possible, however, by a sort of theorizing that hinges upon the principle of causal dependence, to insist that every given characteristic trait of the mind will correspond to a specific formation of the skull. A justification of this, of course, involves a careful and punctilious correlation of the two aspects. To be sure, the phrenologist's very function as a scientist impels him to pursue this correlation without exposing himself to the danger of superficiality, artificiality, and arbitrariness. But the richer and the more complex is the subject's idea of the mind, the more difficult it becomes to relate the given aspects, even if it were reasonable to assume that there are just as many hollows and bumps on the skull as there are cerebral functions in the brain and mental properties in the mind.

The utter impossibility of the phrenological project, however, comes to light only when the subject deliberately refuses to ignore the fact "that the mind's original primordial being consists merely in *dispositions*, which mind has to a large extent under its control".[25] Evidently, human spirit makes itself and activates itself continually. But the skull as an ossified thing is hardly capable of registering mind's continual growth and self-determination. And if the skull does indicate that which is merely potential, there is absolutely no guarantee that the latent disposition of the mind will ever become realized. The notion of the potential disposition clearly implies that the given individual is actually not what he ought to be. Accordingly, the actual marks on the skull might proclaim him to be what in reality he is not and perhaps never shall be.

Therefore, it does not seem legitimate to speak of phrenology as having succeeded in linking the inner and the outer. Exhibiting the existence and form of a bare thing that lacks transparency, the skull cannot make the individual's nature either intelligible or meaningful. Further progress in observation, then, is inconceivable, for if man's inwardness does not reveal itself in the most concretely observable object, one cannot expect to find it revealed anywhere else. And so, "the last stage of reason's function of observation is its very worst, and for that reason its complete reversal becomes necessary".[26]

Despite the urgency of the issue, the occurrence of the promised reversal did not come to the subject immediately as expected. The very fact that the

[25] B., p. 363. *Phän.*, p. 247.
[26] B., p. 366. *Phän.*, p. 250.

observational process has terminated its development seemed to imply
that phrenology should pass into opposite and more closer to the subject's
inwardness. Thus, it is rather remarkable that, having prepared the ground
for a smooth transition, Hegel paused for an afterthought. Obviously,
there was more than one motive playing upon his mind for this unexpected
pause. It is necessary, we believe, even at the risk of tediousness, to touch
upon some of these reasons and their implications.

Apparently one reason which prevented Hegel from plunging immediately
into a new dialectical chain, was that he felt the need of stressing the significance of the whole process which seemed like an intolerable waste of time
and effort. According to Hegel, it should not be assumed that persistent
failures of the rational subject invalidate either the distinction between
the inner and the outer or their mutual connection. Recurrent failure may
have strengthened the subject's conviction that mental traits cannot be ascribed to any corporeal part of the individual; but it can hardly remove their
intrinsic dependence which is certainly not open to observation.

What has initiated and necessitated this long and ambitious process
was the subject's deeply-rooted conviction that the rational and the real
are identical. Although the subject was precluded from proclaiming a
complete and unconditional identity of the two, the essential principle
requisite for such identity has been established. The claim to validity for
this principle was derived from the impossibility of retracting the causal
dependence between the inner and the outer, in the sense that the first
partakes of the second. Thus, the rational (*geistige*) individuality if
it is to have an effect (*Wirkung*) on the body must as cause be itself bodily
(*leiblich*).[27] The law of causal dependence — which appears to be the only
valid law so far — defies all attempts at explaining it away. This idea not only
demands that we acknowledge the unity of mind and body, but it offers us
the basis for a genuine identification of rational subjectivity and mere
objectivity. Certainly, to assert that the being of man is his skull is to assert
something that is dangerously near nonsense. This danger, of course,
arises from the belief that the statement ascertains a complete reduction
of rational subjectivity to thinghood or to a sort of objectivization of subjectivity. Once this assumption is set aside, it becomes clear that Hegel had
every right to insist that the mind is at least *as objective* as a bare thing.
Crucial here is the fact that the subject has found the most elementary type
of objectivity in its own individual being, but without having to renounce
its rational depth and its spiritual potentialities. In a sense, the subject

---

[27] B., p. 352. *Phän.*, p. 238.

has turned itself into something whose very nature was formerly conceived as opposed to consciousness, rationality, and freedom. It seems safe to say that the subject has always sought to measure its being in terms of a rational thing and finally this intent was brought to fruition by the observational performance.

Having achieved objectivity whose inner meaning is essential subjectivity, the subject can refuse to set itself over against the objective existence of a mere thing. What is more, the notion of objectivity now receives a new connotation, for it no longer means something belonging to an alien impersonal reality. The subject is at least as objective as a corporeal thing or a material entity. Thus, the initial identity of the rational and the real does not lead Hegel to look upon the subject's acts as embodying and exemplifying the thinghood and nothing more. The objectivity of the subject is, professedly, richer than the objectivity which is proper to a mere thing. But to present this conviction in an irrefutable manner, the subject must move from self-examination to self-realization.

CHAPTER XII

THE SELF-REALIZATION OF THE RATIONAL SUBJECT

It seems logical to assume that, having exhausted the cognitional potentialities of the observational reason, Hegel should advance to the performances of the practical reason for the sake of exhibiting the volitional capacities of the subject. Such transition, then, is conditioned by the alleged distinction between the cognitional and the volitional approach to self-consciousness. Therefore, it seems proper to make here a few remarks regarding that distinction.

Let us first of all note that rational observation has a cognitional function. Hegel describes this activity as a detached and abstract (*begrifflos*) process, not, however, without adding the qualifying note that the subject engaged in such process "seeks to find itself immediately". Nonetheless, by interpreting self-consciousness as a reality that consists in the skull-bone, the rational subject has no clear understanding as to what that judgment really involves, and "does not grasp the determinate character of the subject and predicate in the proposition and of their relation to one another".[1] Thus, exposing the shortcomings and limitations of the observational reason, the subject finds itself compelled to depart completely not only from the theoretical procedure, but also from the attempt to find itself immediately. And this departure appears to the self-conscious subject indispensable for the very sake of realizing "itself by its own activity". Hence the process of the practical reason is a process of self-fulfillment, and the volitional activity appears as the sufficient condition of the possibility of that process. In short, observation is replaced here by practical operation. This sort of operation we can qualify as "voluntary", in the sense that it is a manifestation of what Hegel calls the "will-process",[2] which is expected to reveal a new dimension of the rational subjectivity.

---

[1] B., p. 371. *Phän.*, p. 352.
[2] Cf. B., p. 380. *Phän.*, p. 260.

If allowance for the specification of the self-realization is made, the conception of the individual subject must be reformulated in terms of the mundane being who steps into the world to meet other mundane existents. Now, according to Hegel, the subject steps into the world "with the intention of duplicating itself in the determinate form of an individual, of producing itself as this particular individual, and creating this its own existential counterpart, and thus becoming conscious of this unity of its own actual reality with the objective world".[3] To be sure, leaving the process of observation, the subject has the awareness and certainty of its unity with the external reality. But at this point, the concept of unity does not reveal itself in complete transparency. Still, however vague, indeterminate, and obscure this unity may be to the observing self-consciousness, it is improper to characterize it in a merely negative manner solely by stressing the absence of explicit determinations.

It is worth noting that the dismissal of the theoretical approach entails not only a new orientation, but also a new insight. By virtue of this insight what is given in the very decision to seek unity is considered as gratifying. From the very beginning, then, the project of the practical reason receives the index of being able to procure for the rational subject the experience of satisfaction and happiness. Certainly, this fact should not come to us as a surprise, because hand in hand with the search for unity, goes the desire for happiness. It is safe to say, then, that desire for unity is a desire to complete one's subjectivity, and ensuing upon that desire is the expectation of happiness.

With this the ground is prepared for the dialectical argument advanced in the section, entitled *"Pleasure and Necessity"*. The heading suggests a quite adequate idea of the content of what follows. Here again, however, it is the dense argument and the detailed exposition, and not the general themes, which give a special coloration to the content.

Turning from cognitional to practical sphere, the subject leans upon its deep-seated desire to seek completion and find happiness in doing so. Desire is thus essentially an invitation to initiate a new process. But in order to come to a concrete starting point which would be both feasible and phenomenologically justifiable, the subject must be cognizant of its starting position. Now, it is readily apparent that the rational mind is explicitly aware of being an objective reality, even though its objectivity is as yet merely the notion of self-consciousness. This simply means that self-consciousness has objectivity within itself, but it does not enjoy an actual independent

3 B., p. 380. *Phän.*, p. 259.

existence. Small wonder, then, that existence (*das Sein*) should appear to the subject as a reality distinct from its own (*als eine andere Wirklichkeit*). Granting and stressing the distinction between what self-consciousness is "for itself" (*für sich*) and what it is "in itself" (*an sich*), the subject is led to regard the latter as a reality other than its own and, therefore, as an ideal that implicates both aspiration and purpose. Because the subject allows for self-realization as purposive process, it cannot escape the demand of turning this ideal self-consciousness "into its own self". But, seen in a strictly phenomenological way, what does this opposition mean, and how does it express itself in the dialectical manner?

Since the subject desires "to see itself as another independent being", one may assume that it should make an attempt at grasping what this really means. Accordingly, one would expect that the examination of this opposition would be recognized as the primary concern of self-consciousness. One is, indeed, justified in asking whether the ground for the affirmation of an actual and independent self-consciousness is to be sought for in the subject's awareness that it has not yet accomplished its objectivization — in which case the proposition would be mere anticipation; or whether the concept of existentially secure self-consciousness is derived from an actual *an sich* — in which case the proposition would imply that the subject has already encountered another self-conscious being who "is essentially itself". It cannot, to be sure, be asserted or even assumed that the artless self-consciousness has to impersonate another self-consciousness which has surpassed the first in existence, maturity, and experience. From the strictly phenomenological position, this view is untenable. And so, the second alternative collapses under its own weight. But if we retain the first alternative, the alleged difficulty does not disappear, for the introductory proposition merely states the problem which awaits a dialectical explicitation and solution. Evidently, the issue here positively and resolutely clamors for elaboration and clarification. To be sure, the reality which stands in opposition to the practical mind is a conception constituted, professedly, by the subject longing for unity and happiness, but there follows, as evidenced by the text, no explicit explanation and no attempt to eliminate the imminent danger of ambiguity. Instead of that, the rational subject is suddenly led into a very concrete situation, into the whirl of sensible existence, where the individual "takes to itself life much as a ripe fruit is plucked, which comes to meet the hand that takes it".[4]

As if beginning anew, Hegel turns to concrete existence with the intention

---

[4] B., p. 385. *Phän.*, p. 263.

of stressing the subject's interest in the world and its "fruits". If, then, we assume with Hegel that the individual self-consciousness plunges into life in order to carry out its longing for happiness or pleasure, the main issue of the section becomes intelligible and we can easily follow its course. Surely, the point of view from which the subject considers the world must be grasped in its specific character. If the subject is confronted with the realm of life, it is because this realm reveals itself through certain cognitive acts. But if the subject is *interested* in the world, it is because this world presents itself *as gratifying*, as responding to the needs and aspirations of the subject. In brief, the subject is interested in the world, not to perceive it or to scrutinize it, but to enjoy it.

Abiding by this standpoint and this orientation with respect to the realm of life, the rational subject assumes the attitude of a pleasure-seeker. Undoubtedly, the pleasure-seeker's contention is precisely this, that there is nothing more evident than the experience of desire, and nothing more important than its gratification. Still, the object of desire is so vague and the experience of gratification is so indefinite that the general contention that it belongs to the very nature of man as an individual that he should be happy gives us no information as to the kind of happiness or pleasure which is sought. What complicates the issue is the fact that the practical reason, having turned its back on the "grey shades of science, laws and principles",[5] which alone stand between happiness and the mind, is precluded from making value judgments and from identifying its object. Accordingly, a longing from which reflection is excluded can never distinguish between happiness and pleasure, between hedonism and sensualism. However, the practical self-consciousness experiences one permanent, stable conviction : that the individual subject is objectively and irrevocably ordered toward happiness, and this belief is simply accepted, implicitly and unreflectedly as a rule. But despite this unreflected commitment, the search for pleasure is involved in all activities of the subject in a rather articulate form. Still, this is not so much a general thesis or a general philosophy, as J. N. Findlay seems to suggest,[6] but an indispensable activity entailing search for individual identity. According to Hegel, the attachment to the pursuit of pleasure serves the purpose of rendering explicit the essential condition of the subject to become a fully objective reality. On this point Hegel's thought

---

[5] B., p. 385. *Phän.*, p. 262.

[6] *Op. cit.*, p. 108. It might be well to note here that Hegel grants hedonism philosophical significance, but as a problem, not as a constituted doctrine. This means that the doctrinal claims of hedonism remain open to consideration, doubt, and criticism.

is very explicit. He writes : "The pleasure enjoyed has, indeed, the positive significance that the self has become aware of itself as objective self-consciousness".[7] Still, this achievement is almost trifling, for it signifies little more than the confirmation of the mind's initial conviction of being an objective being. There is, however, considerable significance in the fact that the "pleasure enjoyed" can supply the subject with an effective means of realizing itself as an individual. The subject plunges into life and seeks pleasure as if its whole nature as an individual consisted exclusively and solely in that activity. Seeing no other possibility, the subject has the impression that this path leads to the discovery and realization of true individuality.

However, whether the subject can retain this position and remain on the original path is a question that is to be decided only through the consideration of the negative significance of the pleasurable enjoyment. So, what must be stressed is not primarily the positive significance of the pleasure-seeking activity. More important is the reference to its negative import which arises from "nothing else than the notion of what this individuality inherently is".[8] Obviously, this is an obscure statement, and it verges on the inconceivable because it is an epitome awaiting dialectical argument. But despite all the obscurity involved in presenting negativity in such a manner, one fact is beyond any dispute : One is confronted here with the problem of the relationship between the individual as it appears and constitutes itself through the search for pleasure and the individual as it implicitly and inherently is.

It was no stubborn pedantry or preconceived plan that made Hegel proceed to seek for the nature of the individual through the self-correcting process. All of which comes to one thing : the discovery of interrelated insignificant acts does more for subjectivity than the discovery of an isolated power. In Hegel's eyes, the development of individuality is a process of gradual experimentation. Perhaps one could add that the general orientation and direction of this process is defined by the ideal of complete rationality and utmost existence. Under whatever aspect the individual has thus far presented itself in the course of its volitional process, there are, at every phase of the development, references to the ideals of utmost rationality and existence. Of course, this does not mean that from now on the subject will seek to realize its individuality by appealing to some illusory and imaginary ideal. If phenomenology meant only this, it would hardly represent a dialectical development. The truth is, however, that the individuality must be

---

[7] B., p. 386. *Phän.*, p. 263.
[8] B., p. 386. *Phän.*, p. 264.

allowed to follow its course and provide its own justification, which it can do if it attends to the immediate issues and succeeds in purging itself of relativity and limitation. While the rational self-consciousness anticipates and places projects before itself, it cannot leap to their immediate solution. So, the most urgent interest of the practical reason is always directed not to the ideals or anticipations but to the issues that are already present and are somehow given.

Now, it is obvious that pursuing and enjoying self-centered happiness, the subject is destined to become a self-centered individual to whom nothing matters except personal gratification. Eventually, the individual subject in search for pleasure comes to regard itself as self-sufficient, pretending to have achieved the being-in-itself and genuine individuality. By Hegel's own explicit admission "this individuality is, however, as yet the poorest form of self-realizing mind; for it is to itself still simply the abstraction of reason, or is the merely immediate unity of being-for-self and being-in-self".[9] Thus, instead of having reached its goal of utmost rationality and existence, the subject finds itself in a state of mere relation of "pure unity" and "pure difference". Undoubtedly, the experience of pleasure develops the individual and contributes to its growth, but precisely the same experience brings the subject into conflict with other subjects, for the self-centered individualism militates against intersubjectivity and precludes the subject from any mutual, positive communion with others.

The other individual is, for Hegel, an independently existent being. Since the rational subject fully participates in the concrete life, the question concerning the existence of other subjects cannot be considered as problematic. In other words, the pleasure-seeker's awareness of other individuals forms part of "vital" experience. For life itself is the irrefutable revelation of the differentiation of multiple subjects. But obviously, there is nothing exceptionally new in all this, for already in the descriptive introduction to the present section, Hegel has warned us that the rational subjectivity, upon entering the sphere of practical activity, breaks into numerous entirely independent beings.[10]

Although we may be dismayed at an argument so dogmatic and abrupt, we

---

[9] *Ibid.*

[10] "Reason appears here as the fluent universal substance, as unchangeable simple thinghood which yet breaks up into many entirely independent beings, just as light bursts asunder into stars as innumerable luminous points, each giving light on its own account, and whose absolute self-existence (*Fürsichseyn*) is dissolved, not merely implicitly (*an sich*), but explicitly for themselves (*für sich*), within the simple independent substance". B., p. 376. *Phän.*, p. 257.

have here a hint of the mutual contact between solitary individuals. To be sure, speaking of the pleasure-seeking as being equally essential to all individuals, we have in view the possibility that this important preoccupation will assume enriching, elevating, and other character. But the matter turns out quite differently. Though reason demands that what the subjects do should be rational, consistent, and meaningful, the search for the self-centered pleasure brings solitary individuals in conflict with one another. Awareness of the mutual collision intervenes in the search for the subjectively satisfying, and the experience of hostility suddenly disturbs the pleasurable enjoyment. More properly, however, this intervention is one of those conditions which determine the subject's surrender to the incomprehensible fate (*Schicksal*). Thus, individual subjects, gathering some comfort from the hope that pleasure-seeking also would lead to genuine individuality, were given somber warning by the antagonistic collision that they should abandon their unrestrained subjective pursuit and follow the dictates of the overpowering necessity. In a sense, this transition from the realm of pleasure to the realm of fate is performed by a leap which is founded upon a different evaluation of life. The pleasure-seeker was convinced that the worldly existence is attuned to his personal longings and needs, including the deep-seated concern to attain true individuality. But after his disappointing experiment with the continuous stream of self-centered enjoyment, the individual comes to regard life as adverse and inimical. When the subject's attention is caught by the concept of necessity, characteristic features of that concept receive prominence and the subjective desires appear rather irrelevant. More precisely expressed, the very rise of the problem of necessity and its formulation motivates the fatalistic resignation and, hence, the abandonment of the individual as such. So, what began as a promising search for the true individual has ended in discovering no individual at all.

Hegel touches here a very important point, namely, the danger of presenting the individual as a being entirely alien to itself. In pursuing the subjectively satisfying, the subject runs the risk of developing a pseudo-individuality with the corollary danger of losing forever the authenticity of its individual identity. Thus, the struggle for genuine individuality at length wears itself out and "appears consequently in such form that the individual is simply reduced to naught".[11] Still, what Hegel is attempting with this ruthless reduction is not so much to transform the subject into some lifeless substance as to establish a new line of thought which could provide

---

[11] B., p. 387. *Phän.*, p. 265.

an evidence that fate or necessity is essentially an expression of the subject's universal nature itself.

Owing to the permanency of self-consciousness and its inherently universal nature, the subject can never lose sight of itself. Nor can the subject permit its living unity to degenerate into an alien and lifeless mode of existence. It should be clear, too, that the experience of danger can induce the subject to ask questions and awaken its determination to preserve itself from destruction. Thus, when the subject dwells upon this grave threat, the premise from which it has been derived is given not only as having been greatly exaggerated, but also as able to be restored into a positive step foreward.

To see the significance of this we must remember that the crucial task before the subject is the explicitation of the concept of necessity. Initially, the idea of necessity was conceived as a "relation bare and simple, but imperturbable, irresistible, and immovable, whose work is merely the nothingness of individual existence".[12] Seen in this way, the category of necessity opposes the rational subject and works against it. But the transition — one would like to say, transformation — of the subject's "living being" into "lifeless necessity" is an abstract reduction which is accomplished without a mediating factor. Its absence is the basic reason why the subject views the attempt at reduction as unjustifiable. And its specious character is the reason also why the subject regards the argument as perverse; and realization of this perversion is, finally, the reason why the subject denounces the fatalistic causality and places the principle of necessity within its own proper nature. Thus, we are brought before that very phenomenon which, when disclosed and rendered explicit, finds its expression in the law of the heart.

What we have before us is a complicated argument whose primary characteristic is that it moves from the pleasure-seeking to fatalistic resignation and from the fatalistic resignation to a kind of sentimentalism. Such an argument contains many difficulties and obscurities, and the suspicion arises that Hegel's procedure is essentially arbitrary. Now, if we remain at present in the sphere of general principles, we can ask ourselves the question whether it would be possible to find a less arbitrary transition. Obviously, Hegel himself would be the first to say that the disillusioning experience of the life of pleasure is the crucial point of the present dialectic. But if disillusionment with the self-centered gratification constitutes the problem and supplies motivation for the decision to accept the mysterious, impersonal necessity, the solution can hardly be confined to a fatalistic

---

[12] B., p. 387. *Phän.*, p. 264.

resignation. Seeing that the self-centered pleasure suffers an eclipse and ends in mutual conflict and disappointment, the subject should recognize the urgent need to break through the circle of a life which is of boredom, hostility, and self-imprisonment. In other words, having failed to achieve a purely subjective pleasure, the subject should aim at the objective happiness. Now, there can be little doubt that this is altogether in keeping with the gradual constitution and self-realization of true individuality. If the constant enjoyment of the subjectively gratifying *isolates* the pleasure-seekers from one another, the pursuit of the authentic happiness *liberates* the individual from self-imprisonment and discloses the social dimension. Thus, the disillusioned subject could confidently decide that an approach other than the merely subjective is really possible without the necessity of referring to the fatalistic attitude. Besides, several outstanding historical doctrines are available to illustrate the career of the subject in search of subjective pleasure as well as the subject's longing for an objective happiness.[13] What is more, this would abbreviate the process and eliminate so many details. But Hegel has decided on a different course and has chosen to illustrate the sentimental pursuit of the practical reason in terms drawn from the works of Goethe and Schiller. Though one is puzzled by Hegel's decision, one feels that in the so-called law of the heart he saw a relevant exemplification of a special type of individuality. Apparently, with the concept of individuality Hegel has never lost his patience and was well prepared to torment himself and his reader with the most intricate details.

As we saw, in this "new attitude self-consciousness regards itself as the necessary element"[14] and takes its self-existence as universal. These two statements are not only complementary, but imply the third, namely, that self-consciousness contains within itself a law, which we can qualify as "immediate", for it is not yet actual and explicit. When we add to this the contention or conviction that the law in question is the law of the heart, which stands in opposition to the concrete reality of life, we have a galaxy of impressive ideas replete with farfetching implications. To whatever extent these ideas are vague and indefinite, they are referred to as constituting a professedly complex starting point.

---

[13] We are thinking here of the doctrine of pleasure proposed by Aristippus of Cyrene and the notion of a lasting happiness introduced by Plato and elaborated by Aristotle. The name of Epicurus must be mentioned, too, although there seems to be no reason for tagging him as an egoistic hedonist. Prof. Norman W. DeWitt describes the teaching of Epicurus as "a higher hedonism". See his *Epicurus and His Philosophy* (Minneapolis : University of Minnesota Press, 1954), p. 31.

[14] B., p. [391]. *Phän.*, p. 266.

Passing on from hedonistic pursuits to sentimental concern for the well-being of mankind, the subject does not depart from the original attitude of desire that certainly includes a longing for the perfect individuality. The basic volitional tendency thus proves to be on a par with the necessities of the law of the heart. There is, of course, a considerable change in the subject's immediate interest, which has been aroused by the discovery that the world of concrete life is an intersubjective world, common to all individuals, in which they not only live together but also orient themselves in their actions with regard to one another. By virtue of such a significant recognition, the subject's interest is withdrawn from the subjectively satisfying to be shifted to the entire social order to which it has not previously been directed under the predominance of selfishness. Being modeled on the altruistic ideals, the dialectic takes a new turn, with the assumption that the sympathetic concern for mankind contains within itself all that could be said about the true individuality.

The heartfelt concern for humanity implies that the actual state of mankind is deplorable, calamitous, and unjustly oppressed. For the subject, then, the whole of mankind appears to be subjected to an alien and oppressive factor. To deal with the world, therefore, purports being presented with a certain range of data which, on account of their relevancy to the subject's altruistic concern, constitute the notion of external necessity. This assertion, however, seems at variance with the previous one that the principle of true and really meaningful necessity lies in the subject. Still, the presence of external necessity is a phenomenological datum and must be recognized as such. But recognizing and emphasizing the external necessity, the subject must not overlook the fact that it contradicts the law of the heart and vehemently opposes rational subjectivity.

If we continue to examine the oppositional character of this strange necessity, we will see that it alone is responsible for the suffering and misfortune from which humanity must be delivered. But obviously, the subject cannot overcome the grievous necessity except by carrying out the law of the heart, that is, by declaring the heart to be the universal promise and salvation of mankind. To say this, of course, implies saying that the law of a particular individual should be transfigured into a "universal ordinance". If so, the subject imbued with the desire for universal welfare must ignore itself as particular and recognize the realm of independent universality.

With this attitude, isolated from itself as individual, the subject takes on another complexion and suddenly finds itself on the road of self-alienation. Put in his own words, Hegel is saying that the "law of the heart ceases through its very realization to be a law of the heart".[15] Now, when the proposed law comes into actual existence, it becomes a universal rule, "which holds this particular 'heart' to be a matter of indifference; so that the individual, in establishing his own ordinance, no longer finds it to be his own".[16] Thus, instead of realizing the law of the heart, the subject gets involved, entangled, and enmeshed in an ordinance, which appears as detestable to all the other subjects, for they do not find that ordinance to express the law of *their* hearts. Here begins the collapse of individualism, for the desire to reshape the world in accordance with the law of the heart alienates the subject from its own individual self. The subject loses sight of itself as individual in the independent universality, although the latter is the result of its own action. Here begins also the collapse of sentimentalism, precisely because the other subjects find in the proposed law "not the law of their heart fulfilled, but rather that of someone else".[17] Failing to find their own hearts in what is law, they turn against it and also against the legislator. The conclusion of all this is that the pretendedly altruistic, benevolent, and heartfelt intentions of the subject are rejected by other subjects as utterly egoistic, personal, and heartless. However, if others see laws of the heart this way, the subject's self-assurance is not thereby lessened. The subject remains persistent and unbending in its ambitious decision to restore the world. Surely, this same attitude extends itself to the entire society of individuals, where each person encounters all the others revolting and struggling against him. Consequently, when accused of possessing and exhibiting a perverted nature, each and every subject retorts with the same accusation, without realizing that such contemptible action leads to a pitiless and "frantic self-conceit".

The basic intention of the rational subject remains misconceived if one interprets the inner perversion of rational consciousness and the ensuing "war of each against all" as a critique of Rousseau or even as a necessary outcome of "social reform". Accordingly, the struggle of the practical reason cannot be approached from the polemical standpoint; nor can it be adequately fitted into the heroic story of Schiller's *Robbers*. The frenzy of self-conceit marks the opposition that obtains between the immature individual and the true universal. Surely, the concern for humanity directs the individual subject beyond its own narrow horizon to the universal social order. But this road could never lead to the attainment of true uni-

---

[15] B., p. 393. *Phän.*, p. 268.
[16] *Ibid.*
[17] B., p. 395. *Phän.*, p. 269.

versality. "It is the heart, however, or the particular consciousness immediately seeking to be universal, that is thus raving and perverted".[18] That is to say, the perversion of rational subjectivity lies precisely in this that it seeks to achieve universality through a direct leap. But when the subject proposes and then establishes the law according to its own heart, "it finds itself resisted by others because it conflicts with the equally individual laws of their heart".[19] What appears as universal here "is only a universal resistance and struggle of all against one another".[20] Still, if the subject examines the meaning of universality implied in the very notion of universal ordinance, it will find two meaningful aspects of unequal value. The first aspect of universality can be completely and satisfactorily accounted for in terms of restless individuals. Each individual, seeking to establish the law of the heart, is aware of its self as this particular reality. Its intention, however, is to realize itself as universal. Since this is true of all subjects, they must regard their individuality to be unreal and the unattained and unattainable universality as their reality. The other aspect of universality reveals itself in what Hegel calls its inherent and static essence (*Allgemeine als ruhiges Wesen*). This static — one would like to say "ideal" — universality, however, can come into an actual existence only by cancelling or transforming the immature individuality. Thus, the constitution of the true universal demands the destruction of the petty individual.

Indeed, since an isolated, confused, and perverted individual seems to have little, if any, significance from either a social or universal perspective, and since it stands in the way of meaningful self-realization, there can be no reason whatsoever for trying to save it from dissipation or cancellation. Now, according to the nature and status of a particular individual, the act of cancellation must assume a definite specified form. Since the ultimate cause of mutual rejection, contempt, and perversion lies in the individuals' egoistic, personal, and heartless dispositions, it is only the *virtue* that can overcome these vices. The subject is thus led to advance the idea of a purge of the dishonest individuality in terms of noble and idealistic virtue.

One misleading idea which must be avoided in the approach to the category of virtue is that of considering it as a self-explanatory term which has a definite meaning as it stands. Concepts like virtue and rectitude arise only if the subject, while ascribing a noble attitude to itself, reaches over into the world with the intent of perfecting it, or conversely, while perceiving

[18] B., p. 397. *Phän.*, p. 272.
[19] B., p. 399. *Phän.*, p. 273.
[20] *Ibid.*

the triumph of evil in the world, turns to the volitional capacity in order to lay the foundations for the decision to dethrone perversion, dishonesty, and egoism. Initially, then, virtue is "an abstraction which only attains reality in a relation",[21] the one term of this relation being the morally awakened subject and the other the "course of the world". Therefore, all questions about virtue and its meaning lead to the one question about the relation of subjectivity and the actual course of the world. Seen in this way, the law, which receives now moral relevance, represents the element to be preserved and the individuality the one to be eliminated, for this latter has been recognized as the enemy of universality and the source of evil. Without stretching the point too far, then, this means that the universal is expected to receive its alleged reality and significance from the subject turned virtuous.

Convinced that the true meaning of the law lies in goodness and universality, the rational subject may continue its search for self-realization. Perhaps one could say that to explicate the pursuit of self-realization simply means to show in what way and under what conditions the rational subject can ask the question : what is really good or universal? The question is inevitably complicated by the fact that one cannot isolate the notion of universality from the particular individual and one cannot detach the individual from the concrete world process. For universality determines the purpose of the individual turned virtuous and the course of the world is determined by the individual who seeks self-gratification and "wants to be a law independently and on its own account".[22]

Still, one may assume the rational subjectivity to be so strongly convinced of being the instrument of universality and so unconditionally dedicated to the realization of universal purpose in the shape of the good that personal feelings and desires are seen as alienable possessions. Such an orientation is motivated and even necessitated by the virtuous consciousness, and surely, the emergence of the virtuous disposition is accompanied by knowledge as to the importance of universality. When the inner tension of self-consciousness diminishes so that the individualistic aspect loses its predominance, the egoistic attitude prevailing in the subject is superseded by an honorable and righteous attitude. Accordingly, when the subject takes cognizance of its new position, it naturally can claim a moral merit out of its decision and subsequent action in realizing the good in the world which in itself is assumed to have no value whatsoever. With this the path

[21] B., p. 405. *Phän.*, p. 277.
[22] B., p. 403. *Phän.*, p. 275.

is prepared for the subject's conflict and struggle with the world as if this were really opposed to goodness and authentic values.

Despite all the preparation involved in assailing the opponent, the subject turned virtuous finds the world process unyielding and invulnerable. "Wherever virtue comes to grips with the world's process, it always hits upon places where goodness is found to exist; the good, as the inherent nature of the world's process makes its appearance, and where it is real the good has its own existence too".[23] This is no more than to say that self-consciousness has learned in the course of its struggle that the world, which was previously declared to be the enemy of the subject, can no longer be considered as perverted, evil and alien. This shift contains a totally different view, and one may well ask how such a new orientation could have emerged at all. It seems safe to say that the action of the virtuous subject as regards the actual course of the world has rested on an abstract and purely verbal distinctions. Thus, the authentic good was considered to be what is implicit, as opposed to what actually exists. However, it is clear even from this preliminary distinction — which is merely a distinction for consciousness — that it is impossible to draw a sharp line between "implicitness and explicit being".

Whatever tangible effects this new orientation may have had, it was certainly limited. This alleged limitation is quite understandable. The virtuous subject, seeing that it is gradually overpowered by the world process, is content with "a mere sham-fight", which lacks seriousness and dedication, self-assurance and courage. However, this situation gives Hegel the opportunity to invoke the ancient virtue whose significant and fruitful function in the social sphere has precluded it from being "directed against actual reality as a general perversion".[24] It is precisely here that the nostalgia for the Greek way of life in Hegel's *Phenomenology* comes out.[25] What he is equivalently suggesting with this reference to the *antike Tugend* is that dialectical propositions do, indeed, point to the dated events. If so, there

---

[23] B., p. 407. *Phän.*, p. 278.

[24] B., p. 410. *Phän.*, p. 280.

[25] Herbert F. Muller aptly summarizes the nostalgic spirit of the West in this respect : "We are dealing with a great romance. In all history, Spengler observed, no culture has so passionately adored another culture as the Western has adored the ancient Greek. This cult of the classic is a becoming tribute to a glorious people — the most remarkable people in history, I should say — to whom we owe the beginnings of most of the values of our civilization". *The Uses of the Past* (New York : Oxford University Press, 1957), p. 100. For a more specialized analysis of the nostaligic spirit in Hegel and in the thought of German idealism, cf. Jacques Taminiaux, *La nostalgie de la Grèce à l'aube de l'idéalisme allemand* (The Hague : Martinus Nijhoff, 1967).

arises a new paradox of Hegel's teaching, for in asserting that dialectical propositions refer to the dated occurrences, one is not assured that such terms must be understood without any historical connotation. This seems to support G. Fessard's thesis that the Hegelian attitude towards history is characteristically ambivalent.[26] Accordingly, one is tempted to suspect that Hegel's approach to the problem of virtue fails to be properly dialectical, precisely because he straightforwardly ascribes a richer content and a greater significance to the dated ancient virtue than to the one which is supposed to bring to light the fact that universality is "animated by individuality". At any rate, the passage strikes a sceptical note, for Hegel seems to believe that the virtue exemplifying the spirit of his own time "is removed from that substantial life, and is outside of it, a virtue with no essential being, a virtue merely in ideal and in words, and one that is deprived of all that content".[27]

One thing can be decided on the basis of what has been said so far, namely that instead of transforming the world in accordance with virtue, the subject itself becomes transformed into a pompous zealot "who professes to act for such noble ends and indulges in such fine phrases holds himself for a fine creature : a swollen enlargement which gives itself and others a mighty size of a head, but big from inflation with emptiness".[28] Instead of developing the individual, undue distinctions and rhetorical eloquence waste efforts and talents that might be working for the self-realization of subjectivity. We can even suspect of the virtuous consciousness that its attempt at idle moralization could transport it into the realm of imagination or illusion.

But this still enables Hegel to speak of the positive significance of the subject's conflict and struggle. By its very appearance in a definite dialectical framework, the necessary condition of reconciliation is finally fulfilled. Needless to say, the struggle serves to eliminate all those abstract distinctions which only obscured and concealed the true relationship between the individual and the universal. As regards the elimination of individuality, we can sum up the case thus : The realization of values in the world through sacrificing individuality proved abortive precisely because the very reality of individuality constitutes the essence of the universal. At this point, then, the relevancy of the individual comes back into play. Individuality,

---

[26] Cf. Gaston Fessard, "Attitude ambivalente de Hegel en face de l'histoire", *Archives de philosophie*, 24 (1961), 207-241.

[27] B., p. 407. *Phän.*, p. 280.

[28] B., p. 409. *Phän.*, p. 280.

to use Hegel's typical expression, is the "explicit actualization of what is implicitly and inherently real (i.e. the universal); and the perversion ceases to be looked at as a perversion of goodness, for it is just the transmuting of the good, *qua* bare purpose, into actual reality".[29] Perhaps one can add that without the individual and its action, the universal would certainly remain an abstraction which could never be carried into real effect. For Hegel, then, *die Bewegung der Individualität ist die Realität des Allgemeinen.* And this concise statement about individuality seems to be the very core of the problem of self-realization. Now, the individual is victorious simply because it has conquered something unreal and abstract. Conversely, what the subject has lost in the struggle was obviously not anything worth preserving. Ultimately, thus, the conflict emerges as an advantageous gain, leading to the possibility of reconciling the individual and the universal.

Still, at the present stage of the phenomenological development, the reconciliation of the individual and the universal remains drastically incomplete. Actually, it has just begun. The entire chapter on self-realization, then, is no more than the first step toward showing what is implied in constituting the rational subjectivity. Obviously, the individual would hardly merit the name of subjectivity if it did not achieve universality through union with the totality. By the same token, the universal would hardly merit the name of subjectivity if it did not find a way to be particularized in the individual. And so, the subject has finally zeroed in on the principal Hegelian ideal — the expectation of reconciling the individual and the universal.

---

[29] B., p. 410. *Phän.*, p. 281.

CHAPTER XIII

THE TRIUMPH OF THE RATIONAL SUBJECT

"Self-consciousness has now grasped its own principle, which at first was only *our* notion of it, viz. the notion that, when consciously certain of itself, it is all reality. Its purpose and nature henceforward consists in the interpenetration of the universal (*its* 'gifts' and 'capacities') and individuality".[1] Hegel's initial statement [2] indicates the shift of emphasis from an analysis which starts with the opposition between the individual and the universal to an analysis which starts with the individual and the universal as mutually dependent and interpenetrating. The important thing here is that the problem of subjectivity occurs as a concrete unification of two distinct poles. Certainly, the link between individuality and universality had already been anticipated in Hegel's recurrent phrase, "the universal individual". This time, however, the individual subject not only resolutely refuses to be separated from the universal, but categorically demands unification in terms of distinctly concrete forms.

It is clear that these general considerations, taken by themselves, cannot be considered as offering even a hint for the solution of the problem. One important thing, however, is obvious : reconciliation is a topic which quite clearly lies in the center of the subject's direct and urgent concerns. But here emerges the question : what is really meant by reconciliation and how it is possible? Obviously, the subject's attempt at reconciliation must not be construed as an endeavor to explain more fully some of the terms which have been introduced and recognized as significant: nor is it a project which begins with the commitment to remain true to some preconceived ideal. Now, since the word "reconciliation", ordinarily understood as

---

[1] B., p. [414]. *Phän.*, p. [283].

[2] It opens the Section C of the *Phenomenology*, entitled *Individuality, Which Takes Itself To Be Real In And For Itself*. Needless to say, the title is extremely specific, indicating a new and advanced claim of the subject.

"synthesis", does not suggest any specific method or procedure, the subject might be tempted to establish a purely logical synthesis by merely correlating the concepts of individuality and universality. But to do so would be to revert to the abstract connection the rational mind wants to overcome once and for all. That this way out is blocked should not come to us as a surprise, for dialectical reconciliation can never be reduced to a synthesis of fixed concepts. Unlike the logical conception of reconciliation, Hegel's intent never implies formal synthesis or verbal identity. Evidently, to speak of a reconciliation is to speak of further development of the subject, and to this corresponds the attempt at concrete performance. The link connecting the individual and the universal can only be supplied by the evolving subject. Knowing itself as limited and constantly negating its limitation the subject knows what the universal subjectivity must be. It is impossible, therefore, to speak of an authentic universality without relating it to the gradual procedures through which such a universality can be constituted as actual by the subject. Thus, it is the rational subject itself moving towards concrete universality which supplies a hint for the solution of the central problem.

Detaching itself now from "all opposition and every condition limiting its activity",[3] the subject discovers within itself a new link between the individual and the universal; it becomes aware of a novel meaning of individuality which no longer makes it a stranger in its own eyes. Self-consciousness thus unveils a fruitful mediating principle which alone could constitute subjectivity and found it as rational and real. And this is but another way of saying that no universality is an authentic universality unless it springs from the very *activity* of the subject. To conquer the unreality or the abstract character of universality and to eliminate the infantile individuality which characterizes the immature consciousness, such is the decision of the subject, "which takes itself to be real in and for itself".

If this decision appears somewhat singular and promising at first sight, it becomes less so when the subject begins to unveil the implications concealed in the notion of activity. What is more, this unveiling is conducted in such an acute manner that acting individual, questioned by rational consciousness, reveals itself as a transition "from a state not yet explicitly expressed to one fully expressed".[4] This is not to suggest, of course, that the question of activity is a simple introspective analysis. It is rather a question of bringing out, gradually and intelligibly, the implicit conception of individuality in every act of its manifestation. And if it is extremely difficult to

---

[3] B., p. 415. *Phän.*, p. 284.
[4] B., p. 421. *Phän.*, p. 287.

answer the question, What is the nature of individuality?, this is because the nature of the individual is unclear until it has made itself visible by action.

Hegel's repeated insistence upon a thorough investigation of activity is not merely an intention to secure fruitful and lasting contact with universality but also to allow the subject to revert to its negative capacity. According to Hegel, action is a manifestation of negativity.[5] Therefore, when the subject acts, its "specific determinateness" undergoes an unexpected shock which dissipates the individual "into the general process of negation".[6] It is interesting to observe, however, that no sooner is this radical negation accomplished than it shows itself to be as real, supplying evidence for the conviction that the subject is what it does. All this shows us that the question of radical negation and the ensuing dissipation is ultimately rather a positive affirmation. Thus, for Hegel, activity is not merely a fecund capacity to be utilized in pursuing various goals; it is ultimately a condition of self-knowledge. Correctly understood activity, too, is a function of universality, indicating "what is one's own in a universal element".[7] Obviously, activity always originates in the individual subject, but its significance is grasped by the universal subject. In other words, the consciousness which performs the act is the individual consciousness, but the consciousness which becomes aware of the individual in the action is not the individual consciousness but universal consciousness.

We see that for Hegel the activity of the subject, which is permeated by negativity, is clearly a tie that binds the individual and the universal. Never before has it been shown so convincingly that the authentic elements of individuality and universality are consubstantial with subjectivity. Still, it would be rash to assume that the argument has already succeeded in establishing an adequate reconciliation. Accordingly, it would be pointless and idle to dispute with J. Loewenberg about the foreseeable failure on the subject's part to suppress the opposition between the two poles. But we have one reservation about Loewenberg's argument, and it concerns what he calls the deceptive character of the attempted reconciliation. According to him, the section before us describes "a type of individual *deceptively* united with the universal. To unmask the deception is the aim of the analysis that follows".[8]

It cannot be denied that the subject has an overt, ever present, and well justified suspicion with regard to the tie that binds it to the universal.

---

[5] B., p. 420. *Phän.*, p. 286.

[6] *Ibid.*

[7] B., p. 437. *Phän.*, pp. 299-300.

[8] *Op. cit.*, p. 168. Italics mine.

Even if we have not been able to describe in detail the process of the notion of activity, nor completely unravel the conditions responsible for the universal's failure to break in from all sides, at least it appears clearly that at the present stage of the phenomenological process the adequation of individuality and universality is unconcealably disquieting. Thus, the possibility of reconciliation is contested and remains problematic. Clearly enough, questioning and testing of reconciliation is inscribed in the very nature of the rational subject. But to contest the reconciliation by denouncing it as a simple deception would be to assume that the subject has already been convinced of having won the sought union with the universal. However, the subject never arrives at this conviction. Rather, by inquiring dialectically into the concealed implications of activity, the subject comes up with the realization that the anticipated link between individuality and universality is inadequate. Once this is understood — and to understand it is simply to realize that the reconciliation merely intended is not the same as reconciliation actually attained — the alleged "deception" vanishes.

It was impossible to achieve an adequate and immediate reconciliation precisely because the subject could not orient its analysis directly and decisively toward the universal itself. All this, however, has simply demonstrated that the *Phenomenology* has remained faithful to its fundamental principles. We rediscover here the need for the gradual universalization and the mediating process so important in dialectical phenomenology. What is more, we see here the enormous distance that separates Hegel from rationalistic teleology and the Platonic tradition. Hegel could not conceive of universality as being some ideal "telos" introduced by reason or imagination; nor could he conceive of it as belonging to the Platonic world of ideas. In Hegel's eyes, the subject can become universal only when it appears as outcome reached by negation and mediating process. Such an innovation is obviously intriguing and meritorious. Seen in this way, the universal subject is but another term for the individual subject purged of limitation, finitude, and relativity. To speak of unification, then, is to speak of the subject's activity, with the intent of detecting universality latent in it. Obviously, to the extent that the purgative function displayed by action permits the universal elements to appear, and that individuality identifies itself with these elements, the universal subjectivity is already explicitly contained in the concrete action. But since the character of universality is strictly proportionate to the abstract character of action, the subject must turn to more concrete forms of activity. Fortunately, taking into consideration the fact that activity itself is now in the process of being concreted, the subject can expect to find in it some relevant determination that would transform it into a positive performance. Indeed, since the subject's activity advantageously assumes the form of positive and meaningful work, it can be said with full justification that action expresses itself most concretely in and through work. Hegel thus takes another step along the line we have traced up to here : he turns away from the general and professedly abstract notion of action to focus his attention on work. By making not only rational capacities but also work a self-perfective function of subjectivity, it is evident that Hegel has opened up a new direction in the analysis of individual consciousness and also in the search for unification. Thus the dialectical method, which is hardly reducible to an "expository integument",[9] renews the problem of reconciliation by attacking it through the uncovering of the meaning of work.

It is characteristic of work, no matter what its form, to develop the individual and to turn it progressively into a universal subject. Evidently, this is but a reiteration of the insight that every act of work is a conscious attempt at universalization. Just as the slave recognized that an independent consciousness is not possible except as constituted by a self-initiated work, so the rational subject has recognized that only in becoming aware of the individuality and universality of the work that the unification of both could be achieved.

Turning his attention to the new problem, Hegel finds that work is the self-revelation of the subject because, at least at first view, it appears that the individual cannot grasp itself except by the performance of a voluntary deed, by the bringing to light of a "reality which consciousness gives itself" and which up to now had remained implicit and inaccessible. In brief, the individual becomes aware of what it is only by surrendering itself to work and by recognizing it as its own explicit reality. But in this search for the explicit nature of the individual we suddenly come up against two fundamental and interrelated insights whose implications are of a decisive importance for the subject as universal. The first insight could be formulated in this manner : The mind which becomes aware of the individual in the work performed is not the individual consciousness but universal consciousness. The subject thus becomes detached from the particularity and acquires a concrete experience of its universal dimension which it did not have previously. The second insight, which is corollary to the first, bears on the unexpected opposition between work and consciousness in its universal character. The subject, taking cognizance of its work and withdrawing from it, reaches a state of indeterminateness. "It thus goes beyond itself

---

[9] J. N. Findlay, *Hegel : A Re-examination*, p. 358.

qua work, and is itself the indeterminate region which its work still leaves void and unfilled".[10] But by placing the universal beyond the sphere of work and beyond the determinate individual, the subject runs the risk of disrupting its own unity and identity. It is to be observed that the subject feels a certain uneasiness in the atmosphere of the new difficulty, precisely because it is anxious to know "how individuality will retain its universality in the existence of the work".[11]

Obviously, it is not a question here of simply relating the individual to the universal to preserve their unity and to reaffirm the subject's identity, but of re-examining the process of work itself. But if it is the work which makes possible the unification of the individual and the universal, the subject must focus essentially on the distinctions the performed work entails. Certainly there is no reason to contest the fact that in its work the rational subject becomes aware of the distinction between being and acting, willing and performing, purpose and means, intention and fulfillment, effort and result. But in phrasing the phenomenological distinctions in this way, one must not forget that the emerging differentiation is strictly correlative to dialectical consciousness for which these distinctions are merely recognizable constituents and vanishing factors of work. Again, the rational consciousness does not consider seriously the procedure and the result nor the productive activity and the product in isolation from one another, but the very unitary structure of their correlativity and complementarity. This unitary structure stands opposed to the constituents of work only so far as they claim to have a significance in isolation, but is ultimately their very identity. Decidedly, this unity is identifiable with the true work and its fundamental concern (*die Sache selbst*).[12] We might understand this concern as the principal intent of the subject : every act of work is performed by the very fact that the act is purposive and enterprising. Accordingly, we can qualify this concern as "reconciliatory", not only in the sense of being the unifying factor of the opposed aspects of work, but also in the sense of linking the inward nature and actual reality. But this is not all. To say that the fundamental concern of the subject succeeds in cancelling the various aspects of work as isolatedly valid implies saying that these same aspects are valid as "moments" of the universal concern.

Thus, what emerges as alone meritorious and important is the enterprising concern, in which and through which the subject has recaptured its univer-

---

[10] B., p. 426. *Phän.*, p. 291.
[11] *Ibid.*
[12] B., p. 430. *Phän.*, p. 294.

sality and attained an objective conception of itself as substance. Still, this achievement does not necessarily imply a successful and complete reconciliation of the individual and the universal. To recognize the emergence of the subject's "own substance" in the predominant concern does away with the need of establishing an interpenetration of individuality and objectivity, for their actual coalescence is given in the notion of substantiality, but the concern does not transform the immediate substantiality of the subject into a truly real substance (*wahrhaft realen Substanz*) [13] nor does it reconcile the individual and the universal.

Recognized as universal, the concern contains all particular attributes, aspects, goals, and constituents of work, despite the fact that the subject refuses to consider them in radical isolation. If so, what can really claim universality is but the general, indeterminate notion of concern and not its "moments". Although no one is satisfied with indeterminate and abstract concern, the universal remains a reality in which alone different subjects can realize their nature. Recognized as concrete, however, the primary concern is a commitment of *this* or *that* individual whose purpose, procedure, effort, and circumstances are far from being applicable to all the other individuals. Indeed, if the intentional concern remains only concern, it is, of course, enterprising and universal, but containing specific projects, ends, particular purposes, and unique circumstances of the individual worker it is hardly common to all. To speak quite plainly, work has no need of universally recognized goal to promote an individual enterprise to the level of achievement, contribution, and recognition; the realization of a meaningful task is sufficient.

Obviously, all this confusion and ambiguity arises from the fact that work, like action in general, has a universal dimension and an individual character. Now, in the first aspect it cannot be exclusively the individual's own and in the latter aspect it cannot be another's. One could develop the implications of this opposition and dependence still further, but we will limit ourselves here to a brief indication. The subject discovers that both aspects are equally important moments and that the main concern is neither merely a fact, which is opposed to individual work and to work in general, nor an action, which is opposed to essential reality of the individual and to reality in general. But no sooner is this position of the subject elucidated than it shows itself to be contestable and the nature of the primary concern is immediately colored by abstract universality.

In this insight Hegel recognizes explicitly that no one of the given mo-

---

[13] B., p. 431. *Phän.*, p. 295.

ments is the subject, and that the fundamental concern itself "is not yet subject". It is because the particular moments and the concern simply stand *for* the subject and "because they belong to the aspect of individualness",[14] that the universal is neither a true substance nor a genuine subject. Thus the Hegelian subject becomes aware of its lack of universality, of its immaturity, and of its dependence on the individual.

This is not to suggest, however, that with the problem of concern Hegel has lost his patience. On the contrary, his characterization of this type of subjectivity as *ehrlich* — honest, fair, and upright — clearly indicates that the problem of concern is ultimately for him the problem of moral concern, of probity, in the twofold sense we anticipate : on the one hand, the problem of the possibility of performing individual work in a fair and honest manner, and, on the other, the impossibility of pursuing universal goals without personal vanity and egoistic pretentiousness. Without going into the details of this intricate argument, we can say that the subject's commitment to a universally acknowledged goal or value does not eliminate or suppress the awareness of the subject's own personal achievements and merits. If the subjects engaged in edifying work remain mindful of their individual efforts and contributions, mutual struggle appears as a necessary outcome. And this helps explain how it is possible for Hegel to write so grandly on questions which entail a sham integrity : "The true meaning of this 'Honesty', however, lies in not being so honest as it seems".[15]

The conception of "honesty" is one of the turning points of Hegel's phenomenology, as is very clear from the present section. But it now turns out that the principle of honesty, as explained and applied, does not come from any aspect of work nor from any characteristic of universality and individuality; that it is a common-sense notion introduced for the express purpose of providing an expeditious transition and ingress into the moral and spiritual realm. One's suspicion that Hegel did not arrive at his notion of *Ehrlichkeit* through dialectical process but merely specified the character of the subject's concern to remove its appearance of indefiniteness, seems to us well justified. At any rate, the category of "honesty" appears to be introduced just as arbitrarily as a *deus ex machina*. Perhaps this arbitrariness could have been avoided by showing that in the rational subject there is realized a coincidence of primary concern and honest attitude, and that this coincidence is given at the start, but self-consciousness neglects it and passes over it to focus its attention on some goal or ideal.

---

[14] B., p. 432. *Phän.*, p. 295.
[15] B., p. 434. *Phän.*, p. 297.

While interpreting the two concluding sections of the third major part of the *Phenomenology*, the commentators of Hegel have taken for granted that these very brief segments were written to serve as addenda. This explanation, however, seems overly simple and unnecessarily doctrinaire. We think that Hegel's exposition in this respect has a different character and moves in the opposite direction. The two final sections provide a sort of prelude to Hegel's doctrine of the spiritual subjectivity.[16] Supposing that the conception of honest concern is already given to us, we can begin a preliminary investigation of the ethical field, but we cannot append to the previous section unless we assume that the material added to that section is not essential to its completeness, but is attached as an accessory. It is precisely in this sense that we have to understand Hegel's prefatory explanations of moral issues in what it has become customary to call "appendices".

This is not to suggest, however, that in his final essays Hegel has abandoned the decision to reconcile the individual and the universal. On the contrary, in both segments the process of unification remains the primary aim, and it is a return to reason as the source of moral concern. We may briefly call attention here to the conspicuous convergence of reason, moral concern, individuality, and universality. With this convergence, Hegel's philosophy of subjectivity is decidedly headed for a new experience. Firstly, the convergence of reason and individuality marks the decisive rupture with narrow, subjective individualism, for rationality is a distinct perfection in which all individuals participate and which unifies them all. Secondly, the convergence of reason and moral concern consists in this that the first emerges as a lawgiver. Now, if this is a question of reason as moral source, the conscientious individual guarantees an unconditional universality, for by following the dictates of reason every individual identifies itself with the universal. Thirdly, the convergence of rationality and universality aims at putting the individual in possession of itself, for activity in conformity with rationality

---

[16] Hopefully, we can clarify this point a bit more fully by recalling the opening statement of the first section, entitled *Reason as Lawgiver* : "Spiritual essential reality is, in its bare existence, pure consciousness, and also *this* consciousness". B., p. [440]. *Phän.* p. 301.

Hegel is at pains to show that the spiritual reality is not merely consciousness as such, but that it is also a recognizable individual self-consciousness. Now, this spiritual reality unifies both the individual and the universal. Hegel clearly suggest that no individual subject is genuinely spiritual unless he is related to the universal. What applies to the individual applies also to the universal : no universal subject is genuinely spiritual unless he is related to the individual. In a word, the spiritual reality is a unified whole from the very beginning.

is an invitation — and also a command — to act in conformity with the universal concern.

As an immediate view, the attempt at reconciliation is too explicit, too intuitive, and too facile. But as an act that awakens the critical view, it focuses problematically on the unconditional and universal validity of the moral law in which the subject expects to find, unrecognized and unlabeled, certain conditions and qualifications.

As regards the immediate project, the claim of reason is simply that it can grasp the moral law directly and immediately. Thus there evolves with the operation of reason the possibility of a non-mediated cognition of the moral concern, i.e. of the categorical imperative.[17] Now, since the rational subject knows the moral law intuitively or immediately, the law itself is valid for it only intuitively and immediately. Here Hegel raises the important problem of reason's legislative capacity : the legislative deliverances of reason are to be taken as provisional, initial and not as authoritative, final communications. And this helps explain how inadequate, how incomplete, and how inappropriate the proposed moral law is. Therefore, all that we require to remember here is Hegel's own statement : "What is thus given immediately must likewise be accepted and regarded as immediate".[18]

We see that this Hegelian position demands that mediation take the place of the immediate moral consciousness, and that the possibility of mediation hinges on the critical examination of the implications present in the law's very claim for universality. And this brings us to the second consideration which bears on the questionable status of the unconditional law. As if this were not enough of a daring and intricate contrivance, Hegel proposes to examine two celebrated commands : "Every one ought to speak the truth" and "Love thy neighbour as thyself".

Attentive investigation of the first maxim tells us at every turn that we are dealing here with a merely conditional principle, although it is "expressed unconditionally". While one cannot speak of two definitions of the same maxim, and can at most say that the maxim has both an unconditional and a conditional dimension, one can distinguish between what is actually expressed and what is really intended. But exactly how does the subject make this distinction possible? Hegel's own answer is given in the statement

---

[17] Although Hegel does not mention Kant by name and never employs the phrase, "categorical imperative". it is clear from the context that Hegel's critical remarks apply to Kantian ethics.

[18] B., p. 441. *Phän.*, p. 302.

that follows the definition of the maxim, where he says that one is unconditionally commanded to speak the truth only "*if* he knows the truth".
Granted the possibility of such qualification, Hegel insists that the moral
condition demands an adequately articulated maxim as a principle for concrete ethical decision : "Each must speak the truth according to his knowledge and conviction about it on each occasion".[19] Failure to issue an
unconditional command without the specification makes its unconditionality
unjustifiably presumptuous, but the articulate specification of the command
infringes upon its unconditional significance. Clearly, the specification of
the maxim proves only the inadequacy of expression, but Hegel interprets
this as a contradiction in the maxim itself. It is something of a puzzle that
the notion of the moral law should be qualified by a straightforward declaration that truth is contingent or relative. This is perilously close to the sort
of intuitive deliverance and presumptuous leap which Hegel rejected with
regard to the unconditional aspect of the law. This leap, however, permits
Hegel to achieve his primary objective — to deny "healthy" reason the
capacity to legislate univocal and unconditional maxims. Upon the subject,
therefore, who places between expression and intention a gap so wide and
deep that "to speak otherwise than one intends means not speaking the
truth",[20] it is incumbent to accept the fact that the necessity has turned
into contingency or that the anticipated universal content destroyed itself
by exposing its relativity.

Hegel's critique of the second maxim seems to be motivated by the same
objective, for it aims at eliminating from the command precisely that unconditionality which is the reason of universality and hence of moral obligation.
When Hegel describes the command "Love thy neighbour as thyself" as
a "relation of sentiment or feeling", he wants by that to indicate two things :
first, that the above law is reducible to the notion of relation that implies
a merely emotive response; and secondly, that the intention of well-being,
which is ultimately rooted in feeling, refers to an action that seeks to fulfill
a need "which is as contingent as it is momentary". Thus, the effort of
natural reason proves wasteful and leads only to contingency; similarly,
the radical attack on a professedly universal command ends up only sati-
rizing and thus suppressing rationality as the sole agent of moral legislature.

With this the ground is prepared for another function of natural reason
and for another approach to moral laws. Fortunately, here Hegel deals
with the question of transition in a way for which we have been adequately

---

[19] B., p. 442. *Phän.*, p. 303.
[20] *Ibid.*

prepared. Reason as lawgiver can be said to be reducible to reason as tester of laws precisely because the performance of criticizing the laws is concomitant with the performance of laying down the said laws. Paradoxical as it may seem, the rational subject may envisage the possibility of becoming a critic of moral commands precisely because it already exercised the critical function when engaged in establishing and sustaining such commands. In order, however, that the legislative claim of reason become definitely suppressed and in order that the justification be given to the subject's analysis of the principal criteria in terms of which every morally significant maxim could be tested, it was simply necessary to perfect that critical spirit which would enable the subject to become a full-fledged critic who decides "whether a content is capable of being a law or not, i.e. whether the content does not contradict itself".[21]

The rational subject, leaving the problem of the origin of existing moral laws unsolved but accepting the role of the moral critic, may insist that any intelligible testing of moral commands must be such as to make univocally clear that these are rational and universally valid. This being so, the subject could not describe moral criteria as dependent upon any determinate content or any specific situation. Reason as judge is thus led to the idea that the standard of moral valuation must be extracted from reason itself, for only in this way would it be possible to apply a rigorous test with regard to the existing moral commands. Seen in this light, then, the problem facing the subject is to explain rational activity and moral activity as being one and the same. If so, the subject may be said to be in the position to return to the issue of the identity of thought and reality, for the moral law conceived by rational consciousness is the same law that becomes real through action.

It might be maintained that what the rational subject is primarily committed to is the avoidance of contradiction, incongruity, and inconsistency. Thus, by examining the basic posture of the subject, Hegel finds that rationality involves essentially the demand for consistency. Therefore, those criteria of conduct can be rationally and consistently adopted which are such that every rational subject could employ in testing any given maxim and utilize them in resolving the conflict arising from opposite commands. This gives Hegel the evidential basis for his account of the formalistic derivation of universally valid laws. First of all, no law is a universal law unless it satisfies the requirement of consistency. Secondly, Hegel does not certify the validity of a command by reference to a specific content. He appeals

---

[21] B., p. 445. *Phän.*, p. 306.

rather to the formal definition of such a command, where contradiction is allowed to be merely an abstract and theoretical criterion.

On the supposition that moral laws can be tested on the basis of consistency, reason is expected to guarantee the universally obligatory norms without appealing to anything outside the field of rational thought itself. The principle here is logical and very convincing, but the point is that, if consistency has its origin in reason, then it is endowed with an *a priori* mark and has nothing to do with the experience of moral obligation and has no bearing whatever upon the task of concrete application. It is not surprising, therefore, that the principle of consistency does not establish the necessity of any course of action, nor take away the ambiguity of any proposed moral maxim; since it is incapable of any *a posteriori* proof and gets its justification only from its formal, *a priori* nature. What is perhaps more important, however, is the sense in which the dual and opposite claims about any presumably moral concept can be construed as consistent and workable. What is decisive here is that reason simply demands consistency; it is not an agent descriptive of moral relevance. Thus, taken by themselves, the concepts of property, justice, sex do not contradict themselves, nor do they indicate in any positive way what specific course of action should be adopted. With regard to these concepts there are numerous and contrary courses of action which are all plausible in the sense of not being inconsistent if universally accepted.

In face of this, Hegel proposes not to correct Kant's categorical imperative but only to explain the irrelevancy of the principle of contradiction to morality. By examining the formal character of this principle, he refuses to identify it with the universally valid moral law. The universally obligatory character of the moral maxim cannot be determined by ascertaining what reason alone holds to be in accordance with the principle of contradiction, in its application to the presumably ethical notions.

What Hegel is also attempting with his analysis of reason as a critic of moral principles is not so much to expose the limitations of the rational consciousness by declaring that these principles simply "*are* and nothing more" as to provide an ingress into the personal sphere of subjectivity. Although one can challenge the rational subject to indicate a single uncontested case in which it has really succeeded in achieving a significant victory, one cannot reasonably conclude that the entire rational process has been in vain. Despite all the uncertainty involved in describing the subject's efforts as peremptory and meritorious, one thing is unmistakable : the rational process — and especially the "appendix" of the third part of the *Phenomenology* — has a lot to do with the radical transformation of the subject and has bearing upon the issue of transition from mere rationality to true personality. Seen in this way, the triumph of the rational subject consists precisely in this that the insights attained through the process have succeeded in transforming subjectivity into a spiritual being (*das geistige Wesen*). True enough, at the very outset the subject's spirituality is essentially artless and rudimentary. Nevertheless, it has the distinct stamp of a personal agent, and this novel character of the subject leads us to inquire into its meaning and structure, into the renewed efforts in its gradual constitution and self-criticizing activity.

Part Five : The Spiritual Subject

CHAPTER XIV

THE RISE OF THE PERSONAL SUBJECT

When we turn from reason to spirit, we are rather hesitant in accepting the latter expression in the sense of reason being suddenly "raised to the level of truth",[1] even though it remains true that the presentation of the last part of the *Phenomenology* does not diverge fundamentally from the preceding one. It is clear that, especially because of the latter fact, the final portion of Hegel's work is not a chasm away from the portion that has gone before. Still, the new part which begins with the phrase, "reason is spirit", shows a somewhat different character. As opposed to the previous analyses which proceed from the distinct cognitive acts as they appear in and through consciousness, Hegel sees no difficulty in the transition from the "abstract" consideration of such acts to their presupposition and grounding principle — spirit.

The emergence of spirit was already indicated in the immediately preceding movement of consciousness, where the subject developed and attained moral awareness. Hegel probably had the insight there that the spiritual awakening of the subject owes its origin to the consciousness of moral problems. Thus, all questions about morality lead to the one question about the subject's spiritual mode of existence. The problem of morality then constitutes the point of departure of the phenomenology of spirit. In phrasing the problematic of the present part in this way, however, one must not forget that the presentation of the spiritual reality given in the *Phenomenology* is social and anthropological in character. In this way the development of the new line of thought is relatively independent of the previous process — and thus necessarily constitutes a completely different stage.

We must begin, then, by rehearsing Hegel's shift from the individual sphere to the social sphere. As we saw, the entire weight of the rational process rested on the formal principles of reason. Precisely because the legis-

---

[1] B., p. [475]. *Phän.*, p. [311].

lative and the critical functions of reason were essentially theoretical and primarily derived from the individuality as an isolated agency, the ethical interrogations of reason remained on the surface of the problem and missed the fact that moral laws are operative only in the context of concrete social life. For Hegel, then, true individuality is only realizable through the union with other individuals. Now, if this suggests anything, it definitely suggests that spiritual existence and social life belong together. In other words, organized community is the proper setting wherein man becomes himself, and it serves to specify both the personal character of subjectivity as well as its strikingly unconditional universality. By this "socializing" process, according to Hegel, there could be secured an answer to the issue raised by the rational subject of how to guarantee the universal moral laws without appealing to anything outside the established community itself.

Hegel's procedure rests upon a solid and significant principle; the only criticism that can be brought against it is that he starts not with the social relations which are requisite for the organization of various communities, but with the social attitudes springing from the communities already in existence. As Hegel sees social action, it is an expression of a previously experienced communal life. In order to understand how such a notion of sociality is conceivable, it is necessary to grasp the inevitability of the social order. For Hegel, the social order is above all a fatalistic one; and the law operative in that order supplies the genuine foundation for all relations and duties of its members. To be sure, Hegel's procedure is rooted in the conception of a communal order established on natural and biological foundations. By thus approaching the social problem, Hegel made it possible to concentrate on family and state as depending on sexual differentiation and thus to concentrate on the different laws governing these communities.

Before we proceed to the discussion of family and state, there is still one doctrinal difficulty to be overcome : It concerns Hegel's description of spirit which seems to diverge from the phenomenological procedure. Hegel's introductory statements to the effect that spirit is the "self-supporting absolutely real ultimate being (*Wesen*)", and that the previous stages of "consciousness are abstraction from it"[2] convey the impression that his battle against doctrinal presuppositions proved futile and that the phenomenological method is simply a handmaid for his dogmatic metaphysics. If one accepts that "spirit is the immovable irreducible basis and the starting point for the action of all and every one",[3] we can no longer believe that the phenomenological procedure can be taken as a guarantee for the avoidance of

---

[2] B., p. 459. *Phän.*, p. 314.
[3] B., p. 458. *Phän.*, p. 214.

all dogmatic issues. Indeed, to describe spirit as the "self-contained and self-sufficient reality" is to make use of one's metaphysical conviction and to proceed in a straightforward manner. To employ such a method, however, is to jeopardize the phenomenological principle that an analysis of the spiritual subjectivity may be accomplished without prior assumptions about its structure and nature. Even where Hegel speaks of the act (*die Handlung*) that "divides spirit into spiritual substance on the one side, and consciousness of the substance on the other",[4] he fails to warn the reader that this should be understood without any dogmatic connotations. Shifting the subject from the strictly individualistic mode of existence to community, Hegel burns the bridges before he comes to them. It seems that he intends to rest his exposition upon certain preconceived principles, giving thus the impression that they can elucidate or increase the intelligibility of the arguments to follow. Obviously, this assumption is not worthy of Hegel, but then so it is with almost all of the narrative prefaces in the *Phenomenology*.[5]

Perhaps the reason Hegel has persuaded himself to expose his philosophy of subjectivity to this reproach is his intention to initiate the reader into the sphere of spirituality by offering the descriptions which constitute no integral part of the phenomenological analysis. In this sense, then, Hegel's introductory annunciations constitute a simple preview of the social structures soon to appear. Although this may not be satisfactory to those who believe that Hegel's personal and direct comments are out of place in connection with gradual exposition, it is really doubtful whether his straightforward presentation destroys the phenomenological basis on which the gradual emergence of the spiritual subject is made to rest.

Spirit, so Hegel contends in the prefatory section, has the peculiar power of inspiring individuals to form social orders and of determining the goals of communal life. Hence a twofold effect of spirit on family and state : spirit is the motivating force of social action and the purpose of all organized communities. Although Hegel introduces the notion of "spiritual substance" ahead of time, he does not imply that spirit is prior to social orders. To be sure, Hegel himself would be the last to claim that it is permissible to speak of a spiritual reality without relating it to the concrete

---

[4] B., p. [462]. *Phän.*, p. [317].

[5] Still, it is not primarily Hegel's prefatory remarks which might induce one to reproach him for abruptly introducing the spiritual reality and the distinctions pertaining to it. The reproach is inspired by the descriptions which he seeks to endow with an immediate intelligibility and validity. By Hegel's own standards the validating effect pertains only to a dialectically structured analysis and exposition.

social activities through which such a reality can be realized as actual
and as concrete by the society-oriented individuals. There is simply nothing
prior to what the subject actually and presently is. To say this is to reiterate
the basic principle that the only reality which can have undeniable significance in the *Phenomenology* is a progressively evolving reality of the subject.

Likewise, what Hegel is affirming here is the indissoluble link between
spiritual reality and personal subjectivity. One of Hegel's definitions of the
person is the capacity to transcend himself and to create ever new modes
of existence. Thus, if it were necessary to describe the emerging personal
being both socially and morally by his aspirations and intentions it would
have to be in terms of these two : he is a mature individual irrevocably
devoted to communal life; he is a responsive agent passionately committed
to moral laws present and operative in that life.

In *The Ethical World*, significantly subtitled "Law Human and Divine :
Man and Woman", Hegel depicts the subject taking a giant step forward
to a new stage. Probably no explanation is necessary that the relationship
to the other constitutes the very essence of the person. Whenever this relationship occurs, there is question of common interests, of universally recognized goals. These interests and goals can so absorb men and women that
they lose sight of themselves as isolated individuals. To say this implies
saying that isolated individuals can become conscious of being personal
subjects only insofar as they identify their needs and ideals with the needs
and ideals of others. From this it follows that the personal mode of existence can only be reached through the social, familial, national, and moral
experiences of conscious beings living in community. To put it differently,
the social order is the reality in which alone the different selves can find
their *personal* identity.

From all this it should be clear that Hegel can approach the problem
of community because he recognizes a person's openness for the other with
whom he shares the same ideals and goods. Now, since these common goals
are multiple and also diversified, the concrete manifestation of the social
spirit can take several forms. In the face of this, however, Hegel proposes not
to explain certain primitive interpersonal acts requisite for bringing men
into social contacts and lasting unions but to re-examine the social units
of family and state. What is decisive here is that the communities of family
and state arise mysteriously, spontaneously, and simultaneously. Evidently,
then, family and state appear together, or they do not emerge at all. This
doubling, of course, is not only a bifurcation of humanity and of the "ethical
substance", but the return to the ubiquitous problem of individuality
and universality. Being centered around the individual person and expressing

an intimate concern for the other as the other, the familial community represents the individualistic principle whose herald and guardian is the woman. On the contrary, the state arouses a quite adequate idea of universality whose safeguarding and promotion is entrusted by nature to man. Obviously, what Hegel is attempting with this dual structure is not so much to distinguish different forms of social participation as to establish a basis which will provide a guarantee for the emergence of divided loyalties and the ensuing socio-moral conflict. Hegel is anticipating, then, that the community of family must be recognized for what it is, but it cannot be treated independently of the community of state.

While interpreting the phenomenology of society, the commentators of Hegel have taken for granted that different social laws or powers, conceived as manifestations of both the divine and the human spirit, can be understood only by describing them as arising from two irreducible sources. However, it suffices to read Hegel with just a little attention to find a completely different orientation. What really challenges the position of Hegel's interpreters is the fact that "human law as a living and active principle proceeds from the divine".[6] The term "proceeds" (*geht*) does not necessarily imply temporal priority, nor does it necessarily signify a causal determination, but since the familial community lies at the foundations of the state, the law governing the first underpins and determines the communal life of the latter. Paradoxical as it may appear, the duality of the sources of divine and human laws are hardly as pronounced as the duality of the laws themselves. Therefore, it would be pointless to dispute with Hegel's scholars about the fact that divine and human laws exhibit distinct characteristics; and it would be rash to assume that the chapter before us explicitly indicates their common origin. Though these different laws must be stated in terms of distinction and discrimination, Hegel has recognized the need to prevent them from freezing into isolatedness and hastened to reject their claim to self-sufficiency.[7] In this, we believe, consists Hegel's notion of mutual relation — one would like to say, dependence — of both laws. Accordingly, in examining the incompleteness of each law, Hegel has realized that the law of the state is related to the law of the family not only by mutual relation or dependence but also by complementarity.

There is, of course, considerable significance in the fact that Hegel's notion of relation of the communal laws reflects the relation which exists between the categories of immediacy and mediation, and without stretching the

---

[6] B., p. 478. *Phän.*, p. 328.

[7] "Neither of the two [laws] is alone self-complete". B., p. 478. *Phän.*, p. 328.

parallel too far, one may say that the family law hinges on immediacy, whereas the state law depends on mediation. Indeed, by focussing attention on the family life, we discover that the divine law neatly fits in the order of immediacy. To say this implies saying that the family law appears and functions as the "simple immediate essential being of the ethical order".[8] Now, the immediacy and the piety manifested in the divine law affect not only the content of that law or its ethical significance, but its intelligibility as well. Precisely because this law appears in the form of immediacy, it resists every attempt at formal description and conceptual explication. It is from the immediate nature of the divine law that Hegel derives its unconscious character [9] and its emotive quality.[10]

By the same token and in the same manner, we can relate the human law to the category of mediation. Like the first, the human law enjoys authoritative validity and negates the independence of the individual. But unlike the first, the law operative in the state exhibits an intelligibility which is "openly and unmistakably manifested"[11] and claims an uncontested universality. In order to understand how such a conception is conceivable and justifiable, it is necessary to remember the role mediation plays in the constitution and production of both intelligibility and universality. First, that is truly intelligible which has been disclosed in accordance with the requirements and procedures of mediation. And secondly, that is truly universal which has been established in accord with the principles of mediation. Seen in this way, these two issues are basically one : significant intelligibility and authentic universality are what they are only through the mediating performance of the subject.

There can be no doubt that this question played an important and decisive part in the present chapter, even though this division receives certain modification in the concluding paragraph, where Hegel speaks of the "untroubled transition" from the one of the communal powers to the other and of

---

[8] B., p. 467. *Phän.*, p. 319.

[9] "The family, as the inner indwelling principle of sociality operating in an unconscious way, stands opposed to its own actuality when explicitly conscious: as the basis of the actuality of a nation, it stands in contrast to the nation itself; as the *immediate* ethical existence, it stands over against the ethical order which shapes and preserves itself by work for universal ends; the Penates of the family stand in contrast to the universal spirit". B., p. 468. *Phän.*, p. 320.

[10] "The reverent devotion (*Pietät*) of husband and wife towards one another is this mixed up with a natural relation and with feeling, and their relationship is not inherently self-complete; similarly, too, the second relationship, the reverent devotion of parents and children to one another". B., p. 475. *Phän.*, p. 325.

[11] B., p. 476. *Phän.*, p. 325.

the "immediate permeation" of the one law with the other.[12] In this way, the immediate character of the divine law becomes less pronounced because one recognizes the mediating capacity of woman in whom this law is individualized and exemplified. Accordingly, the human law ceases to be less and less dependent on its mediating character, since in the immediacy of the divine law it discovers its own foundation, substantiation, and confirmation. Thus the problem of distinct laws transforms itself into the problem of the possibility of mutual dependence and permanent harmony. However, all questions about dependence and harmony finally lead to the one question about the "union of man with woman", because this union alone "constitutes the operative mediating agency for the whole".[13] All of which brings us back to the social significance of sexual differentiation.

However much this union may contribute to the "stable equilibrium of all the parts" and however firmly it may tie into one process the twofold movement of social powers, the duality of laws can never be retracted and continues to be a constant threat to communal harmony and tranquillity. In other words, the union of man and woman, which is only a mediating act, is for Hegel an inadequate agency to prevent social friction and conflict.

The other significant sign of the possibility of communal conflict proceeds from the occurrence of action. To say this implies saying that the problem of communal tension begins only with the question of action. As Hegel sees social confrontations and conflicts, they simply do not arise until the members belonging to different communities decide to act. But to claim this implies saying that organized communities precede action or that their coming into existence can dispense with action. Still, despite the imminent danger and prospect of excluding every form of activity from community organization, Hegel's presentation of the cause of social conflict can be reconciled with his slightly conspicuous description of the social order. There is no doubt for Hegel that all primary communities are and remain in some sense independent of personal actions. The communal powers strive to organize social orders and thus in these spheres mere action does not dominate. Rather only the communal laws which the emerging spiritual subjects accept have force, thus reducing action to the level of pure means. But the significance and function of action change as soon as we consider action, not simply as instrumental but as moral — only Hegel did not explicitly discuss it. The moral and not only the dynamic character of human action constituted the decisive motive of Hegel's orientation.

---

[12] B., p. 481. *Phän.*, p. 330.
[13] B., p. 482. *Phän.*, p. 330.

If, then, we agree with Hegel that there can be no reconciliatory committal to both laws, the social conflict becomes unavoidable. For instead of acknowledging both laws as truly complementary, the acting subject wants to remain faithful to the law of his choice and thus to the community which he recognizes as his own. While the individual person believes that he can realize moral good in no other way than by adhering to one law or to one set of duties, opposition and tension arise through this belief in an exclusive pledge. Accordingly, if one definite law is recognized as possessing morally relevant status, an irrelevant character must be ascribed to the other law.

To be sure, it is the shortsightedness of the immature subject and his lack of knowledge that decisively causes him to interpret the accepted law as demanding exclusive obedience. Perhaps one could even say that this is accomplished by holding the other law as negligible, not on the basis of its irrelevance, but rather on the basis of confusing its distinctiveness with opposition and thus on the basis of ignoring its complementarity. Still, that the other law does not in this case become intelligible is no reproach but rather unavoidable error, which is due to the myopic condition of the subject.

However, with this exclusive committal that keeps itself free from other allegiances the subject becomes involved in a serious moral problem. If the only choice the subject has is between ignoring the duties of the family and ignoring the duties of the state, then the attempt to avoid moral blame seems impossible. Small wonder, then, that at this point Hegel calls all of the subject's actions morally objectionable — a view that appears to run counter to his previous characterization of them as conforming to prescribed communal laws and therefore deserving moral praise. All this, however, is in tune with the dialectical procedure, for a praiseworthy action with regard to one particular law is a blameworthy action with regard to the other. Evidently, it cannot be satisfactory when a person, adhering to one definite communal law, toys with the idea of self-righteousness. Still, only on the assumption of the obligatory nature of both social powers can the actions of the subject be regarded as containing guilt and merit. To say this is nothing more than to recognize that moral merit and guilt are concomitant qualities. The frustrating experience here is that, since the social subject has not effectively realized moral good, he cannot lay claim to the title of spiritual subject.[14] What is more, if the person is to avoid

---

[14] To say this, of course, does not imply saying that the subject as an individual person is held morally responsible for his actions. Even where Hegel speaks of guilt and crime as a conscious experience, he hastens to assure the reader "that it is not *this* particular individual who acts and becomes guilty. For he, *qua* this particular self, is merely a shadowy unreality; he *is* merely *qua* universal self, ..." B., p. 489. *Phän.*, p. 335.

this paradoxical fusion of good and evil — and this the subject is really tempted to do — he must withdraw from action and sink into the idle, lethargic mode of existence.

To get back to the predicament allegedly affording no escape, we must focus our attention on the subject's experience of guilt and merit as concomitant moral qualities. To speak of guilt and merit as concomitant qualities is to recognize the opposite laws — the divine and the human — as concomitant imperatives. This, of course, does not involve exalting or elevating in rank either; instead, it involves neutralizing their hostile tendencies and suppressing their isolatedness. Seen in this light, the opposed imperatives are recognized as constituting a uniform law but a law revised in accordance with rationally sound and just principles. With this as the initial insight the subject can then concentrate on the juridical meaning of right which will define the social law and which will be legal in every sphere — private and public.

Though it is difficult to see how the category of right could be so suddenly introduced, Hegel suggests that this concept was already operative during the very social conflict. It is the function of right, so to speak, to attain the equilibrium between the opposed social laws; and Hegel insists that only "in the equal subjection of both sides that absolute right is first accomplished, and the ethical substance, as the negative force devouring both sides, in other words omnipotent and righteous Destiny, makes its appearance".[15] The significance of this assertion, of course, does not stop here, as can be seen from Hegel's description of the conflict between two brothers [16] who have equal right with regard to the power to rule the state and who "find their destruction reciprocally through one another".[17] On account of its vulnerability, the rudimentary notion of right finds its dissolution in the category of the legal status and thus gives place to a revised notion of right — Rechtszustand. Consequently, all the difficulties of the primitive and artless community fall to the ground because they rested on a primitive and inadequate conception of right.

Once the concept of the legal right is grasped, however generally, as characterizing the genuine social law, the subject's ingress into the juridical sphere is an irrevocable fait accompli. And with this the way is prepared

---

[15] B., pp. 492-493. Phän., p. 337.

[16] This probably refers to the two sons of Oedipus : Eteocles and Polynices who agreed to rule alternate years, but at the expiration of the first year, the older brother, Eteocles, refused to give up the throne, whereupon Polynices, the younger, induced the Argive chiefs to espouse his claim. Be that as it may, this is no more than a concrete illustration.

[17] B., p. 494. Phän., p. 338.

for another notion of the individual and for another conception of morality. Indeed, when the idea of right appears on the scene, there is no longer a danger that the spiritual subjects will be reduced to what Hegel calls "shadowy realities" and will be forced to continue to perform their duties in accordance with the prevailing customary rules. Evidently, the notion of right is a principle exerted against the custom as the only guidepost of social life and against the narrow concept of duty which refuses to grant any privileges to man as a person. Although society preserves itself only by suppressing the spirit of individualism, it can no longer be maintained that the members of society have only categorical duties and no personal rights of any kind. Once this is grasped — and to grasp it is simply to understand that the mere assertion of duty passes over into the question as to whether a person can have any duties without possessing certain basic rights — the emergence of a legal personality is affirmed. Now, demanding certain legal rights, the subject orients himself towards a novel society, a society which is governed by legally and explicitly formulated social laws. In this way, the individual's total fusion with the ethical substance is prevented by his being legally recognized as a social unit. And only within a juridical recognition thus understood can we comprehend Hegel's contention that the ethical substance is destined to "split up into the atomic units of a sheer plurality of individuals".[18]

Accordingly, the emerging juridical realm can quite immediately and justifiably take the univocal legal right as the model of the moral imperative, since this explicitly defined right remains the sole obligatory maxim governing private and public spheres of activity. If so, morality becomes reducible to legality, for the juridically constituted law can neither recognize nor tolerate any other norm. Thus, that is moral which is legal or which corresponds to the impartially constituted legal system or legal code.

Obviously, all this has the advantage of assuring equal rights and equal treatment to each and every individual member of the society, since the new social law is conceived as being inspired by the spirit of impartiality and as recognizing the identity of human elements in which all are sharing. Still, if we continue to examine legalism as it is presented to the social subject, we will see that the consideration of both the legal personality and the legal morality is bound to exhibit the experience of confusion, frustration, negation, and unhappiness, just as was the case in the dialectic of stoicism, scepticism, and self-estranged consciousness.

Now, assuming that "Stoicism is nothing else than the mood of conscious-

---

[18] B., p. [501]. *Phän.*, p. 342.

ness which reduces to its abstract form the principle of legal status, the principle of the sphere of right",[19] one can quite innocently claim that it resembles the position of legalism, in which the right of the person is still an abstraction, for its meaning remains detached from the essential and substantial reality of the individual. To put it differently and in negative terms, just as the stoical consciousness has failed to link its independence "to anything that exists", so legalism has failed to link the right of the person to the inner, substantial nature of the individual. And just as the stoical consciousness toppled over into the sceptical thought in which the subject had to presuppose its own autonomous being and yet was forced to negate every kind of independent existence, so, too, the legalistic thought passes over into a similar state of confusion, into an incoherent position, which while recognizing that the legal right and the "abstract unit of the person" are grounded in a richer or more powerful existence of the individual (*ein reicheres oder mächtigeres Dasein des Individuums*),[20] ignores and tacitly negates that substantial and truly personal subjectivity. True enough, this negation is neither explicit nor radical, for defining personal subject in terms of concepts drawn from the juridical sphere, legalism recognizes and acknowledges its indifference to the inner person. But it is precisely this recognition which leads the consciousness of right to the experience of the "loss of its own reality".[21] Only thus can we understand Hegel's contention that the legal definition of the individual in terms of personality is simply an expression of contempt (*Verachtung*).

Whenever Hegel spoke of the loss of the subject's own reality, to which he ascribes the central significance, he logically had to assume also that true personality which remains inaccessible to the legal law had to be depicted as estranged from the abstract person; but at the time he did not need to spell out the latent drama of alienation. At most one can look upon this experience of loss as the rudimentary insight out of which the cultural alienation developed, but not as a fully constituted alienation itself. However, to intensify the subject's awareness of division and to expose the implications latent in the legalistic spirit, Hegel had to turn his attention to the triumphant absolute person who exemplifies the universal might and

---

[19] B., p. 502. *Phän.*, p. 343.

[20] B., p. 502. *Phän.*, p. 344.

[21] "Consciousness of right, therefore, even in the very process of making its claim good, experiences the loss of its own reality, discovers its complete lack of inherent substantiality; and to describe an individual as a "person" is to use an expression of contempt". B., p. 504. *Phän.*, p. 345.

who takes himself to be the gigantic (*das ungeheure*) self-consciousness.[22]
There is a succinct discussion of this issue in the passages devoted to the
"lord and master of the world", where it is said that the "absolute plurality
of dispersed atomic personalities is, by the nature of this characteristic
feature, gathered at the same time into a single centre, alien to them and
just as devoid of the life of spirit (*geistlos*)".[23]

Hegel did not simply assume that legalism had failed to express spiritual
subjectivity; he tried to show that it did, and in doing so he realized that
he had to introduce the concept of continuity (*Kontinuität*) as the mediating
link between the emperor and his subjects. To have overlooked this relational principle or to have omitted it for the sake of simplification would
have left unanswered the pressing question, how can the absolute person,
for whom there exists no higher type of subjectivity, prepare the stage
for alienation in the social realm. It was, of course, no historical pedantry
that made Hegel proceed to seek for the experience of alienation in the
negative relation between the Roman emperors and their subjects. He
was looking primarily for the "spiritual union and concord in which the
various persons might get to know their *own* self-consciousness".[24] Now,
as the emperor exemplifies the "principle of connexion and continuity",
while his subjects are "dispersed atomic personalities", one must logically
look for the source of the spiritual unity in the emperor.

Considered in this way, however, continuity is something more than
a mere legal bond. Continuity is the "essential being and content" of dispersed legal personalities, precisely because the absolute person represents
the entire content, and hence is taken to be the very realization of their
aspirations. However, since the "lord of the world" — who is the "essential
being and content" of juridical personalities — treats his subjects exclusively as legal entities and resolutely refuses to recognize their independent
selfhood or their self-conscious existence, his negative attitude cannot provide
the spiritual link requisite for the further development of social personality.
At first Hegel seems to have considered whether the singular legal personalities could be connected with the absolute person, in order to ensure their
continued growth on the social scale. But he also became aware that the
one aspect of subjectivity which loomed beyond the reach of the legal law
or code and which was completely ignored by the emperor — was the concrete personality itself. Consequently, this concrete person, reaching out

---

[22] B., p. 505. *Phän.*, p. 345.
[23] B., p. 504. *Phän.*, p. 345.
[24] B., p. 505. *Phän.*, p. 346.

into his own depths and locating his true and essential center above and beyond the sphere of legal rights, inevitably recognized his legal status and his juridical personality as an alien reality.

It is from this point that Hegel goes on to say that all legal personalities exist "in a merely negative relation, a relation of exclusion both to one another and to him, who is their principle of connexion or continuity".[25] Admittedly, then, the experience of alienation derives all the actuality it has from the fact that each personal subject withdrawn into his own concrete existence becomes estranged not only from himself, but also from the absolute person and all the legal personalities constituting the entire social order. To say this, of course, is to admit that there are in Hegel's thought and argument some significant insights which prepare the ground for the spiritual subject's itinerary that will be marked by alienation. The insight that clearly comes to the fore is the one which reveals that social consciousness, driven back into itself out of the legalistic sphere, makes the said sphere an object of thought, realizing that the concretely manifested objectivity of the legal consciousness is a reality estranged from it.[26] A few phrases and explications could, to be sure, lead the reader to discover and to locate the starting point of the new dialectic. Instead, Hegel simply says : "This objectivity is the universal actuality of the self as well — it is the loss of its essential being".[27] Still, once the subject's social performances are recognized as having objectivity and intelligibility of their own, the step to a recognition of the whole cultural realm as alien to the immanent personality is not a difficult one, though, what precisely the cultural world will consist of can only be anticipated.

Before entering more in detail into the new development of the alienated subjectivity, it seems necessary to attempt a brief characterization of Hegel's social phenomenology. Now, Hegel's position about the dialectical structure of the social sphere raises two questions. For one thing, even assuming that Hegel is right in believing that the connections forged between the artless morality of Greek tragedy and the Roman jurisprudence were not tenuous, do the insights drawn from the ancient sources explain the development of social personality? For another, what is Hegel's justification for unduly narrowing the social field and for straightforwardly selecting family and state as the point of departure of the phenomenological analysis?

As regards the gradual development of social personality depicted by

---

[25] *Ibid.*
[26] B., p. 506. *Phän.*, p. 346.
[27] *Ibid.*

Hegel, this could not be achieved without some simplification and even cheating. The primitive morality and the legalistic spirit were capriciously tailored to fit the aspirations of a subjectivity which, while pretending to be completely and authentically spiritual, bifurcated itself in self-alienation. As regards Hegel's point of departure, it is primarily the failure to examine certain basic social contacts and relations which induces us to reproach him for selecting family and state as the initial problem.

And even if we just waive these two issues, there is a sense in which Hegel's social phenomenology appears paradoxical. Those who expect from Hegel an elaborated or relatively complete social philosophy must feel disturbed by its fragmentary character and cannot be convinced by the ideas derived from *Antigone* and the Roman jurisprudence, while others who demand a purely phenomenological treatment of the social problem do not seem to be pleased with Hegel's complex doctrines and abrupt maneuvering.

CHAPTER XV

THE DUAL LIFE OF THE SPIRITUAL SUBJECT

The conclusion reached in the preceding chapter is that the inner person is the essential and the principal subject, precisely because he has attained consciousness of being more than legalism cared to acknowledge. Although the person can never know what he really is until he realizes himself through action, his own inwardness and concrete personality is the uncontestable evidence, present to consciousness in the very act that drives consciousness back into itself.

This, however, is still not enough for the determination and recognition of the subject's true personality; the person thus affirmed is but a "bare self-existence without any content".[1] If no more than the mere inwardness is posited, then no new insight has been attained and, consequently, no advance can be made. Fortunately, the emerging spiritual being rejects his isolated mode of existence and refuses to be shut out from the legal sphere, for he knows that "it is his [own] work". However, if we look at the inner self-conscious personality not as an "insular self" but as an agent indissolubly connected with his work of laws and cultural values, we have before us the constitutive elements of an integrated subjectivity, but which can easily break apart and culminate in mutual alienation. The reason behind all this is very simple. Despite the fact that the objective and spiritual world of civilization is the "work of self-consciousness", it appears to the inner self both as an order that exists independently on its own account and as an alien reality. If so, there is given a concrete person, who has self-consciousness, but possesses no recognizable content, and a spiritual realm, which has both actuality and content, but is deprived of a living "spirit self-established and indwelling within it".[2] Now, despite the fact that the objective world of laws and cultural matters becomes intelligible only

---

[1] B., p. 505. *Phän.*, p. 346.
[2] B., p. 511. *Phän.*, p. 349.

through the self-conscious subject and this concrete, conscious subject recognizes his spiritual content in the legal codes and cultural values, both aspects of the spiritual subjectivity "take each other to mean and to imply alienation".[3]

By the very logic of his radical and sharp distinctions, Hegel has been led to the problem of division and alienation. The importance of all this, however, is that the occurrence of alienation places the subject in front of a new and dramatic experience : the experience of the dual life. This experience makes new relations occur, relations which can hardly be compared to those of the unhappy consciousness. Still, it is the spirituality of the subject and of his cultural environment Hegel is here principally concerned with. Indeed, the central reality is for him the spiritual : an inward self, who grasps himself as a concrete spiritual agency and the realm of cultural values, which are spiritual in the sense of being created to provide the necessary conditions for a spiritual-rational life. Now, with the spiritual element as the common denominator, the subject's dual experience becomes a genuine metaphysical problem : how the objectively existing spiritual values could be reconciled with the spiritual subjectivity, whose actuality remains almost intangible? What is more, the actual and the objective sphere of culture, emerging out of the overpowering insight into its independent mode of existence, can very easily threaten to undermine the supremacy of the spiritual subject, who, although he is immediately certain of himself and of his self-identity, remains vague and indefinite, and just as indefinable as the concrete existence itself.

Probably no justification is necessary that culture in its essential sense exists for the explicit purpose of serving as a spiritualizing force, as an educational agency. Seen in this light, culture is intended to offer an explanation of personal growth which has definite advantages over legalism. And it will hardly be denied that the cultural order is a setting wherein the person becomes himself, and it serves to identify both the creative character of the subject as well as his universality. Culture, then, is the subject's salvation, for it promises to elevate him to a higher mode of existence. What the subject must do, however, is not merely to deepen his awareness of cultural values or to surrender to their meaningful call, but to comply with the conventional standards prevailing in the given civilization. But a description which does not entail all characteristics essential to what is described, is incomplete. The equivocation is that "culture" in the one sense means the "development of individuality *qua* universal objective being",[4]

---

[3] B., p. 510. *Phän.*, p. 348.
[4] B., p. 516. *Phän.*, p. 352.

while in the other it is not edifying at all, for in conforming itself to cultural standards and rules, consciousness empties "itself of its own self".[5] But with this new and deeper awareness of cultural conditions and their transforming influence the inward subject and the cultured subject break apart. Understood in this way the problem of alienation is traceable to the fundamental attitude of the culturally oriented subject. It is when this subject allows himself to be shaped by cultural factors and wants to promote them for the whole social order, and ceases to seek anchorage in his inward self that he begins to experience his truly dramatic predicament.

Still, the genuinely decisive factors in the subject's acute experience of conflict and dual existence lie deeper. It is safe to say that the event of alienation took on especial importance for Hegel because he refused to ignore and to repress the natural self lurking at the very roots of subjectivity. There can be no doubt that this position is extremely fruitful, for it permits Hegel to ascertain the immediate grasp of the inner person and to prepare the way for the mediated understanding of the indefinable self. And though the inward self cannot be defined, he can easily be identified. Where there is self-affirmation, where there is rebellion against the uniform and conventional behavior, and where there is belief in an order other than the cultural, there is found authentic subjectivity. Thus, Hegel's subject remains aloof and speaks out in opposition to the threatening artificial order contrived by art, education, and other cultural efforts. For Hegel, the entire cultural order "is negative as regards the [inner] self",[6] precisely because the subject cannot look upon culture and cultural formation (*Bildung*) as compatible with true subjectivity and spirituality. And here lies the fundamental reason why the natural self condemns conventionality, uniformity, and conformity, seeing that these categories emanate from the artificially construed order. The inner subject's development, then, goes away from an artificial order in favor of a natural order. All this, however, merely intensifies the feeling of alienation and sharpens the opposition between the civilized person and the natural person.

It is evident that, with the widening of the gap between the two selves, the urgent question about the unification of culture and personality was bound to become increasingly problematic. Being forced to lead a dual life but retaining freedom to question the primacy of the inner self and the meaning of the civilized mode of existence, the perplexed subject wastes no time in trying to find the solution of the conflict in the direction of

---

[5] B., p. 517. *Phän.*, p. 353.
[6] *Ibid.*

critical evaluation. Thus, the primary issue flowing from the experience of bifurcated existence is the realization that the distinct and opposite modes of life cannot possibly embody the same worth. Since each given mode of life has its own specific nature, in the sense of having a recognizable value and meaning, and has a determinate reality as against the other, it is only logical to express this distinction "by means of the absolute opposites of 'good' and 'bad', which are poles asunder, and can in no way become one and the same".[7] Furthermore, since the alienated subject identifies himself with the simple, self-identical reality, it is the natural self which at first appears good, "badness" being ascribed to a cultured being, "a being partly sacrificing itself for another".[8]

This distinction, however, being too radical and one-sided, does not take us very far; it simply emphasizes opposition and reaffirms alienation. Be that as it may, the distinction and the application of good and evil cannot stop here. Remembering that the very essence of what is initially determined and fixed consists in its gradual transition to its contrary, we can anticipate that Hegel will re-examine the subject's valuations in such a manner as to make them vanish into their opposites. Before undertaking this task, however, Hegel unexpectedly turns to the determinants of culture with the intent of applying to them the categories of good and bad, and his only justification for doing so is that in culture these categories "appear as moments that are objective".[9] Still, by thus broadening the applicability of value judgment, Hegel has made it possible to examine the universal conditions of culture, and thus to determine their possible contributions to the development of the spiritual subject.

Hegel's analysis of the determinants of culture — the power of the state (*Staatsmacht*) and the wealth (*Reichtum*) — carries the stamp of an original phenomenological work. There is no doubt that in relating these two conditions to each other and to the self he has contributed many valuable insights, but in confining himself to the issues of state, wealth, and language, he has unjustifiably restricted the scope of the cultural problem. Measured in terms of the intricacy and vastness of the cultural realm, what Hegel singles out for detailed analysis is only a fragment. And consequently, the evaluation of cultural conditions is essentially such that it becomes clear from the very beginning that both, precisely as indispensable conditions, are equally important and resisting any devaluation. Nor is it really evident

---

[7] *Ibid.*
[8] B., p. 519. *Phän.*, p. 354.
[9] B., p. 519. *Phän.*, p. 355.

that the valuations thus accomplished are necessary for the transition from the categories of good and bad to the subject's attitudes of nobility and baseness, for the argument merely confirms the prior assumption that each cultural condition is as important as the other. In Hegel's eyes, however, a lengthy analysis — which gives us impression of being a needless detour — was necessary to overcome the radical antithesis of the state power and the wealth. Thus, when the two pairs of opposed value judgments occur in relation to state power and wealth, the alleged contradiction cracks under its own weight. In other words, when "there is an opposite relation established towards both the essential realities", that is, towards the determinants of culture, "we must pass judgment on these different ways of judging"[10] and take cognizance that the power of the state and the economic resources possess the same importance and enjoy the same status.

With or without an elaborate argument, the transition here discussed is simply from the evaluated cultural conditions to the evaluating consciousness itself. Now, to say this implies saying that the conscious life of the subject, assuming the attitude of agreement or disagreement in relation to the principal conditions of culture, becomes itself characterized as noble (*edelmütige*) or as base (*niederträchtige*). The conscious subject becomes noble when he accepts the "public authority of the state"[11] and looks upon wealth as something essential to his overt life, being convinced that these conditions place him "under a debt of obligation".[12] We may, then, recognize that there is a certain amount of rather significant implications contained in this double proposition. One thing must, to be sure, be emphasized immediately which cannot be overlooked, if we want to grasp the doctrine of nobility in Hegel's own spirit. The noble attitude springs from and pertains to the cultured subject. It is rather obvious that the cultured subject, precisely as cultured, identifies himself with the government of the state, for it safeguards, promotes, and fosters the cultural realm and its values.

It is from these points that Hegel goes on to say that the essential mark of the cultured person is nobility. Threading through the present section of the *Phenomenology* the theme rises and develops, ambiguous in some passages to allude to the life of aristocracy and its peculiar heroism, unmistakably clear in others to stress its importance, subtly varied by the demands of alienation, but constantly it is there : culture and nobility are discovered together, or they are not recognizable at all. Indeed, what is really novel

---

[10] B., p. 524. *Phän.*, p. 358.
[11] B., p. 525. *Phan.*, p. 358.
[12] B., p. 525. *Phän.*, p. 359.

in Hegel's treatment of alienation is precisely this fusion of cultured life and noble attitude. Now, the reference to the heroism of aristocracy suggests very distinctly that this noble attitude is particularly suited for sharpening the tension between the cultivated subject and the natural self. By taking up a positive relation to the political and economic foundations of culture, the subject heroically renounces his natural self and "sacrifices [his] individual being to the universal, and thereby brings this into existence".[13] At this stage, then, self-sacrifice is assigned the task of realizing the universal, even if the price to be paid is the radical self-suppression and the univocal identification of subjectivity with the civilized personality. However, it is something of a paradox that the posture of self-sacrifice should accentuate self-importance. Although the noble subject, being dedicated to the promotion of universality through culture, sincerely negates his personal needs and interests which the inner self constantly activates and fosters, his very act of sacrifice explicitly affirms the presence and the value of the personal subject. In other words, the subject's awareness of his heroic effort only confirms his self-importance.

What emerges from all this is that the heroic service (*der Heroismus des Dienstes*) that the cultivated subject intends to carry out has an abortive character. The self-sacrifice of the cultivated person becomes a failure, for, rendering service to the political power, the self-consciousness "sacrifices merely its existence to the state, not its essential nature".[14] It should be noted, then, that there is a subtle distinction in Hegel's thought between the "sacrifice of existence", which designates the very *Dasein* of the overt subject, and the "sacrifice of essential nature", which expresses the *Ansichsein* of the natural self. Now, it is unquestionably not sufficient that the sacrifice of the *Dasein* be unconditional, if that does not also mean that it is complete. And it is precisely here that the meaning of complete sacrifice in Hegel's thought comes out. As he sees it, the possibility of complete sacrifice cannot be entertained without evoking the notion of heroic death. In Hegel's own words : "The sacrifice of existence, which takes place in the case of service, is indeed complete when it goes so far as death".[15]

This thought, however, leads the subject to a deeper and a more cautious consideration, for the issue is far from being univocal and obvious. The first problem to be met is the "endurance of the danger of death which the individual survives".[16] In this case, to be sure, the subject retains not only

[13] B., p. 527. *Phän.*, p. 360.
[14] B., p. 528. *Phän.*, p. 361.
[15] *Ibid.*
[16] B., pp. 528-529. *Phän.*, p. 361.

the "inner secretly reserved spiritual principle", but also "a separate individual will as against the power of the state".[17] The second problem, as
is clear from the text, refers to the heroic motivation and the eventual
death of the noble servant. In this case, however, the dead hero cannot
survive his renunciation and passes directly into the opposite which is beyond any possibility of reconciliation. Since the self-sacrifice achieved
through death turns out to be an irrevocable self-destruction, this act does
not remove self-estrangement and, therefore, it should not be attempted.
Thus, after a considerably long detour, the subject comes to the point
from which he has started, the experience of alienation. But the subject
does not look upon this as a final defeat and refuses to abandon the attempt
to attain reconciliation through sacrifice. If so, the previous efforts were
not in vain, precisely because the analysis of death has helped to unveil
the possibility of true renunciation. "That alone is true sacrifice of individuality, therefore, in which it gives itself up as completely as in the case
of death, but all the while preserves itself in the renunciation".[18] It must
be noted, however, that this interesting passage reads somewhat differently in the original, for Hegel describes sacrifice (*Aufopferung*) as an act
that involves the externalization (*Entäusserung*) of the inner self.[19] It is
precisely the attempt at externalization which brings into clear light the
principal guidepost of further development.

As Hegel sees sacrifice, it hinges on the inner self's ability to come into
the objective existence, so that the "secret spiritual principle" of the subject
becomes "something for others". If this suggests anything, it suggests that
only by externalizing his inner self is the subject able to renounce and to
preserve himself. Now, it seems clear enough that such a double function
of preservation and renunciation characterizes language. The particular
subject as such, Hegel insists, is non-existent unless he expresses his inwardness and his inner life by means of language. Through the spoken word,
then, he manages to reveal his interiority and thus to show his concern
for the social order and cultural values. It is not likely, indeed, that any
thinker would question Hegel's contention that "in speech the self-existent
singleness of self-consciousness comes as such into existence".[20] Unlike
every other mode of expression, speech contains the "ego in its purity"

---

[17] B., p. 529. *Phän.*, p. 361.

[18] B., p. 529. *Phän.*, p. 362.

[19] It should be noted, too, that in this passage the concepts of *Entfremdung* and *Entäuss-erung* appear together for the first time. In Baillie's translation, however, this important occurrence remains undetectable. Cf. *ibid.*

[20] B., p. 530. *Phän.*, p. 362.

and in its essential content. Small wonder, then, that language is the only means for expressing one's loyalty to the state and one's readiness to serve or give advice. What is more, embodying laws, formulating commands, and conveying advice, language assumes the role of a mediator. Surely, this sort of mediation can be qualified as "spiritual", not only in the sense that language is a spiritual agency and a conscious link connecting the natural self and the cultivated subject, but also in the sense that "through the mediating process spirit comes to exist in spiritual form".[21] Hence Hegel's own statements leave us no room for doubting that language is more than an image or symbol of spirit. This, of course, is a somewhat inadequate way of putting it, and the explication which follows is hardly transparent; but it all shows Hegel's hesitation to reduce language to a few secondary and instrumental functions.

The role of language is evidently not confined to mediating between the distinct aspects of the same subject, because through language the personal being can establish a direct contact with others. We stand here before a problem of intersubjectivity and thus before a complex issue. It is through language alone that the inner self can convey the knowledge of his inwardness to others. But others apprehend the self only in terms of universality. Thus through speech the subject proceeds beyond his original natural status of particularity and isolated individuality. To say this, however, implies saying that, by becoming object to others, singular consciousness becomes aware that "its existence is itself dying away".[22] In other words, the assertion that language "kindles a universal consciousness of self" has for its correlate the insight that the subject, as a self-conscious Now (als selbstbewusstes Jetzt), has no subsistence, and that he subsists only through his disappearance. This sounds like a sacrifice again; but the subject sacrificed is the base self. The conscious subject thus acquires a sort of universal mode of existence : he abandons his particularity and nothing can ever restore it. Therefore, it is precisely in language, where there seemed to occur a simple externalization of the self, that the subject becomes aware of having "passed into another self".[23]

Up to this point Hegel's analysis of language might be considered as a sustained effort to remove alienation and to promote the universal character of the subject. Since, however, Hegel is primarily interested in the heroic sacrifice of the noble consciousness, he finds that language is an

[21] B., p. 531. Phän., p. 363.
[22] B., p. 530. Phan., p. 362.
[23] B., p. 531. Phän., p. 363.

appropriate medium and the most suitable means for expressing and rendering service to the power of the state. Because language is always transforming by the mediating criterion, Hegel seems to have supposed that there were good motives for appealing to it in relation to the state power. Oral mediation between the individual subject and the state authority raises the latter "into its transparent, purified universality".[24] But it is obviously not sufficient that sacrifice to the state be effective, if that does not also mean that it is sacrifice to a monarch. Now, what the noble subject abandons through the laudatory language is his personal thought, and with it, the subjectivity itself. And once it has been admitted that laudatory language gives the monarch "his proper name" and puts this individualistic consciousness on its pinnacle, "the heroism of dumb service passes into the heroism of flattery".[25] Hegel connects this new type of heroism with a penetrating psychological observation. It occurs to him as an important fact that all flattering praises of the noble class are themselves positive and formative. *Heroismus der Schmeichelei*, consisting solely of panegyric phrases, contributes to the personification of the state authority and assures the monarch that his power is as unlimited as he claims it to be. What is more, flattery is a rewarding activity, for the noble subject, in return for the self-sacrifice, dedication, and services rendered, receives the proper share of the state power which he himself has helped to establish.

Still, the heroism of flattery is not so heroic and not so selfless as it may appear. Confessedly, flattery is a base and selfish preoccupation. And Hegel finds a quick solution by appealing to the flatterer's experiences occasioned by his laudatory performance; it is their verdict that flattery is essentially egotistic, because it produces the most intense and the most enjoyable feeling of personal satisfaction. But through these subjectively satisfying experiences the noble subject rediscovers his inwardness : by finding gratification in and through flattery he manages to reaffirm his inner personality and thus to give his natural self the importance which was previously suppressed and denied. One thing, then, becomes very clear : while the position of the cultured subject gradually deteriorates, the situation of the natural and invisible self is bound to improve. This improvement, however, leads the subject to a deeper estrangement, because the inner self can posit himself only by breaking away from the cultivated self. There is for the spiritual subject a chasm into which he is forced to gaze. What is more, he gives up all concern about state power, all interest in economic

---

[24] B., p. 533. *Phän.*, p. 365.
[25] B., p. 533. *Phän.*, p. 364.

resources, in order to concentrate on his dramatic predicament. Heroism turns into hypocrisy, sacrifice into selfishness, and dedication into self-interest, precisely because the spiritual subject begins to look upon the world of culture as something artificial and vain and turns to the "realm of pure consciousness, of thought".[26]

And so, the subject sees himself ultimately led to a point at which merely linguistic reconciliations no longer suffice in order to silence the inner self. Even the devastating talk, in which everything is reduced to vanity, is no longer an obstacle for self-assertion, for such senseless performance reduces itself to vanity and collapses under its own absurdity. Its disintegrating action only confirms its own vanity and prepares the way for a positive approach. Under these circumstances one's inner self emerges as an objective being, "having a truly universal significance and value".[27] Thus the self's feeling of being ignored and misunderstood gives way to a feeling of self-confidence. The spiritual subject therefore raises himself to a new dialectical phase in which he no longer has confidence in the cultural realm, in its basic conditions, and in its means.

The return to the inner self brings us to the essential issue upon the settlement of which depends both the determination of a new point of departure and the passage from culture to enlightenment. Now, since the inner life of the self hinges on thought, the subject must take a long and profound look at the act of *insight*, exploding the term to include the activities of doubt and criticism. Accordingly, since the subject truly believes in the reality of his own self, his primary attitude must be an act of faith (*Glaube*). These are perfectly clear statements. But what we have to consider at the moment is why in his exposition Hegel should emphasize the fact that the act of belief is religious in character.

The answer to this problem need not be long, for, as if anticipating the question, Hegel hastens to warn the reader that religion does not appear here as it is in itself and for itself.[28] This explanation is in no way startling, since of religion proper there can be no question at this level of the phenomenological development. But it seems safe to say that the religious connotation of the act of faith here considered is basically the same as in the case of unhappy consciousness : it is secular in character and analogous in meaning.

---

[26] B., p. [549]. *Phän.*, p. 376.

[27] B., p. 547. *Phän.*, p. 376.

[28] "Wie hier die *Religion* — denn es erhellt, dass von ihr die Rede ist, — als der Glaube der Welt der Bildung auftritt, tritt sie noch nicht auf, wie sie *an und für sich ist*". *Phän.*, p. 377.

But there is another aspect to the matter, and it has to do with the relation between alienation and belief. Hegel was obviously not unaware that the experience of alienation and the act of faith occur concomitantly. It is for this reason that he spent so much time and effort in trying to relate the two. Upon this issue much might be said, but we will limit ourselves to two brief remarks. One is that the subject's search and longing for the unconditional subjectivity is similar to the quest of the religious for the Absolute Being.[29] The act of faith exhibits better than any purely cognitive act how urgent and how significant is the subject's profound belief in his own unified and complete reality. The other remark is that belief is an act that arises in the estranged subject. To be aware of one's inner reality is to have evidence in its regard; but to be aware of this essential subjectivity as irrevocably estranged from its existential mode of existence is to aspire to the "concrete actuality of spirit directly present to itself".[30] But since such a reality remains for the estranged person "an inner principle, which is all and effects all, but never itself comes to the light",[31] he can become one with it only through faith.

Different and deeper understanding of faith reveals itself in relation to insight. Now, we may think of the connection of the act of belief to the act of rational insight as a complementary relation, precisely because they are two acts of one and the same consciousness. However, another mode of connection is demanded and sought here. Thus, seen in the immediate perspective, the two forms of the same consciousness appear as involving tension and quarrel. The distinct acts of the alienated subject are no longer placed in a complementary relation; rather, the exact opposite occurs : "the peculiar object against which pure insight directs the active force of the notion is belief".[32]

From one point of view this can be looked upon as the rational critique of belief. Expressing the rationalistic principle, insight attacks belief for two obvious reasons. First, consciousness dominated by insight regards faith as a questionable attitude, since it fails to realize that the absolute subjectivity which the rational thought seeks to attain is also the final goal of all aspirations and efforts of faith. Secondly, insight, identifying itself with the rationalistic principle whose aim is to turn everything "into

---

[29] To be sure, "this pure consciousness of Absolute Being is a consciousness in estrangement". Still, belief constitutes only one side of the estranged self-consciousness. B., p. 551. *Phän.*, p. 378.

[30] B., p. 556. *Phän.*, p. 381.

[31] *Ibid.*

[32] B., p. [559]. *Phän.*, p. 383.

conceptual form", recognizes only rational evidence and assumes that belief does not possess that type of evidence. What is really peculiar in all this, however, is that the entire argument is not univocally carried out but is rather intentionally rendered ambiguous by a subsequent line of thought which emphasizes the religiousness of the attitude of belief. According to Hegel, "pure insight is born of the substance of spirit, it knows the pure self of consciousness to be absolute, and enters into conflict with the pure consciousness of the Absolute Being of all reality".[33] This conflict is extraordinarily conspicuous. Previously the act of belief was conceived as the act of the estranged person aspiring to his own unconditional reality; now suddenly the same act is represented as designating the consciousness of the Absolute Being of all reality (*Bewusstsein des absoluten Wesens aller Wirklichkeit*). However, the earlier line of thought is not given up. That is confirmed in the following paragraph, where Hegel says that "the reality in the case of belief is a thought, not a notion, and hence something absolutely opposed to self-consciousness, while the reality in the case of pure insight is the self".[34] This shows with how much subtlety Hegel knows at this point how to differentiate between insight and belief. But it is questionable whether the phrase "the reality in the case of belief is a thought" militates against the religious character of the act, and whether he does not rather intend to say that belief in the Absolute Being is initially vague, abstract, and exposed to superstitions. Be that as it may, insight and belief can no longer be seen as standing in a merely "formal opposition;" rather, this twofold vision constitutes a novel schism in the spiritual consciousness and the subject continues to experience estrangement, unhappiness, and immanent tension.

We are here dealing with a variant of dual life of the spiritual subjectivity the character of which is determined by an insight that seeks to be "resolved into universal insight".[35] The Hegelian phrase *die allgemeine Einsicht* is a striking illustration of the complementarity of both terms : universality that is not grounded in authentically rational insight is abstraction without recognizable content; insight that is not intersubjective is incomplete and ineffective. Thus insight develops into a truly universal attitude and begins to build a universal movement precisely by getting all subjects deeply involved with the task of rational enlightenment. Indeed, where there is complete surrender to reason and intelligiblity, where the radical purge of

---

[33] B., p. [561]. *Phän.*, p. 385.
[34] *Ibid.*
[35] B., p. 560. *Phän.*, p. 385.

the irrational is desired by all, and where there is radical repudiation of "superstitious prejudices and errors", there is found the spirit of enlightenment. This spirit of enlightenment is not one of the spiritual manifestations : it is the very life of subjects who resolutely appeal to rationality itself. And though enlightenment cannot be identified with the dated movement bearing the same name, it can be related to the latter as exemplifying historically the essential traits of the intersubjective vision.

Armed with negativity, insight is prepared to attack belief and to discredit all its irrational elements. The importance of this rationalistic assault, however, is not so much in the ruthless critique as in the self-realization of insight. This is really a significant truth, though not completely evident to the subject engaged in the rationalistic evaluation of belief : "What is not rational has no truth, or what is not comprehended through a notion, conceptually determined, *is* not. When reason thus speaks of some other than itself is, it in fact speaks merely of itself; it does not therein go beyond itself".[36] Evidently, there is no real difficulty in the first statement of this argument, and it seems safe to say that we have here an assertion of the identity of truth and existence : what is not intelligible is not (*was nicht begriffen ist, ist nicht*). In other words, that which is intelligible (*vernünftig*) is true (*wahr*), and that which is true is real. Negatively stated, the unknowable cannot be affirmed as real. If so, the only meaningful intelligibility objects have is that which they have in pure insights. So far, then, we have no real problem. But one is justified in asking whether the basis for the claim that whenever reason "speaks of some other than itself is, it in fact speaks merely of itself" is to be sought for in the first statement — in which case the argument is logically unified; or whether the notion of self-actualization is incapable of being deduced from the identity of truth and existence — in which case the argument is cut up into two independent fragments.

Now, if we investigate the first proposition of the argument, we will find that it does not contain any traces of a transition to the second statement, and the absence of these traces in the argument divides it up into two lines of thought. Still, what Hegel means by his second proposition is far from being obscure. One thing, however, is too little stressed : that the constitution of intelligibility implies in its meaning a reference to consciousness, to cognitional activity. Therefore, when the subject declares that something is, or that something is intelligible, he intends to claim — at least implicitly — that the object affirmed cannot be known independently of consciousness. It is indisputable, of course, that the rational subject

---

[36] B., p. 566. *Phän.*, p. 389.

can say "is" or "is not" in many different ways. Therefore, the other or the opposite to which the existential reference is made does not have to be something other than the subject or the subject's own act. To put it more concretely, the opposite of insight is not necessarily something other than itself. Thus, when the rational insight speaks of belief and declares that the Absolute Being professed by belief is a reality that comes from belief's own act, it speaks originally of itself and seeks its own actualization.

The unfolding of insight is slow and gradual, stealthy and silent. Having lost sight of itself in its own negative activity, the insight does not realize that this "absolute negation of itself" constitutes its proper and ultimate nature. "But this silent steady working of the loom of spirit in the inner region of its substance, spirit's own action being hidden from itself, is merely one side of the realizing of pure insight".[37] The other side of this self-realization, however, makes "its appearance in the form of a great noise, and a violent struggle with an opposite as such".[38] Here insight no longer spreads out unnoticed but attacks passionately belief because rational thought cannot help but regard it as an attitude belonging to "unreason" (*Unvernunft*).

Hegel makes it clear that the renewed attack on belief has been inspired by its alleged idolatry, irrationalism, and uselessness. And the subject fights nothing so relentlessly and forcefully as these three manifestations of belief, seeking evidence and support in the fact that they are open to direct observation and description. Quite obviously, this critique of faith becomes intelligible only in terms of the fundamental assumptions of the rational subject. First, reliance on external object of religious worship precludes the rational subject from grasping the authentic significance of religious rites and liturgy. Therefore, the subject develops his critique in such a way that the truly religious worship becomes reduced to worship of graven images. Secondly, since the subject recognizes only the rational type of evidence, he leaves no room for an evidence of another sort, for spiritual evidence. Thirdly, the subject takes cognizance of the utility principle and, in the course of the dialectic of enlightenment, he develops this principle more sharply and stresses it increasingly. All values thus are reduced to the category of the useful which derives its total significance from the individual it serves.

Whenever the subject appeals to these rationalistic principles for confirmation of his position, he clearly admits that the act of insight is nothing else

---

[37] B., p. 565. *Phän.*, p. 388.
[38] *Ibid.*

but an act of faith in reason. However, through the same principles the rational evaluation of belief becomes restricted. The entire problem of belief's inwardness, of the spiritual evidence, of the subject's immediate relation to the Absolute Being in the act of faith — all of this remains foreign to reason and insight. For the believer, then, insight, which is bound solely to rational criteria and observable expressions of belief, fails with the problem of the nature of belief.

Still, the rationalistic critique and explanation, superficial and restricted as it remains, does help to modify the attitude of believing consciousness. Although the believing subject refuses to recognize the unconditional validity of the principles of rationalism, the spirit of enlightenment achieves at least partial victory by instilling in him the desire to arrive at a more meaningful understanding of faith. And with this remarkable victory the step into the realm of rational religion is finally ventured.

It is important to recall that the whole doctrine of the enlightened consciousness does not intend to render intelligible the errors and prejudices of the belief but rather intends to clarify its true nature. Now, the enlightened belief implies in its meaning a reference to a supreme being. However, guarding itself against irrationalism and superstition, the religious consciousness can conceive of the supreme being only as "an unknown and unknowable Absolute".[39] What the subject means by this cautious statement is, of course, sufficiently clear. Of the Absolute Being recognized by pious consciousness nothing else can be said than that it is a predicateless (das prädicatlose) reality. Still, one "predicate" is applicable to the supreme being without contradicting rational thought and without exposing oneself to the danger of anthropomorphism. The supreme being is the ground of utility which is the only valid category of worth. Therefore, man's every relation to this being embodies and expresses the utilitarian value.[40] Naturally, the rational consciousness regards this clarification as a positive and lasting contribution and, consequently, ceases discrediting belief, because it suddenly recognizes itself in the newly formed conception of religion. To the religious subject, however, this new conception of rational religion is an appalling distortion. Belief "finds itself utterly wronged by enlightenment",[41] since its authentic experience cannot be penetrated, understood, and appreciated by the natural light of reason.

---

[39] B., p. 589. *Phän.*, p. 407.

[40] "The relation to Absolute Being, or Religion, is therefore of all forms of profitableness the most supremely profitable; for it is profiting pure and simple; it is that by which all things stand — by which they have a being all their own — and that by which all things fall — have an existence for something else". B., p. 580. *Phän.*, p. 400.

[41] B., p. 581. *Phän.*, p. 400.

However, what the spirit of enlightenment really wants to usurp is merely the right to relate itself to belief, to reveal to belief its own thoughts, and to overcome the constant inattentiveness and forgetfulness of belief.[42] To say this, of course, implies saying that the self-realization of belief is only possible through insight, although this truth is not immediately obvious to the believing consciousness. Let us look at this confusing issue more closely.

Though the enlightened subject can easily be accused of being an usurper, insight strives to free the believing consciousness from the unavoidable limitations of forgetfulness and one-sidedness. However, insight in this function does not give up its right against the believing mind and reminds belief of the opposite of its separate moments. At first insight stresses the fact that the notion (*Begriff*) of belief is an act of consciousness, which, being immanent, ascribes no extrinsic connotation, no transcendental reference, to the absolute reality it ascertains. Seen in this context, then, "the absolute Being belief accepts is a Being of the believer's consciousness *qua* a self, or that this absolute Being is produced by consciousness".[43] The activity of the believing consciousness is only the contingent action that insight sees itself forced to regard as being wrapped up in itself and deprived of all objective and transcendental significance. In short, the activity of the believing consciousness is only the creative activity of representations that have no being in themselves (Vorstellungen, die nicht *an sich* sind).[44]

It is, indeed, true that the insight just made depends upon the voluntary movement of the subject's attention. It is not surprising, therefore, that when the subject's attention shifts to "the moment of otherness which the notion involves",[45] we can expect from insight a diametrically opposed message. Involved in the significance of otherness is the necessity of thinking of an "essential Reality" that is foreign and totally unknown to consciousness. And reflection upon this fact brings to light what the believer regards as his own position, for what his reasoning comes to is simply this : that from the absolute Being — who remains unsearchable (*unerforschlich*) and unattainable (*unerreichbar*) — he receives the assurance of his own self.

---

[42] Hegel explains : "Enlightenment merely brings together and presents to belief its own thoughts, the thoughts that lie scattered and apart within belief, all unknown to it. Enlightenment merely reminds belief, when one of its own forms is present, of others it also has, but which it is always forgetting when the one is there". B., p. 581. *Phän.*, p. 401.

[43] B., p. 583. *Phän.*, p. 402.

[44] B., p. 584. *Phän.*, p. 403.

[45] *Ibid.*

Gradually, then, the continual action of insight transforms belief into a secular attitude, convincing belief that it operates with the elements which belief itself contains. Therefore, believing grown secular appears as the conscious attitude that brings itself to fruition by the very fact that it finds within itself the very principles to which enlightenment merely gives rational clarity. But "belief in this manner has in fact become the same as enlightenment — the conscious attitude of relating a finite that inherently exists to an unknown and unknowable Absolute without predicates".[46]

Except by a reference to the experience of satisfaction or dissatisfaction, we could not differentiate a religious consciousness from a rational consciousness, the belief from the insight. The fact that belief remains an "unsatisfied enlightenment" seems to suggest that insight has failed to purge belief of its mysterious character and to bring it to a clearer consciousness of its own principles. Appealing to the world of sense and sticking to it, the rational insight has brought to light "only what is individual", leaving the believer in the state of sheer longing and unhappiness. To be sure, insight alone must be held responsible for "this stain of unsatisfied longing" and has to see to it that the "stain" be removed through the renewed intellectual effort to clarify the *être suprême*.

The accomplishment of this task places the rational subject in front of a new concept : the truth of enlightenment. But obviously, we are here dealing with a variant of enlightenment the nature of which is determined by quasi-metaphysical constructions of reason. To put it differently, the subject ventures a step into an area of creedal speculations in order to extend the sphere of insight and to remove from the believing mind the "stain of unsatisfied longing". The cognitive insight, however, does not direct itself toward the authenticity of the act of belief in order to reveal its spiritual significance. Rather, insight reverts to its original principles and seeks to explore the notion of an *être suprême* by its own efforts and procedures. But evidently, to assume such a position is simply to proclaim one's faith in reason. In other words, the act of insight moves to cognitions that are creedal in nature. Therefore, in virtue of this principle and intent that reason places before the insight, the latter becomes for the first time completely aware of the fact that its speculations are religious in character.

Taking the point of departure from the notion of a supreme being, the insight indulges in abstract thought with the intent of grasping the nature of the predicateless Absolute. Now, to define the Absolute as the predicateless Being is to employ a designation which is admittedly inarticulate,

---

[46] B., pp. 588-589. *Phän.*, pp. 406-407.

indeterminate, and vague. On the other hand, to propose a specific attribute is to invite limitation and thus to contradict the absoluteness of the supreme being. Therefore, since it is impossible to find a positive predicate which would serve to identify the transcendent being, the subject has to accept the view that strikes an agnostic chord : he must affirm the existence of the supreme being and declare that its nature is unknowable. But this is abstract and for the subject it is a position that cannot be thought out in more detail.

However, another possibility for knowledge of the Absolute by an enlightened subject is conceivable : through a rational consideration of sensible objects. The subject can "infer" to the essence of the supreme being through material beings by abstracting from their sensuous qualities. However many properties the subject might recognize as inherent in the substance of matter, the real nature of materiality remains inscrutable and unknowable. But the absolute matter, which is "something neither felt or tasted",[47] fits the description of the predicateless being, for it is the unidentifiable inner being of real things. Only in this way can the mind claim knowledge of the supreme being which it does not deduce from agnosticism but which stands next to it.

Apparently nothing stands in the way of designating being here as "being-for-self" (*Fürsichsein*), for nothing qualifies as intelligible unless it is related to the self-conscious subject. But here the concern is not with the objective and disinterested nature of being as it reveals itself to the subject but rather with being's utility and serviceableness for the individual. For "being-for-self" is deeply bound up with the individual as conscious of a profitable use, as availing himself of an object as a means to an end. To be sure, this utility is regarded here as an objective capacity of being for serving as means. But beyond the natural capacity of the means as such there is the user's interest or need, which is the reason for which he uses things and ascribes utility to them. All this demonstrates that the concept of utility, insofar as it implies a relation to the self, must appear as a category marked by relativity and dependence, since it is always determined by the individual subject.

This section thus returns again to the position of radical utilitarianism and, more particularly, to the unfettered individualism. In reverting to the doctrine of utilitarianism, the issue confronting the subject consists in the necessity of determining and pursuing that which is useful. But what is considered useful may arbitrarily be expanded, for the aptitude of objects

---

[47] B., p. 593. *Phän.*, p. 410.

to serve as efficacious means for the ever new interests and needs is the sole measure of evaluating everything. Needless to say, personal interests and useful ends presuppose individual users involved in their identification and determination, and in growing conscious of his ability and liberty in determining them, the user becomes the sole judge and the unfettered arbiter. Thus, the subject is suddenly led in a new direction, into the position of unrestrained liberty, which Hegel sketches in the next section, entitled "Absolute Freedom and Terror".

Hegel, as we will recall, designated the problem of freedom as the central theme and as the final goal of the subject's self-realization. Accordingly, he did not simply suppose that freedom had social implications; he tried to prove that it did, and in doing so he realized that he had to test it in a framework of an organized society and in the context of the "self-opposition of universal and single will".[48]

No thinker has emphasized more than Hegel the fundamental distinction between the individual and the universal while at the same time asserting their mutual implication and complementarity. This basic difference is essential here, but being considered in abstract terms it forces the self-alienated mind to run its course from absolute freedom to terrorism. What Hegel wants to show in this section of the *Phenomenology* is that the subject, after he has succeeded in uncovering the possibilities of complete self-liberation in the concept of utility, does not feel himself limited by the social institutions and refuses to draw away from the position he has achieved. By letting freedom manifest itself in its entire inner force, however, the mind inevitably assumes the attitude of annihilation, since "there is left for it only negative action; it is merely the rage and fury of destruction".[49]

The freedom of the individual constitutes the source of all his actions and decisions. However, in exercising his freedom each individual subject is not only acting in the name of the universal will and not only representing this will — his personal will *is* the universal will. But the attribution to single individuals of absolute freedom has its origin in the abstract derivation from the principle of utility, which does not impose any rules and restrictions for a fruitful participation in the universal will. Small wonder, then, that a society composed of free individuals, who intend to retain their unconditional freedom, refuses to recognize any government and to obey any law. Therefore, every attempt to transform this unruly and turbulent society

---

[48] B., p. 610. *Phän.*, p. 422.
[49] B., p. 604. *Phän.*, p. 418.

into a governable state must inevitably result in bloody revolution and senseless killing. "The sole and only work and deed accomplished by universal freedom is therefore *death* — a death that achieves nothing, embraces nothing within its grasp; for what is negated is the unachieved, unfulfilled punctual entity of the absolutely free self".[50] Indeed, the aspirations of the free individual are in principle like those of any terrorist intent upon liquidating all social institutions and destroying anyone and everyone. And so, absolute freedom, seeking support in pure negativity, which is itself devoid of content and mediation, turns into a self-destructive, self-abolishing power.

The only result of Hegel's eloquent sketch seems to be the message that absolute freedom, which leads to nothing but capriciousness and death, has transformed the emerging spiritual subject into a senseless criminal. Through this it acquires an awakening power, warning the subject to safeguard freedom in the sense of its spiritual content against mere universalization and false absolutization. In other words, what is needed is to envisage freedom apart from its absoluteness and to get it into relation with the inner self. The reason is that the essence of freedom never lies in doing what one pleases, but rather in the very impartiality of the doer. The individual achieves his spiritual fulfillment, not by abstract freedom, nor by an arbitrary restriction to social action, but rather in his morally oriented consciousness. It follows that the subject must abandon the self-destructive position of the terrorist and look for positive ways through which to exhibit his mature spirituality and freedom.

[50] B., p. 605. *Phän.*, p. 418.

CHAPTER XVI

THE MORAL SUBJECT

Opposed to the previous modes of spiritual consciousness, which, incidentally, hardly reflect any genuine spiritual content, stands moral consciousness.[1] That depth of the spiritual being which could not be discerned in social action comes to light when the subject overcomes alienation and apprehends himself in the self-imposed moral responsibility. Here the person acquires certainty that his volition is not a merely "ethical" or determined choice but is in fact an expression of that depth of subjectivity which is not susceptible to any external influence or coercive force.

Having experienced brutal terror, revolution, and the shipwreck of freedom in the social sphere, the spiritual consciousness flees from the troubled world and hastens back into itself. But with this return to the self, freedom comes to assert its importance and indispensability again.

The very essence of freedom lies in the volitional capacity of the subject. Inasmuch as freedom is not a passive perfection, but remains the true source of conscious intentions and decisions, Hegel often speaks of "moral consciousness", which he describes as that which is a "willing of pure duty".[2] Unconditional freedom and complete autonomy of the will are interchangeable concepts. To be subjectivity is to be free, and to be free is to be conscious of moral obligation. Freedom, for Hegel, is not one of the moral principles : freedom is the very life of the morally conscious subject. Freedom lifts the acting person out from every determinism of the customary laws and sees him face to face with a pure concept of duty.[3]

---

[1] To this we must add : though the developed personality and some of the most basic characteristics of spirituality are absent from the previous modes of consciousness, one can find in them clear indications of the presence of "spiritualizing "forces, including negativity and desire for freedom. In becoming conscious of itself as what it is in itself, the personal subjectivity spiritualizes itself.

[2] B., p. 621. *Phän.*, p. 429.

[3] This squares with Kant's categorical imperative, but there is no need to exaggerate

Hegel blasted the concept of duty as an abstractly conceived principle as perhaps no one before him; but, in the final analysis, his dialectical argument is not against duty, but in its behalf. Initially and essentially, moral consciousness signifies nothing but awareness of moral obligation. But herein lies the strength as well as the weakness of the concept of pure duty. It appears as a strength to him who seeks an absolutely autonomous principle of action, which he himself posits and legislates. Evidently, duty, expressing the true vocation of man, must spring directly from the subject's volitional center. But what first appears as strength is actually weakness, because only in conformity to nature, which is devoid of spirituality, can moral duty be realized. Duty is duty only when done in conformity with nature. Still, were the subject to ignore nature, the only course open to him would be formal and ineffable duty. Therefore, that there is duty at all is identical with the idea that there is natural order, because the subject can conceive of morality in no other way than as conformity to nature. Human consciousness cannot call itself moral, unless harmony between two distinct orders is secured. Seen in this way, then, nature alone is the condition of the possibility of duty, and, consequently, of all morally praiseworthy actions.

Hegel's specification of the meaning of "duty" is, of course, more than a matter of dialectical expediency and more than a critical argument against Kantian ethics. It is the outcome of a logical consideration, which shows that moral duty is not intelligible, unless it is seen as implying some sort of conformity to a norm. This also shows that the subject cannot determine the nature of morality by simply trying to deduce it from pure obligation; rather, it becomes possible for him to act morally only after he has discovered and recognized the specific norm of moral goodness. To say this implies saying that to become morally conscious is to enter into a process of differentiation by opposing and relating duty and nature. Moral obligation assumes the character of duty only when the subject takes cognizance of the fact that the natural order alone can provide the required norm. At this stage, then, the subject assumes that the category of "nature" is sufficiently clear, failing to see that nature as norm offers the same problems as the notion of pure duty.

What Hegel here deals with is neither a moral attitude nor a specific moral theory, but a self-correcting activity of the will. Striving and failure, crises and new beginnings, positing and displacing opposite views are inher-

---

the importance of this analogy. For a comprehensive definition of the Kantian imperative see H. J. Paton, *The Categorical Imperative* (New York and Evanston : Harper, 1967), pp. 115, 127.

ent in the very nature of moral consciousness. But it is precisely this decision to oppose and then to relate morality and nature which leads the spiritual subject to conflict, frustration, and hypocrisy.

Let us begin by saying that the subject, devoting all his efforts to moral issues, never places nature on the same plane as duty. "While experience must necessarily bring to light the disharmony between the two aspects, seeing that nature is detached and free, nevertheless duty is alone the essential fact and nature by contrast is devoid of selfhood".[4] Duty as such is a moral and spiritual notion, nature an ontological concept. Accordingly, duty is a free and conscious decision, nature a state. Admittedly, then, the natural order is indifferent to and cut off from the moral realm. Now, the point of this impressively dualistic contention is that the subject learns and matures by introducing unsparing opposition which in turn gives rise to a reconciliatory act.

The subject hesitates to claim an immediate reconciliation, and with good reasons. If morality has for its goal the concordance of duty and nature, the activity to which moral value is ascribed must terminate when this harmony becomes realized. Thus, the search for complete and perfect harmony between duty and nature culminates in the actual abolition of morality itself. If the moral subject had had to believe that the moral ideal was authentically real and not merely apparent, the realization of it could have meant much to him. But the point is this : whereas the moral act has as its corollary the unity of duty and nature, the attainment of this ideal has as its corollary the irrevocable termination of morality. Thus, harmony proves to be a dubious means of establishing morality, and the efforts at unification are too easily employed to destroy moral values instead of enhancing them. Therefore, in order to save morality from dissolution, the subject must be prepared to regard it as an endless progression and to postulate the permanent disharmony between duty and nature. In other words, sensing a lapse in the preceding moral awareness, the subject holds that the necessary character of morality is a perpetual tension and struggle. There is a striking peculiarity about morality which renders every advance towards ideal harmony impossible. Seen in this light, morality is not the sort of enterprise which the subject can progressively exhaust by dutiful action, and this new conception launches him on a relatively different course.

One suspects, oddly enough, that the new position is as untenable as the preceding. Indeed, the idea of endless progression offers the same difficulties as the postulate of complete concordance. If morality consists in end-

---

[4] B., p. 617. *Phän.*, p. 426.

less struggle, the activity of the subject becomes a wasteful and pointless process. The weakness of process without end is that it is irrelevant and unrealistic. In the end, it proves to be guilty of the most feared evil : it is sterile. Be that as it may, the moral subject finds himself facing a question which is both paradoxical and bizarre : how to avoid the realization of harmony between duty and nature? The question which the morally concerned agent raises is a logical one : may not nature as norm be inappropriate to the moral ideal? Evidently, one way to prevent the occurrence of harmony and to maintain the required tension between duty and nature is to specify the latter as expressing and representing man's sensible essence. To be sure, man's sensibility is not only resistance to be controlled by the rational will, but is itself rooted in the quite other realm, and it revolts therefore against the control which is the subject's task and duty. Thus the determination of moral goodness is dependent on the understanding of the sensuous nature of man. Moral duty is thus opposed to man's spontaneous impulses, passions, inclinations, and sensuous desires. And since the decision to oppose all these sensuous tendencies is arrived at only through reflection which is the product of reason, duty becomes the highest fulfillment of reasonability. But if duty is a true expression of man's spiritual nature and since sensibility represents his sensuous nature, the subject becomes divided and the emerging dualism is simply the condition of the possibility of morality. Still, it is the aim of morality to suppress the sensuous nature of man and to secure a harmonious unity. In passages that illuminate as well as confuse, Hegel tells us how the subject oscillates between the necessary condition of morality and the projected goal of moral action. The real weakness of the initial moral consciousness lies in its inability to reconcile the two, precisely because both are seen as indispensable and as incompatible. It is not surprising, then, that moral consciousness must perforce develop into a trivial and flippant position. Seen in this light, a struggle without a serious respect for the moral ideal is not worth having. In the end, morality is not meant to be realized. At its best, it is an abstract exercise of the will, not a realistic guide to concrete life.

This is not, however, Hegel's last word on morality based on postulates or rational demands. For from this same moral consciousness it is possible to initiate a truly concrete movement of the will which compensates for its abstract character by a "process of acting". In the concrete action, however, the subject wants to accomplish something definite and begins to direct all his efforts on the manifold actuality, and thereby emerges a moral posture "varied and manifold in character".[5] Hence arises the plurality

---

[5] B., p. 621. *Phän.*, p. 429.

of duties, each duty exhibiting a specific and determinate content. What is more, all these duties strive to accomplish that which only one can possess. Thus the positing of many moral laws develops into an unavoidable rivalry between competing duties, for to say that there are many determinate obligations implies saying that all of them have the same pretentions. Therefore, while the subject hopes for the survival of morality as the indispensable mode of spiritualization, he continues its dissolution by his conception of conflicting duties.

The moral action becomes even more complicated when the subject reactivates the experience of pure duty, which he assumes to be necessary, valid, and "absolutely sacred". But the same duty which the subject recognizes as absolutely valid and sacred he espouses as transcendent, as constituting the content of the "sacred lawgiver". Evidently, the actual consciousness, regarding itself as imperfect (*unvollkommne*) and contingent, cannot locate pure duty within itself. In other words, experiencing contingency and being immersed in concrete situations and multiple cases, the subject must go beyond the actual consciousness and affirm the existence of another consciousness, in order to postulate pure and absolute duty. In this way, the opposition between specific duties and pure duty is not one of exclusion or contradiction, but one of relation and mediation. On account of his imperfection, however, the subject cannot claim to possess the power to connect the two, but must ascribe it to "another consciousness, which thus mediates or connects determinate and pure duty, and is the reason why that specific duty also has validity".[6] Consequently, when the subject succeeds in locating moral consciousness in this unconditional form, he is convinced that he has arrived at an understanding of the absolute being which alone can have relevance for him, for only God can distribute "happiness according to 'worthiness', i.e. according to the 'merit' ascribed to the imperfect consciousness".[7] God thus becomes the sustenance of morality. It is God's existence which gives morality ground and promises to bring it to fruition.

And yet this sustenance of morality can prevail only at the level of abstract consideration, since the Absolute Being is "just an object of thought, and is something postulated beyond the actual".[8] At its best, this transcendental postulate marks the triumph of the formal duty over the diverse and the multiple cases. But this mere formality of duty is at the bottom of

---

[6] B., p. 623. *Phän.*, p. 430.
[7] B., p. 624. *Phän.*, p. 431.
[8] B., p. 623. *Phän.*, p. 431.

all uneasiness which attends self-consciousness in its diversified moral decisions. If so, the hypothesized harmony between the absolute lawgiver and
the concrete individual constitutes an unsparing expatriation of the content
of duty. The necessary content is shattered at the very level of concrete
life, exploding into irreconcilable commands which remain in perpetual
competition with one another.

One might assume that with this the ground is well prepared for another
approach to morality, since the puerile conception of moral *Weltanschauung*
based on postulates has already exhibited its insurmountable difficulties
and follies. But the succeeding pages of the *Phenomenology* contain yet another episode, the sophisticated performance of moral consciousness which
refuses to give up the conviction to be a unified whole, a single unity independent of diversity. Rather than immediately retreating within itself,
the moral consciousness chooses to re-examine the experiences which determine the entire structure of the present *Weltanschauung*. This, of course,
does not imply that here the subject seeks some new knowledge about
the collapsing moral attitude by reliving his previous experiences. Rather,
it means that the subject tries to find a novel ingress into his own self
through a conscious shuffling which consists in passing from one recognizable position to the next, thus becoming aware that the opposite moral
attitudes — that the validity of duty has its ground beyond consciousness
and that it springs from the actual consciousness — are essentially the
same, since both proceed from the same subject. Charting the collapse of
one moral postulate after another, the subject takes comfort in what Hegel
calls the "fusion" (*der Synkretismus*) of opposed attitudes : the tendency
of contradictory positions to displace one another and, at the same time,
to neutralize each other. Still the synthesis of contradictions cannot be won
easily. The shuffling of the subject is fraught with a threefold exigency :
that of equivocation of harmony between morality and nature, that of equivocation of disharmony, and that of equivocation of duty. The first equivocation is that "harmony" in the one sense means the goal of moral action,
while in the other it signifies the abolition of morality. The second exigency
is similar to the first : the equivocation is that "disharmony" in the one
sense functions as the condition of the possibility of morality, while in the
other it leads to everlasting struggle and tension. And the third exigency
cuts across the two : the equivocation is that duty in the one sense is pure,
unconditional, and encompassing, while in the other duty explodes into
many determinate and rivalry duties. And so, the shifting of positions
brings the subject to a radical dilemma. If, on the one hand, shuffling deviates
into a noncommital attitude, which the subject regards as unavoidable,

then the moral consciousness transforms itself into a flippant posture. If, on the other hand, the subject decides to avert his frivolity, which tends to suppress moral motivation and precludes true commitment, then he exposes himself to the danger of hypocrisy. Whether by way of non-committal posture or by earnest disposition, every attempt to realize moral values falls short. Thus, the impasse is without solution, and the impossibility of morality seems to be the last word of self-consciousness. From this radical impasse one can understand the orientation of the subject toward *conscience* rather than toward new postulates. Moral conscience carries the subject out of frivolity, out of hypocrisy, and leads to the very center of subjectivity.

Conscience lies at the center of the moral philosophy of Hegel [9] — as of every moral philosophy which stresses the primacy of the subject — though without laying exclusive claim on the personal judgment, intentions, and motives. According to Hegel, the right of giving recognition to what the individual person grasps as reasonable and dutiful is the indisputable right of the subject. This line of thought is clearly discernible in Hegel's early writings, especially in his theological essay *The Spirit of Christianity and its Fate*.[10] Though the moral doctrines sketched in Hegel's early works differ in a number of ways from those presented in his *Phenomenology* and the *Philosophy of Right*, the emphasis on conscience is the same. Conscience, expressing the value judgment of the individual, is an attitude to will what is unconditionally good, and as such it is absolutely incontestable.

Still, the importance of conscience should not be exaggerated. That an act proceeds from conscience is a necessary condition of its being morally good, but this is not the only condition. To insist on the subject's personal decision against what can be determined by reason and objective norms is to exalt and to promote subjective opinion. The primary thing, then, is no longer action as it relates to the "absolutely rational element", but the affirmation of individual caprice, intention, desire, etc. Then the question is less to be moral than to be free and to follow one's personal intentions and whims. For this motive the rational power cannot give recognition to conscience in its private form as personal knowing and judging. Though

---

[9] It is safe to say that the doctrine of conscience, like all the other particular issues investigated in the *Phenomenology*, is an episodic moment in the constitution of subjectivity rather than a building block of the science of ethics. The *Phenomenology*, being a science of experience and of self-constitution, can never claim to be the science of any particular sector of reality.

[10] The pre-phenomenological ethics of Hegel has been examined by H. Eber in his *Hegels Ethik in ihrer Entwicklung bis zur Phänomenologie des Geistes* (Strassburg, 1909).

conscience designates cognitive certitude within the individual moral subject, "what is right and obligatory is the absolutely rational element in the will's volitions and therefore it is not in essence the *particular* property of an individual, and its form is not that of feeling or any other private (i.e. sensuous) type of knowledge, but essentially that of universals determined by thought ...".[11] Deprived of its function of determining morality, conscience appears to be no longer a "sanctuary which it would be sacrilege to violate",[12] but a merely sensuous type of certitude arising from the self. In this sense, then, the certitude springing from conscience is analogous to the primordial sense certainty, notwithstanding the fact that conscience is a manifestation of the spiritual subjectivity. Therefore, seeing himself standing at the elementary level of moral awareness, the subject fully realizes that it is more important to be torn from the inner self and the immediate type of moral cognition than to remain a solitary and self-sufficient legislating agent.

Now, in the perspective of the *Philosophy of Right*, it is remarkable to see how conscience becomes "subject to the judgment of its truth or falsity",[13] and is replaced by the legal "laws and principles" of the state. In the *Phenomenology*, however, the "successor" to conscience and personal certitude is not a "mode of conduct which is rational, absolutely valid, and universal",[14] but the religious consciousness. Even in the initial phases of the dialectic of conscience whose manifestation is characteristically phenomenological, one can clearly perceive the moral issue slipping directly into the religious issue. Still, the impression one gets is that Hegel's transition from morality to religion is quite arbitrary and incredibly abrupt. It is hardly conceivable that a truly religious attitude could grow out of the subject's dissociation from personal self-legislation, which, owing to its individualistic character, is contrary to the universal aspirations of the same subject. To be sure, the subject can seek universality without leaving the moral sphere. In support of such a position, one could say the following : the tension between the self who experiences solitude and is at variance with what he wishes to be and the self who constantly strives towards universality and spirituality can be resolved into a novel position which remains moral in character. Hegel was perhaps right to claim that the religious attitude ranks higher than the moral one and that the first might

[11] *Hegel's Philosophy of Right*, trans. T. M. Knox (Oxford : The University Press, 1942), p. 137.

[12] *Ibid.*

[13] *Ibid.*

[14] *Ibid.*

prevail over the second, but he had little or no justification for assuming that religious consciousness immediately replaces mere conscientiousness. Nor did he explore as he might have done very easily the possibility that there could develop an intersubjective moral attitude which was objective without being rigoristic. But he assumed too readily that conscience, the beautiful soul, the experience of evil and its forgiveness are the final and terminal moral attitudes.

Perhaps the best way of clarifying the subject's assent to religious consciousness is to concentrate on the highlights in the self-correcting process of conscience. As is well known, in focusing attention on conscience, Hegel proceeds in a new direction, different from traditional philosophy which has always sought to show that warning against going morally astray is the fundamental purpose of conscience. But Hegel's methodology does not allow him to indulge in any such outright proposition. For Hegel, the relationship between conscience and subjectivity is never static, but forever in process, in continuous flux. It must remembered, too, that the central point here is that the subject has freed himself from morality founded on rationalistic demands and appeals now to conscientious conviction instead. In this decision the subject allows himself to be guided by the voice of conscience alone and resolutely seeks to determine his course of action out of consideration for nothing but personal motivation. Thus, duty is no longer the categorical imperative appearing over against the self and seeking to constrain the self from without. "It is now the law which exists for the sake of the self, and not the law for the sake of which the self exists".[15] To recognize this is an important matter, and Hegel is ready to admit that conscience becomes the source of the moral law. Finally, then, the dictates of conscience must be absolutized, while all objective and universal norms must be declared to be irrelevant and futile. The moment, then, in which the subject resolutely rejects all universally valid moral principles or rules is the moment in which he rises to the level of self-dependence, achieving thus the supreme triumph of individualism.[16] The subject, however, may insist that speaking about conscience is not the

[15] B., p. 649. *Phän.*, p. 449.

[16] Hegel offers the following explanation : "Conscience for its own part, finds its truth to lie in the direct certainty of itself. This immediate concrete certainty of itself is the real essence. Looking at this certainty from the point of view of the opposition which consciousness involves, the agent's own immediate individuality constitutes the content of moral action; and the form of moral action is just this very self as a pure process, viz. as the process of knowing, in other words, is private individual conviction". B., pp. 648-649. *Phän.*, p. 449.

same thing as speaking about the individualistic caprice. Touched by the concreteness of conscience and duty, the subject wills authentic goodness. And as long as volition confines itself to self-legislation, it is valid, and, as such, at one with moral ideal. But, whenever it assumes objective forms of concrete expression, so that it becomes a factual fact alongside other factual events, it becomes ambiguous and open to scrutiny and interpretation. In other words, though the agent's motivation and moral decisions dwell in the silence of personal loneliness, the act he performs is subject to critical judgment and unsparing evaluation. Evidently, motivation occurs immanently in the inner sphere of the subject, which, by definition, is personal and incommunicable. But the act proceeding from the decision acquires an objective mode of existence, carrying, as it were, the immanent content directly into the world. Only if conscience finds expression in the observable form can it become an object of scrutiny and valuation, but it can never be so in a direct way.

Still, this does not mean that the content of conscience and the act that follows from it are identical. Therefore, for those who observe the act, it is difficult, if not impossible, to know whether the action reflects a morally praiseworthy or a morally blameworthy decision. In any case, the act performed contains a cognitional feature of uncertainty, being for the observer an ambiguous manifestation, to say the least. The act is either an articulate expression of conscientious decision, or it is an intentionally contrived disguise, concealing selfishness and wickedness of the doer. Indeed, no one can know anything with any certainty about the interior life of conscience which always recedes behind observable action, and no one any longer sincerely believes that only goodness must follow from personal decisions. To be sure, conscientiousness is an original feature of spirituality, inasmuch as it is intention projecting itself on moral values in order to bring them to actual fruition; but in the objective mode of existence the activity of conscience is not completely transparent and becomes exposed to the assaults of doubt and suspicion. Against such assaults no concrete and effective refutation, but only verbal defense, is conceivable. The reason for this is that conscience is always associated with the objectively uncertain and that motives cannot be proved, but only communicated through the medium of language. Therefore, the moral agent is compelled to defend his self-righteousness with only linguistic weapons. And this is the point at which the subject will begin to insist that he acts out of consideration for nothing but the dictates of his conscience and that he communicates out of consideration for nothing but the moral duty to speak the truth.

One would expect that the emerging possibility of intersubjective communication would diminish the prevailing mutual mistrust and lessen the tension between individual selves. This is, as a matter of fact, what actually happens. For the linguistic pronouncements are relevant not only to the defense of behavior grounded in personal conscience, but to the mutual agreement among individual subjects. When the subject is acting from conscience, he is actually ascribing universal validity to the form of the act, but not to the content of the act. Therefore, "it is this form which is to be affirmed as real : the form is the self, which as such is actual in language, pronounces itself to be the truth, and just by so doing acknowledges all other selves, and is recognized by them".[17] In this way the equality of individual subjects becomes established. And with this reciprocal recognition, which opens up a way to mutual approbation in moral matters, the disturbing condition of tension and mistrust falls away. It is most striking, then, that the purpose of language is to make the form of the conscientious act appear as a universally valid moral principle and to make conscience itself receive assurance of being the decisive and "essential fact" in morality. This assurance coming as it does from all individual subjects may also guarantee that conscience is a sort of moral genius (*moralische Genialität*) and a mouthpiece of the divine voice (*göttliche Stimme*). Now, from this new shift one can more clearly understand the whole orientation of the present dialectic of Hegel toward religion then toward morality grounded in objective norms or in the universally valid content of the act.

Laying exclusive emphasis on the formal aspect of action, the subject allows his conscience to put "whatever content it pleases into its knowledge and willing".[18] In like manner, the moral consciousness lays claim that God is immediately present in the self and that His voice is operative in conscience. Indeed, enjoying absolute freedom to put whatever content he wishes into his acts and responses, the conscientious subject becomes a real *advocatus Dei*. In the attempt to clarify this by going more into detail, the subject naturally has to cling to the mediating capacity of consciousness, which "knows the immediateness of the presence of ultimate Being within it to be the unity of that Being and its self".[19] Thus it is not surprising that the spiritual subject guided by conscience alone had to come upon the idea that his apprehension and knowledge is religious in character. And so Hegel did eventually come with a certain consistency to the attitude of the "beautiful soul".

---

[17] B., p. 663. *Phän.*, p. 460.
[18] *Ibid.*
[19] B., pp. 664-665. *Phän.*, p. 461.

With this the path is prepared for another posture of conscience and for another conception of individualistic morality. A strange desire for self-importance and self-righteousness seems to be the principal concern of the beautiful soul. To be sure, the conception of conscience here tends toward the aesthetic sphere, but it still stands close to morality and religion. Now, the important thing is not so much to determine whether conscience can best be termed aesthetic, moral or religious — there are sufficiently good reasons for calling it either — but whether these aspects can be dialectically related. How this alleged relationship is possible and what it means Hegel does not explain. But what he does explain is this : "that the very difference between the terms is abolished in the *immediateness* of the relation of the self to the ultimate Being".[20] In the same paragraph Hegel goes on so far as to say that "a relation is mediate when the terms related are not one and the same, but each is a different term for the other, and is one only with the other in some third term : an immediate relation, however, means, in fact, nothing else than the unity of the terms".[21] However, this type of relation is hardly applicable to the aesthetic, moral, and religious aspects of conscience. It is safe to say that the distinction between the aesthetic and the moral cannot be construed as equivalent to the distinction between the opposite terms constituting a dialectical relation. Hegel himself has placed the aesthetic aspects of conscience side by side with the moral and the religious ones. Therefore, what is decisive here is not the dialectical interplay and the mediating interconnection of different aspects : there remains rather only the working out of the various tendencies in the self-centered subject whose primary concern is the purity of the heart. The relationship which occurs here apparently refers not to the dialectical connection of diverse experiences springing from the inner life of conscience, but merely to the fact that the "self-willed importance" of the solitary subject leads him to self-adoration, self-righteousness, and the service of God in solitude of soul. The aesthetic aspect, which presumably beautifies the self, lies in the alleged purity of good intention. This aspect, of course, does not infringe upon what is moral. Therefore, the moral consciousness calls itself conscience precisely because it recognizes the unconditional universality of the self as the legislating agency. Finally, since the subject knows that God is present to his conscience, he regards moral action to be a genuine divine worship. As a result, the self-sufficient subject "flees from contact with actuality" and occupies himself with "yearning", which is essentially empty

---

[20] B., p. 664. *Phän.*, p. 461.
[21] *Ibid.*

and sterile. Thus, the moment in which the subject seems to proclaim his moral triumph is the moment in which he sinks to the level of futile activity.

Another occurrence must also be mentioned. The self-sufficiency of the subject definitely turns the accepted equality of particular individuals toward defeat. This extreme individualism was bound to assert itself when knowing and acting of one subject proved to be different from another subject. It is natural, therefore, that the equality, which was previously established and guaranteed by means of language, bifurcates into the "inequality of each individual existing for himself".[22] As a consequence, the reciprocal recognition of each other as acting conscientiously must be suppressed and revoked once and for all. But this inequality of individuality to other individuals awakens opposition and fosters mistrust. It is inevitable, then, that the intersubjective relations are bound to become a whirlpool of mutual suspicion and reproach. Consequently, language appears as a pseudo-solution to the problem of morality, for the subject turns his back on pure duty and declares that *die Pflicht liegt nur in den Worten* — "duty is merely a matter of words".[23]

Here again we have the intersubjective conflict and the mutual disagreement involved in the pursuit of morality. Hence it is through intersubjective opposition alone that continuity of moral action is possible, and, therefore, it is through it alone that evil and hypocrisy can be identified and unmasked. But the contest between an individual subject and other individuals is not the only contest. Since conscience draws its content from the individuality of the self, it exempts itself from what is universal and stands opposed to it. This opposition is further complicated as soon as we realize that the universal here designates nothing else but the universal consciousness, which is present and operative in the individual subject. If this is so, it is certain that the opposition in question will find its expression in the inner life of the subject. Thus, over against the conscientious certainty of self there stands the universal consciousness, which regards the first to be hypocrisy.

The judging consciousness, proclaiming that conscience refuses to act in accordance with universality, takes cognizance of the fact that what "ought to be universally acknowledged, is something not acknowledged and recognized".[24] As a result, it must accept the dichotomy between the "ought" and the "is" and must treat conscience as something actual,

---

[22] B., p. 667. *Phän.*, p. 463.
[23] *Ibid.*
[24] B., p. 670. *Phän.*, p. 466.

as having the right to follow its own commands. Now, since the judging consciousness remains passive, but hypocritically intends to see its moral valuation taken for the real deed, it stands in contradiction with itself and assumes the burden of guilt. Surely, if one denies the power of the judgment to act, one denies the power of the judgment to be moral. In effect, one denies the power of the judgment. More precisely expressed, the act of judging always involves attitudes of a non-judicial origin, e.g., attitudes related to self-righteousness, pride and vanity. Now, these attitudes can serve as guides to an explication of the hypocrisy of consciousness, which "wants to find its mere words without deeds taken for an admirable kind of reality".[25] Because of this it is unavoidable to identify moral valuation and personal decision, for hypocrisy is the common characteristic of both. Obviously, however, the identity of judgment and decision implies one significant element, one without which the unity of the subject would be neither possible nor actual : a dissolution of the opposition between consciousness and conscience.

Although the disappearance of opposition goes together with the subject's open admission of guilt, this personal confession cannot be construed as universal and intersubjective. The unflinching confession of moral evil, which admittedly occurs in one individual subject, does not mean that this morally relevant admission may be interpreted as mutual — mutual, that is, in the sense of being reciprocally recognized, in the sense of expressing factual continuity with the other subject. The fact that the individual subject's judging performances and conscientious decisions are identical in being equally blameworthy, offers no guarantee that the open admission of one's wickedness will be "followed by a reply making a similar confession"; but there is, nevertheless, at least an expectation that this might be realized.

The question may arise, however, whether this "open confession" is not really intended by every subject, since all individuals are aware that their immoral disposition is an open secret, and whether therefore it could be described as potentially, implicitly universal. However, the essential point would thus be missed. For what really matters here is the *isolationist* attitude of the other subject, the attitude which prompts the other self to keep himself to himself. In short, the other subject prefers the uncommunicative mode of existence, for he resolutely refuses to renounce the position initially assumed by the "beautiful soul". Still, this is not a question of purely psychic stubbornness but an admission of self-sufficiency and self-sustaining mode of existence. But such an isolationism, as the only acceptable way of being,

---

[25] B., p. 673. *Phän.*, p. 468.

precludes communication or, as Hegel puts it, "continuity with the other". It is not too far-fetched to presume that this perseverance might turn spirituality toward defeat. Hegel makes this unequivocally clear when he says that the isolationist attitude "proves itself to be a form of consciousness which is forsaken by and denies the very nature of spirit; for it does not understand that spirit, in the absolute certainty of itself, is master and lord over every deed, and over all reality".[26] Here we find what may be called the "highest pitch of revolt" to which a spiritual subject can reach and the display of destructive madness. Nevertheless, it is conceivable that the empty longing might be advantageous to the subject. Indeed, the present situation is neither hopeless nor desperate, for only on the basis of meaningless longing can the subject realize that the insistence on his own isolated existence is as meaningless as his longing. To put it differently, the posture of the "beautiful soul" cracks under its own weight and thus liberates the subject from self-centredness. Still, the act of liberation remains obscure and problematic so long as we ignore the subject's spiritual essence and potentialities. Indeed, the fact that soulless and isolated self-existence could not be sustained for any considerable length of time can be understood from the unique nature of spirituality : the subject's actions and deeds are vulnerable and perishable, but his spiritual power is boundless in endurance.[27] The subject is thinking, deciding, and acting. But the subject is also more; he is the possible ground for free self-realization. And in this sense the subject is — implicitly at least — spirit.

Since the renunciation of self-sufficiency and solitude presents itself as the most significant achievement in the moral sphere, it is rather safe to say that this victory marks the point of departure of the final stage of moral phenomenology. What is more, this same achievement draws attention to the interpersonal aspect of morality, which replaces conscience and leaves no room for strictly personal ethics. This thrust into the intersubjective sphere is primarily the search for unity and reconciliation, rousing in the subject the moral concern which enhances forgiveness and reciprocal recognition.

But whereas the situation is clear here, there remains un uneasiness in regard to Hegel's abstract treatment of evil, as well as in regard to his

---

[26] B., p. 675. *Phän.*, p. 469.

[27] Hegel himself phrases this somewhat differently : "The wounds of the spirit heal and leave no scars behind. The deed is not the imperishable element; spirit takes it back into itself; and the aspect of individuality present in it, whether in the form of an intention or of an existential negativity and limitation, is that which immediately passes away". B., p. 676. *Phän.*, p. 470.

abstruse distinctions and interactions between the opposed consciousnesses, where the first displays the "power of spirit over its reality" and the latter appeals to the same power of spirit to bring about "its constitutive, determinate notion". The question might arise whether the distinctions here introduced are of moral attitudes which are actually and concretely held rather than arbitrarily set up. Hegel's analysis of diverse moral aspects and intersubjective responses seems to be both artificial and extremely difficult to relate to any distinct and familiar experience. The bewildering and paralyzing obscurity of the last dialectical chain forces one to recall Hegel's own remark on his deathbed : "Nobody has understood me except one; and he did not understand me either". This might be an encouraging and comforting thought, but, frankly, it does not take us very far. And we should note in passing that a very similar impression flows from Prof. Walsh's lamentation : "If only he [Hegel] could have matched the vigour of his thought with skill in self-expression ...".[28]

Although the significance of Hegel's dialectical circling about the problem of unity cannot be recognized to its full extent, and although it is not clear exactly how his subtle maneuvering can prepare the way for the religious consciousness, the main points of his position are easily distinguishable. First, that the opposition, no matter how radical, revelant, and necessary, is bound up with the anticipated identity of the subject, for it is through opposition that the unity can be recognized and realized at all. Second, that demand to respond to moral duty is essentially a universal and spiritual demand, and owes its effectiveness to the recognition of intersubjectivity. Third, that evil actions, though by no means all of an intentional and deliberate character, demand an act of forgiveness, even if this implies that evil loses its acuteness. Fourth, that the morally conscious subject may find himself in the other without surrendering his own identity and selfhood. Fifth, that moral consciousness liberates the individual subject from selfish and extreme individualism and awakens in him the sense of true universality. Sixth, that the subjects who know themselves in this form of knowledge are apt to find a novel experience which is religious in character. In its initial mode, however, this new experience cannot be fully articulated in all its implications, and therefore must pass through a series of progressively richer forms in order to attain maturity and completion. And so, the transition to the religious realm can be said to be finally established — perhaps for the sake of a more spiritual mode of existence but surely with scant regard for the smooth passage.

---

[28] W. H. Walsh, *Hegelian Ethics* (New York : St. Martin's Press, 1969), p. 39.

In a certain sense, Hegel's moral phenomenology can be regarded as an introduction to systematic ethics or as a first formulation of moral philosophy. But this view is hardly defensible, because it ignores the fact that the *Phenomenology* was not intended to function as a grounding description of moral principles or to lay the foundations of ethics and, for that matter, of any other philosophical discipline. This, of course, does not contradict the fact that in the *Philosophy of Right* Hegel prolongs the interpersonal theme and develops an ethics in relation to the state, which synthesises the objectivity of the factual and of the rational.[29]

It can be fairly claimed that Hegel's *Phenomenology* is simply the exposition of morality as a phenomenon. Still this exposition remains deplorably reductive and concise. To be sure, if Hegel takes a reductive, even though not particularly simplified position toward morality, the reason seems to be that he regards morality as episodic experience rather than as constant posture towards life. But even if one regards this episodic moral experience as the distinct point of view of the maturing consciousness, that is, as a stage in the development of subjectivity, it still shows incompleteness and remains detached from the axiological frame of reference as well as from its wider historical background.

---

[29] That the category of intersubjectivity dominates the moral philosophy of Hegel has been shown and emphasized by W. H. Walsh. He writes : "First, there is the point throughout insisted on that morality is primarily a social rather than a personal phenomenon, something which can be understood only if we see the individual as part of a wider whole or a series of wider wholes". *Op. cit.*, p. 77.

CHAPTER XVII

THE SUBJECT'S FINAL QUEST FOR SPIRITUALITY

In the *Phenomenology of Spirit* Hegel spoke of religion several times : in connection with his theory of unhappy consciousness, especially in his subtle and elaborate doctrine of self-alienation, and in connection with ethical order, culture, faith, and insight. In the penultimate chapter he returns to religion again and speaks of it in connection with the final self-realization of subjectivity. For Hegel, religious experience marks the terminal stage in the subject's self-constituting growth, since the subsequent form of consciousness designates the emergence of complete spirituality, which is no longer an episodic awareness but a permanent, mature, and absolute standpoint.

It is most striking that the development of religion follows the rigorous plan of the preceding phenomenology. All this, of course, might give the impression that Hegel seeks here to elaborate a new and special phenomenology which runs parallel to the secular phenomenology. There is no question that in reproducing the architectonic of the previous process Hegel has decided to present religious consciousness in the familiar forms of consciousness, self-consciousness, reason, and spirit, but these forms are such that it becomes extremely difficult to call them merely secular or merely natural, to say the least. Now, since religious consciousness does appear in the old forms of the dialectical process, we cannot claim that we stand here before a completely different phenomenological structure and thus before a special phenomenology. Still, Hegel's insistence upon the same division is not merely an attempt to guarantee continuity to dialectical process and method; it is rather a search for a crowning stage that recapitulates and re-enacts briefly the principal steps of the phenomenological process, demonstrating that the very possibility of what appears now depends on what has appeared before. And it is for this reason alone that the chapter on religion does not deserve the title of a special phenomenology, much less of a noumenology.

Religious consciousness, appearing as a genuine experience of the spiritual subject, can reiterate the previous forms of the dialectic without giving the impression that the entire final stage of the work is merely a replica of the secular phenomenology. It matters little whether the old forms are defined as secular or as natural. Since religious consciousness is *de facto* presented in those forms, this suggests that Hegel has conceived them as universal and as overreaching. It is not surprising, then, that consciousness, self-consciousness, reason, and spirit re-echo throughout the entire chapter. Accordingly, the formative development of religion involves the continuous passing from standpoint to standpoint, for the self-correcting action is precisely what is requisite for the gradual self-realization of spiritual consciousness. To say this implies saying that the terminal mode of consciousness, as every other mode before it, cannot possibly view its own growth in a manner completely different from that by which it actually lives and experiences.

While one cannot speak of two distinct modes of the phenomenology, and can at most claim that the *Phenomenology of Spirit* has both a secular and a religious aspect, one can discern a host of novel elements in its religious aspect, elements which illuminate the subject's rise to full spirituality. The most important element is clearly the category of infinity. Now, the shift to infinity can be said to be gradual and necessary in the sense that moral consciousness "claims infinity to be immanent in its own knowing and acting".[1] Although it is less doctrinaire and much clearer to say that in the conscientious subject the openness to infinity becomes manifest, it remains true that with this shift the subject's perspective had to change

---

[1] Emil J. Fackenheim, *The Religious Dimension in Hegel's Thought* (Bloomington : Indiana University Press, 1967), p. 59. Although Fackenheim's contribution is extremely valuable for the understanding of Hegel's religious thought, he is not the pioneer in this field. Without attempting to compile a complete bibliography we would like to list the following works :

George P. Adams, *The Mystical Element in Hegel's Early Theological Writings* (Berkeley : The University Press, 1910).

Wolfgang Albrecht, *Hegels Gottesbeweis* (Berlin : Duncker & Humblot, 1958).

Claude Bruaire, *Logique et religion chrétienne dans la philosophie de Hegel* (Paris : Aubier, 1964).

Iwan Iljin, *Die Philosophie Hegels als kontemplative Gotteslehre* (Bern : A. Francke, 1946).

Traugott Koch, *Differenz und Versöhnung*. Eine Interpretation der Theologie G. W. F. Hegels nach seiner "Wissenschaft der *Logik*" (Gütersloh : Gerd Mohn, 1967).

Wolf-Dieter Marsch, *Gegenwart Christi in der Gesellschaft* (München : Chr. Kaiser Verlag, 1965).

Joseph Möller, *Der Geist und das Absolute*. Zur Grundlegung einer Religionsphilosophie in Begegnung mit Hegels Denkwelt. (Paderborn : Ferdinand Schöningh, 1951).

because his attention had moved directly to divinity. This much is intelligible. What is less intelligible, however, is the contention that religion erupts from moral consciousness which alone gives grounding reference to all genuinely religious experiences and thoughts. The emergence of religion is in danger of being misunderstood unless the notion of "eruption" is related to the subject's negativity.

We now come to the basic argument — that the subject's negativity is the principal source to which we owe information about the condition of the possibility of religion. To put it tersely, it is the negativity which drove the subject towards infinity. It is hardly necessary to reiterate that all the significant achievements have been accomplished by this boundless power. Being essentially negative, the subject resolutely refuses to ascribe absolute validity to relative and one-sided truths. There is, however, considerable significance in the fact that the same negativity, especially in its mediating aspect, has enabled the subject to preserve his partial insights by including them in the higher positions in his steady and persistent advance towards the unconditional standpoint. Accordingly, exercising the power of negation, the subject had the opportunity not only to re-enact every conceivable mode of cognition, but also to expose its inherent tendency of parading under the garb of the absolute truth. Now, if this suggests anything, it suggests that negation of the relative implies affirmation of the *absolute*, of the encompassing. And this is but another way of saying that the subject has upon himself the stamp of the encompassing, which is the stamp of *infinity*.

Against this background the subject's movement towards religion becomes more convincing. Describing religious attitude as an awareness of totality and as containing all reality within that awareness,[2] Hegel can say that with this realization the subject has reached the standpoint proportionate to and commensurate with negativity. Still, this in no way implies that the negative performance of the subject stops here. The religious consciousness "descends from its universality to assume an individual form through specific determination",[3] and in this descent, which involves differentiation and mediation, the negativity is constantly operative. This point is clear, and it hardly clamors for further discussion. Religion, which is a true

---

[2] This is, of course, the first attempt at introducing the standpoint of religious experience. Concentrating on the nature of religious experience, Hegel writes : "It is merely the conception, the principle, of religion that is established at first. In this the essential element is self-consciousness, which is conscious of being all truth, and which contains all reality within that truth. This self-consciousness, being consciousness [and so aware of an object], has itself for its object". B., pp. 692-693. *Phän.*, p. 479.

[3] B., pp. 698-690. *Phan.*, p. 477.

embodiment of spirit, is real only as the progressive manifestation of those distinct aspects which are implicit and latent in it. It is characteristic of religion, as it is characteristic of every other phenomenon, that it cannot even identify itself without first exploding its immediacy, without first breaking up into its constitutive elements which are expected to appear in the dialectical sequence. And this sort of constitution one can qualify as "presuppositionless" in the most radical sense, that is, in the sense that it does not accept anything except what such a self-correcting experience itself reveals.

We can detect here one disconcerting difficulty. It lies not in the fact that Hegel is concerned with the dialectical constitution of religion, where spirit is said to assume various shapes, but in the fact that progressive revelation of the divine in physical, organic, artistic, and specifically human forms derive their content from the monolithic and immediate experience of the divine, instead of from other sources not reducible to knowledge that has its whole content contained in immediacy. And the problem is further sharpened by Hegel's contention that spirit, which knows itself in the first instance immediately, "has indeed a filling drawn neither from sensation or manifold matter, nor from any other one-sided moments, purposes, and determinations; its filling is solely spirit, and is known by itself to be all truth and reality".[4] In this way, the subject appears to reaffirm his absolute self-sufficiency and immanent creativity in matters properly religious.

We will probably succeed in finding a plausible explanation for this if we fasten upon Hegel's constant references to particular expressions of religion in the course of history. These historical allusions are extraordinarily conspicuous. It is safe to say that in working out his phenomenology of religion Hegel made use of his rich historical and theological knowledge, though he refused to depict the evolution of religion "as a temporal sequence",[5] as a chronological progression. For Hegel, then, the temporal sequence and chronology are irrelevant and trifling, precisely because they do not function as the true determinants of the dialectical structure. This, of course, is by no means a negation of the significance of the historicity of religion. Although the phenomenology of religion is not a history of religion, the latter remains a source of knowledge from which significant illustrations can be drawn and a source of precious information with regard to religion itself. Therefore, one might venture to say that this new cognitional source in both its dimensions is no less important than the monolithic and immediate experience of religious consciousness. But obviously, to

---

[4] B., p. 689. *Phän.*, p. 476.
[5] *Ibid.*

introduce the distinction between the historical and the immediate sources of knowledge in absolutely contrary to Hegel's aim and procedure. Here, as elsewhere in the *Phenomenology*, his philosophizing follows a completely different procedural rule. It must be remembered that for Hegel the historically and geographically situated religions are not cognitional sources to be methodically explored but ways in which the human spirit has already manifested itself, or ways in which the constitutive aspects of the believing consciousness have fallen apart in time from one another, or again ways in which the spiritual subject has sought to achieve his self-realization. In brief, Hegel's primary concern is the generic religious experience out of which the various views of divinity flow in an internally unified progression. Seen in this light, the religious consciousness introduced by Hegel is not an attitude whose principal motive is salvation but a perpetually self-correcting spiritual awakening; it is a gradual self-constituting activity and not a singular vision of the divine in which consciousness can rest forever. Still, there is more than one good reason to suspect that the different forms of religion would have remained inaccessible for Hegel if they have not been mediated by consulting the available historical knowledge and records.

Despite an obvious presence of the historical perspective in the Hegelian phenomenology of faith, one is still faced with a unique and strikingly original arrangement of the various religious conceptions. Therefore, the development of religious experience cannot be treated exclusively under the historical rubric, for in selecting the exemplary forms of belief as typical illustrations of the dialectical process Hegel has taken radical liberties, and in pursuing his objectives he has been guided by principles other than historicity, chronology, and factual sequence. Thus, rather than considering the historical and geographically localized religious views which Hegel found instructive and relevant, it will be more profitable to consider the pivotal dialectical requirements and the chief exigencies of the phenomenological methodology.

Hegel was well aware that in visualizing the structural characteristics of the course traversed the subject is in no danger of sailing an uncharted sea of spiritual experience. Of course, the chart cannot predict whether the subject will experience God as Sun, as Ruler, or as Saviour; his chart, however little detail it expresses, is to be modeled on the idea of a continuous unveiling of the Absolute, on the idea of a cognitive itinerary whose purpose, to use the phrase of David Strauss, is to achieve gloriously much. Needless to say, the driving force of this itinerary lies in the subject's negativity, which is unrest where stagnation appears and a leap where there is a provisional stop. What is more, it prevents rash absolutizations of one conception of divinity by recalling that truth can lie only in the whole. Now, only an artless and the most rudimentary view of divinity can mark the point of departure, for the whole itinerary is conceived as running its course from the simplest conception of God to the most elaborate one. Let us note that the concept of simplicity is extremely important, for it permits Hegel to fasten upon the absolutely first mode of cognition in which the object is experienced as sensible, as sensuously given. Although in the most primitive mode of consciousness the subject knows that the object just is, Hegel refuses to describe the simplest form of natural religion as an unwavering conviction of God's existence. Still, we don't have to suspect here a failure on Hegel's part to observe the rules of the dialectical logic. To be sure, the conviction that God exists must occur at the level of pure immediacy, but since the immediate experience is essentially vague, unspecifiable, and mute, one cannot expect it to represent a recognizable and distinct mode of faith. Hegel demands that the primary concept descriptive of God's nature be sought for in the sensuous realm, for the sphere of sensible objects alone is open to a mind engaged in its first attempt to pin down the essence of the Absolute. Evidently, to select a divine attribute from the sphere of human activities or from the revealed sources is to forfeit the principle of the progressive spiritual awakening, which does permit any abrupt leap or any divine attribute imported from without.

But if this primordial and artless attribute of God is in the order of sensible objects, how can it be recognized among the glaring variety of sensuous qualities which this order exhibits? Obviously, one must proceed on the principle that one particular sensible quality can have priority over others on grounds of clarity and evidence. Understood in this way the primary attribute of the Absolute is traceable to light, particularly when viewed as a divine manifestation appearing under the tangible form which pertains to the inorganic sphere. Although strikingly objective, light seems to transcend the entire sensible realm by taking it out of darkness and concealedness. On the other hand, the religious consciousness can look upon light as God's objectively visible presencing. Thus, the lighting-up of divinity is doubly significant. First, for the religious subject to apprehend God is to see Him in the form of sensuous transparency. And secondly, for God to reveal His presence is for Him to appear as light. In brief, if the attribute of light constitutes the very truth of the religious conception, then the meaning of this truth is, subjectively and cognitively considered, the certainty of the religious subject and, objectively and metaphysically considered, is the lighting-up of divinity itself.

The conception of God as light is only the first step toward religious life, a step which fails to free the subject's consciousness of divinity from the world of things, from crude objectivity. But since the primitive religious consciousness clings to nature and since its attitude towards natural order is one of careful and attentive differentiation, there is only one way for the subject to correct the conception of divinity which became frozen under the concept of light. Further progress in religious awareness, then, consists in the further investigation of the natural order. This, of course, does not involve any new insight or rational effort; rather it involves reintroducing the distinction between the inorganic and the organic. The religious subject naturally takes this basic division into consideration and ascribes to it a central significance. The distinction makes it possible to pierce the tangle of hierarchical structuring, so that the architectonic principle of the phenomenology of religion becomes clear. And it seems safe to say that Hegel has elevated this distinction, along with that between organic nature and human nature, to the position of a fundamental principle of the hierarchical order, suggesting that the higher and the less physical the level of nature, the more adequately it can express the divine nature. Be that as it may, the sequence of religious forms is due to a principle of selection more ordinary and trite than logical and dialectical.

To take this principle seriously means to demand that the more advanced conceptions of divinity and the additional attributes of God be "derived" from the organic and the human spheres respectively. In Hegel's eyes, the entire organic realm, by virtue of its vitalistic perfection, can lead the subject to suppose that life is a characteristic manifestation of divinity. For this reason the believer speaks — in contradistinction to physical and corporeal — also of an organic presencing of divinity. Life, as a manifestive presencing of sensuality, voluntariness, and activity, is a distinct embodiment of the divine and the sacred. Still, the category of life discussed here is not to be mistaken for the "concept" of life, for the notion of life as "genus", or for the idea of "universal flux of life". Since at this level the religious subject is impersonating the percipient, it is the factual and concrete organism which is the basis for being able to think of divinity as living, to express reverence to it or to be afraid of it; and it is the variety of living beings which provides the basis for being able to perceive different embodiments of the Absolute and to select a distinct animal species for the purpose of veneration and profound respect mingled with love and awe.

With this the path is prepared for the third and the last mode of natural religion. Strictly speaking, the culminating stage is more humanistic than organic, more cultural than natural. Here Hegel is guided by the basic conception of the inventive and creative capacities of man. All this is a clear indication of the direction in which Hegel's religious thought is moving. For in practice this new standpoint results in a double approach to the problem of anthropomorphism, one from the side of artificer — the artifact being the first and the most elementary product of human imagination and inventiveness, the other from the side of the artist — the object of art being an expression of man's creative activity. Though these two approaches have a common basis and stand in closest proximity and propinquity, Hegel relegates the first to the third stage of natural religion and allows the second to dictate the terms of religion in the form of art. Evidently, the common basis of the craftsman and the artist is the characteristic productivity and creativity of a self-conscious agent.[6] But to interpret these manifold activities, which are part of the creative character of man's nature, as pertaining to two separate domains, seems only then to be necessary, if one views the artificer as the conscious being who "lays hold, first of all, on the form of self-existence in general, on the forms of animal life" and loses sight of himself in favour of an artifact. Hegel explains this in his own way : "That he [the worker] is no longer directly aware of himself in animal life, he shows by the fact that in reference to this he constitutes himself the productive force, and knows himself in it as being his own work, whereby the animal shape at the same time is one which is superseded and becomes the hieroglyphic symbol of another meaning, the hieroglyph of a thought".[7] However, by thus lowering the position of the artificer, Hegel has made it possible to eliminate the difficult problem of transition, and thus to bridge the gap between natural religion and religion in the form of art.

In contrast to the synthesizing activity and mere productivity of the artificer, creative performance of the artist is the unique expression of a self-conscious maker. The phrase "mere productivity" implies that the genuinely humane representation of divinity is opaque and that transparence is brought about by activity that has grown luminous, subject-centered, and intentionally related to the religious object. Thus, we see that for Hegel artistic action breaks out of "instinctive" productivity in self-recognition. Of course, to say this implies saying that divinity in the form of the person is disclosed only to self-consciousness, and to the creative power that dwells

---

[6] In the section entitled "The Artificer" we read : "With the production of this work, the instinctive method of working ceases, which, in contrast to self-consciousness, produced a work devoid of consciousness. For here the activity of the artificer, which constitutes self-consciousness, comes face to face with an inner being equally self-conscious and giving itself expression". B., p. 707. *Phän.*, p. 489.

[7] B., p. 706. *Phän.*, p. 488.

in self-consciousness. By the very fact that consciousness has become transparent, humane, and personalized, the subject's notion of divinity, too,
must be humanized and personalized. Hence religious life experiences growth
and intensification through the subject's return to selfhood, spreads to
everything specifically human and gives a novel and advanced expression
to divinity. Religion in the form of art, then, according to Hegel, aims from
the outset at humanistic representations of divinity rather than aesthetic
creations as such, at what is divine and absolute rather than what is beautiful.

That the first representation of divinity should be neither a literary
work nor an oral articulation seems easy to understand, since all linguistic
activities and expressions presuppose a spiritually mature subject. The
kind of art Hegel here demands cannot logically be other than static and
mute. Now, it is precisely this consideration which leads Hegel to single
out sculpture as the simplest mode of representing the divine in the human
form. In keeping with the principle of "existence in the state of rest", the
distinction of the different forms of quiescent art should appear here too.
Obviously, nothing would have stood in the way of identifying painting
and mosaic art as distinct representations and "objectivities", which, like
sculpture, are "without the immediate presence of a self".[8] Then the emphasis on sculptural art would have been at least mitigated. One could also
expect a few phrases discussing the musical adoration of divinity. But this
is omitted. True enough, Hegel speaks of the "melody of the Hymn",[9] but
the original wording (... *in dem Strome des hymnischen Gesanges* ...) merely
stresses the stream-like character of hymns. Be that as it may, the adorative
hymn, being an essentially linguistic phenomenon, transcends all types of
silent art and stands in sharp contrast to them. Thus, at this point, we have
clearly the difference between the abstract primitive art, which is objective,
static and speechless, and the abstract spiritual art, which is verbal, articulate, and truly animated. This implies that language produces a great change
in the self-conscious subject, since it opens up to him new possibilities of
existence. Language is at the basis of the subject's direct communion with
himself and it constitutes the "communicated unity of the many selves".[10]

[8] B., p. 720. *Phän.*, p. 498.

[9] B., p. 720. *Phän.*, p. 499.

[10] This phrase has been extracted from the following passage : "This higher element
is that of Language — a way of existing which is directly self-conscious existence. When
individual self-consciousness exists in that way, it is at the same time directly a form of
universal contagion; complete isolation of independent self-existent selves is at once
fluent continuity and universality communicated unity of the many selves; it is the soul
existing as soul". B., pp. 716-717. *Phän.*, p. 496.

Hence through linguistic performances the creative activity of the subject experiences progress and considerable growth. Accordingly, it is safe to assume that once on the road *via* the linguistic utterances, creative power will gradually abandon all formalistic and abstract representations of divinity, crystallizing itself in what might be called the living and the spiritual works of art.

What is perhaps more conspicuous here, however, is the sense in which Hegel's contentions about language can be interpreted as non-phenomenological and purely doctrinaire. Hegel believes that once it has been admitted that the work of art requires language for its richer and genuine existence, he is forced to say that God himself requires language for his own self-revelation. To say this implies saying that language is no longer a phenomenon, but an ontological and transcendental "element". And to make the claim that God takes language as his "medium of embodiment" is to present language and religion from the point of view of the Absolute. What is more, this doctrine seems to be completely unwarranted, for, in describing language as the medium of God's embodiment and self-revelation, Hegel is actually describing the language of the "universal self-consciousness", but for the latter speech is not a manifestation of an alien and transcendental being. Even if it were logical to ascertain that language is a necessary presencing of divinity, this would still be incomprehensible to self-consciousness engaged in creating and singing laudatory hymns. Of course, Hegel can speak of language as "a way of existing which is directly self-conscious existence", but this only underscores the old truth that language is essentially spiritual. And since the speaking consciousness is totally preoccupied with the veneration of the divine, the transphenomenal dimension of language cannot be verified by reference to the hymn that merely kindles devotion and admiration. Incidentally, similar remarks should have been stated a few pages earlier, when Hegel almost unnoticeably passed beyond the frontiers of phenomenology and adopted the metaphysical perspective, describing the Absolute not only from the standpoint of the religious subject, but from the standpoint of the Absolute as well.

About this new perspective, which we may designate as metaphysical, at least two things can be said. First, according to Hegel, the basic character of religion consists in a human-divine interaction and union. Now this must be understood as implying that there is a relation of the human to the divine and a relation of the divine to the human (*die Beziehung des Göttlichen auf das Menschliche*). In other words, since the relation between the self-conscious subject and the Absolute is dialectical, it follows that both realities are reciprocally interconnected and equally active, and the detailed exposition of all this constitutes the subject matter of the phenomenology of religion. Even if it be a fact that the activity of the Absolute remains inaccessible to the evolving finite subject and perhaps to the phenomenologist who wants to describe the process, still he has to carry the heavy burden of enacting the role played by the Absolute being. Second, and what is merely corollary to the first, Hegel's decision is to make language phenomenal as well as transphenomenal — from which it follows that language is an authentic capacity of the subject and a purposeful activity of God. Finally, there is one particular reason why Hegel was led to discuss God's revelation through language. All of Hegel's efforts were bent toward the unique phenomenon of the oracle which played a considerable part in Greek religion.

To be sure, the oracle is a transcendental manifestation and, by Hegel's own admission, "the first form of divine utterance".[11] This phenomenon signifies that it is God Himself who speaks and gives Himself as word. That which in the eyes of universal consciousness sank into the inwardness of the self, is now a clearly recognizable reality, responding to man's needs and concerns. This also implies that the Absolute has attained a novel objectivity and initiated a direct descent from infinite universality into human individuality, uniting thus with finitude.

Still, it is inevitable that the divine utterance through oracle emerges as a restricted revelation and communication. The oracle confronts the self-conscious subject as a contingent, accidental, and relative event. A consideration of the very nature and purpose of the oracle enables one to see where the alleged limitation really lies. The fault lies at the very essence of the oracle which exclusively emphasizes the contingent and completely disregards the important and the reflective. Indeed, no one consults oracles in order to gain knowledge about the fundamental structure of reality or about God Himself. Perhaps, in the last analysis, the religious subject himself is responsible for the relative character of the oracle, since everyone who seeks divine recommendation regarding an urgent decision is beset by a frenzied preoccupation with the trivial. The most one can say is that divine utterance cannot be conceived to be a significant revelation of the Absolute but, rather, to be a sort of practical advice relevant to quotidian life and conduct.

But there is another problem to be met. Though the oracle is a transcendental apparition dependent on the living and conscious mediator,

---

[11] B., p. 717. *Phän.*, p. 496.

it is difficult to find anything specifically aesthetic in it. Therefore, such a manifestation does not appear to fit into Hegel's conception of art. Neither the term "divine utterance" nor the phrase "speech of an alien and external consciousness" serves to designate oracle as a distinct form of art. Just as little as a constituted notion can be called art, so likewise can the oracular activity of the priest or priestess be called art.[12] Now, if Hegel identifies oracle as exemplifying a specific religious posture in the artistic form, the reason seems to be that he strongly regards the linguistic "element" involved in oracular activity as art rather than as a medium or as a vehicle of communication. Needless to say, Hegel runs the risk of losing the authentic meaning of art when he attaches aesthetic and artistic character to any linguistic occurrence without exception. Therefore, at this point one could easily raise an objection. Linguistic expression does not take on the character of art until creative activity of the subject gives it the stylistic shape of poetry, epic, tragedy, drama, and comedy.

According to Hegel, it is the destiny of the oracular phenomenon to vanish in cult, for the latter reconciles the objectified and estranged divinity of the oracle and the devotional attitude expressed in the hymn. It is assumed here that the distinction between the hymn and the cult is already established and clearly understood. But when the feeling of devotion contained in the hymn and the external presencing of divinity through the oracle are brought together, one may ask whether Hegel has not cleverly and arbitrarily isolated the hymn from the other constitutive acts of the cult and then redundantly claimed that both clamor for reconciliation. This is why the harmony of the laudatory hymn and the ceremonial cult could not become one of dialectical reconciliation, but remained one of convenient reintegration. We need only indicate one more point to support the claim that there exists an original kinship between the hymn and the cult. Even if the hymn is admitted to be an exclusive and typical expression of religious inwardness, one can directly perceive this immanent religious feeling manifest in the hymn slipping into the ritual and ceremonial activities of the cult. It might be added that the hymn, once unmasked as a ceremonial expression, remains for the subject an articulate objectivization of religion, although Hegel reserves this function for the cult proper.

However, Hegel treats religion in the form of cult in a manner for which

---

[12] This statement should be read and understood in the light of the following text : "So too, on the other hand, in the religion of art, because God's shape has taken on consciousness and hence individuality in general, the peculiar utterance of God, who is the spirit of an ethically constituted nation, is the Oracle, which knows special circumstances and situation, and announces what is serviceable to its interests". B., p. 718. *Phän.*, p. 497.

the reader of the *Phenomenology* has not been prepared. Apparently he did not remain faithful to his own basic principle, according to which language constitutes the essence of religion that transcends mere naturalism. Indeed, the linguistic expression always gave Hegel the decisive argument against every purely naturalistic and static conception of religion. Clearly, if language is the main factor demanded for spiritual expression, it should be present and operative in every religious form ranking above the oracle. But it is conspicuously absent in the cult. And it is expected that a deep confusion should descend upon the reader and interpreter of this section. Admittedly, one could argue that Hegel's presentation of oral religious postures should be followed by an attitude which is characteristically mute. Such a view is conceivable. It might, of course, be objected that the act of worship which has come about through ritual performances is not in the least set over against linguistic practices. And even if one leaves the "linguistic element" unemphasized, speech must be conceived as means of communication and of common worship. Thus, the celebration of feasts in honor of the deities is still oral; only the inclusion of the sacrificial act and of the graceful movement of body lends it a mute character. At any rate, the spiritual function of language is subordinated to the art of worship and to the quest for unification with the deities. It is obvious that, especially because of the emphasis on the sacrificial ritual and bodily portrayal of gods, the linguistic element had to be relegated to an ancillary position.

The original importance of language re-emerges and is re-affirmed by the subject in the spiritual works of the epic, tragedy, and comedy. Needless to say, language regains its meaning here within the context of and in reference to the creative Greek genius. The first stylistic language of which we can speak, according to Hegel, is the epic. What is really Hegelian in this is that the literary genre of the epic is regarded as an expression of a peculiar relation of man to gods and as the "memory of an essential mode of being once directly present".[13] This implies that the past and the religious outlook rooted in the past is the sustenance of the epic. Viewed from the dialectical standpoint, the subject's activity moves now from the frantic festivities and the "stammer of delirious bacchantic revelry" into the clear and articulate narrative that depicts intimate relations and transactions between men and gods. In the attempt to exhibit the dialectical force of the epic, Hegel naturally had to recognize in it a structure akin to the inferential process (*Schluss*), "where the one extreme of universality, the world of gods, is connected with individuality, the minstrel, through the middle

---

[13] B., p. 732. *Phän.*, p. 507.

term of particularity. The middle term is the nation in its heroes, who are individual men like the minstrel, but only ideally presented, and thereby at the same time universal like the free extreme of universality, the gods".[14]

At this juncture, one could say that the significance of the epic is not so much in the literary genre as such and not so much in the poetic activity which seeks beauty in its own way and for its own sake as in the presentation of a characteristic ancient belief, according to which men and gods do "one and the same thing". By this phrase Hegel wants to point out that the ancient religious view reactivated and presented by the imaginative minstrel is a sceptical, if not a comic, achievement. The seriousness of religious conviction is shattered, because there arises an opposition between the essential nature of reality and activity. The seriousness with which the divine beings engage in earthly action is "ridiculously unnecessary", for this implies a "comic self-forgetfulness of their eternal nature", which is, to be sure, the causal and determining principle. There is an equally comical effort on the part of human beings, whose illusory aspirations and over-zealous projects remain irreconcilable with their finitude, limitation, and mortality. What is even more comical is the fact that in the epic all gods emerge as completely powerless beings, since only man can procure for them an "interest in acting" as well as the "actual reality" itself.

The theme of "contradictory relation" gradually turns the divine-human encounter toward the "unintelligible void of Necessity" and thus toward failure. And this anticipation is confirmed by the fact that the narrative of the epic seems to point to a critical re-evaluation of mythology and anthropomorphism. Demythologizing seeks to take form under the heroic and rationalistically oriented secularism which Hegel calls the "higher language". Indeed, considering the epic in its essential sense, one may claim that in Hegel the extremely imaginative presentation by the minstrel tends to become a truly secular drama, where gods recede behind the chorus, refusing to appear and to act as concrete persons.

This change of perspective is of utmost importance, precisely because it marks the transition of the epic into tragedy. Here the mortal hero replaces active gods, the impersonator replaces the minstrel, human tensions replace nostalgia, and, finally, the personal language replaces the impersonal one. With this is given the refutation of the close analogy that can be drawn between gods and men on the basis that both are conscious and active beings.

In comedy, which represents the final religious posture in the form of

[14] B., pp. 732-733. *Phän.*, pp. 507-408.

art, an unrestrained sceptical view with regard to gods comes to the fore. But in this manner the sceptical attitude transpiring in comedy becomes a kind of contrast to the subject's religious commitment. Accordingly, this seems to suggest that comedy brings the subject to the threshold of atheism. If the spiritual subject remains below the threshold of atheism and resolutely refuses to become a full-fledged atheist, however, the reason appears to be that he regards his unsparing assault on polytheism and anthropomorphism as a purge of religious consciousness and not as an abolition of religion as such. At this point, then, one has to stress the difference between the negation of imagined, anthropomorphic deities and the negation of the Absolute. To speak quite plainly, Hegel suggests that the real Absolute is sought for by no one more persistently than by the sceptic. Rational and relentless critique of puerile religion produces an awakening in the spiritual subject, since it unveils to him new perspectives on absoluteness. And with this the path is prepared for the culminating religious attitude — the revealed religion. The last gigantic step, in which the subject unravels his whole religious life, is one of the most drastic transitions : a bridge that unhesitatingly leaps the gulf between the refutation of deities and Christian revelation — the birth of God-man.

Hegel's discussion of revealed religion is replete with difficulties and ambiguities. The first question with which we have to deal is whether the phenomenology of revealed religion can be regarded as a logical continuation of the religion of art, that is, as arising directly and organically from comedy, or whether, as so many commentators suspect, it is a series of purely dogmatic views borrowed from Christianity. What we have before us is, obviously, a complicated issue and its solution is not quite so simple.

That Hegel was himself aware of this difficulty is rather clear, for at the beginning of the section C he places one significant remark before the reader : "This incarnation in human form of the Divine Being begins with the statue, which has in it only the outward shape of the self, while the inner life thereof, its activity, falls outside it".[15] The passage convincingly shows that Hegel's principal argument hinges on the theme of incarnation — that is *Menschwerdung*. The philosopher apparently believes that the notion of incarnation cannot be restricted to God-man's birth, though he would grant that Christ's appearance is both historical and unique. It seems that all of Hegel's efforts here are bent toward the enlargement and extension of the term *Menschwerdung*. As the result, incarnation of the divine is admitted even at the level of sculpture, where the work of the artist is said

---

[15] B., p. [750]. *Phän.*, p. [521].

to be the first attempt at humanizing the divine personage in the state of rest. Thus the assent to authentic incarnation is being guaranteed from the very beginning. For the moment in which Hegel treats statue as an incarnation of God is the moment in which he anticipates and actually projects the birth of the God-man. The same thought can be expressed somewhat differently. As long as the birth of Christ is conceived to be a dialectical necessity, that is, an event in accordance with the demands of the dialectical process, the notion of incarnation must be traceable to the most primitive type of the religion of art. Still, the matter remains complicated and dubious, and must be considered more in detail.

To be sure, statues, hymns, and various ceremonial rites are positive attempts to represent the deities in the image of man and to establish a vital contact with them. The crucial point is, however, that Hegel places *representation* of divinity on the same level as *incarnation*. Evidently, every effort to represent and impersonate the divine being originates in the religious subject, whereas the event of incarnation presupposes the self-revelation of God himself. It is clear, too, that representation is a phenomenological notion and that incarnation is a theological-metaphysical notion. In Hegel's philosophy, however, representation and incarnation become indistinguishable and convertible. Therefore, from this unverified and unverifiable identity one can understand and judge the nature of the final transition.

At the beginning of this chapter we have ventured to say that Hegel's phenomenology of religion cannot be interpreted as slipping into a noumenology. At this point, however, we are almost forced to revoke that statement or to qualify it, since at the end of its itinerary the *Phenomenology* must face its own dissolution and prepare the way for a new standpoint. Now, the section on revealed religion suggests, and suggests very strongly, that Hegel is adopting a novel perspective, which might be called metaphysical or transphenomenal. Though the stages of the ultimate religion are presented in a strictly dialectical manner, the presentation of the trinitarian nature of God exhibits Hegel's attempt to approach the issue from the viewpoint of the divine being itself. Evidently, the notion of the trinitarian Absolute cannot be reached by means of a procedure which originates in the religious subject alone. And if one moves beyond the subjective horizon one never remains within the properly phenomenological field.

We may ask ourselves : from what motives and reasons can we infer the necessity of a new perspective? Basically from two : first, from the conspicuous fact that the incarnated God must be recognized as possessing a nature of His own; secondly, from the anticipation that the phenomenological approach has to eliminate itself in bringing the subject to maturity. In the first place, what we are urging here is that the revealed religion, being accepted for what it claims to be, should be seen as a metaphysical occurrence. Now, if this supreme religion is regarded as a metaphysical event, the religious consciousness must stop depicting the Absolute from its phenomenological perspective and draw attention to God's own way of being. In the second place, what must be stressed is that in approaching its terminal point the *Phenomenology* must be prepared to submit its resignation. Indeed, the phenomenological process cannot be expected to last forever. And yet, it cannot abandon its own and native standpoint and assume a perspective that is completely unknown and alien to it. But, if not through the self-initiated resignation, how then is the new standpoint reached? Hegel's answer seems to be this : by means of a message which originates with the supreme religious object — the God-man, whose reality is in no way dependent on the phenomenal ways of knowing. Accordingly, the metaphysical presencing of the God-man explodes the phenomenological standpoint of the believing mind and presses on beyond the horizon of the subjective modes of knowing. It must be remarked, too, that this transition from the phenomenal to the transphenomenal had to be attempted in order to shed light on the fact that the self is no longer subject to the relative and limited viewpoints.

What transpires here is the fact that the God of the revealed religion is the real absolute. The very expression "the real absolute" indicates that the religious subject ascribes reality to the divine being not merely insofar as it impinges upon the mind, but in an unqualified sense. Needless to say, this ascription is neither logical nor phenomenological, but strictly metaphysical, and it brings the *Phenomenology* to a close.

Epilogue

If phenomenological investigation has for its ultimate purpose the subject who is fully developed and completely mature, this investigation must terminate when maturity is attained. To be sure, Hegel's transition from religious experience to philosophical speculation remains problematic. One thing, however, is certain : the *Phenomenology* has no need of metaphysics to conduct the subject's consciousness to the level of spiritual maturity; the dialectical explicitation of cognitive, social, cultural, and moral experience is sufficient. And to say this implies saying that the *Phenomenology* is neither philosophy proper nor metaphysics. It is readily apparent that the latter presuppose consciousness that has been brought to complete ripeness and climbed the ladder to the absolute viewpoint. Thus, the *Phenomenology*, without becoming an ordinary introduction or propaedeutic, prepares for and heralds philosophical speculation.

Still, there exists a puzzling problem concerning the *Phenomenology* and its relation to the Hegelian system. Despite the fact that the phenomenologist intends to be a patient observer and wants to begin at the beginning, consciousness issuing the command to conduct a presuppositionless investigation and description of knowledge originates with the subject already enjoying the absolute perspective. Clearly, only the subject who stands at the very threshold of metaphysics can successfully retrace the steps of consciousness coming to full maturity. It will not do, so it seems, to conceive of the point of departure of the *phenomenology* simply according to the analogy of what we know of the evolutionary and generic character of natural knowledge. Thus while recognizing that the phenomenological process is governed by its own logic, we must resist the temptation of locating the point of departure within the sense certitude. Systematically, the *Phenomenology* begins with the most primitive act of knowledge and continues until a standpoint that excludes *Aufhebung* is reached; actually and in principle, however, the course is the reverse. We can say, then, that the *Pheno-*

menology is the movement of subjectivity which traverses its self-constituting process and "reaches its beginning only at the end".

Needless to say, the end of the *Phenomenology* is also the beginning of the *absolute knowledge*. But even at this stage it is not easy to ascribe a univocal meaning to the phrase "absolute knowledge", since within the process of the final transition the various elements are not clearly related. But one could probably succeed in elucidating the character of the absolute knowledge if one fastens upon the formative and constitutive function of the phenomenal cognition. Now, the moments of the latter process have appeared "as determinate modes or shapes of consciousness", which had to move forward by their very nature, in order to constitute consciousness as an integrated whole. All this implies that the phenomenological consciousness was constantly compelled to go beyond itself and adopt a higher standpoint. But this progressive growth in maturity is not a merely additive development. It is a development of self-formation and of self-realization in which the subject advances through apparent, partial, and even deceptive knowledge to true knowledge, where mind knows its object to be itself. Now, it is precisely this self-formative and self-corrective function that characterizes the phenomenal consciousness, but it does not characterize the absolute consciousness. Therefore, the absolute knowledge, arising from the mature consciousness cannot be expected to engage itself in the activity of self-constitution. Grafting itself upon the organic totality of the previously elaborated modes of experience, the absolute knowledge is no longer an episodic form of consciousness, but an activity "in which mind as a whole makes its appearance". Evidently, it would be pointless for the mature mind to distinguish between the knowing self and the objective truth, since now it knows its object to be truly itself. Thus, in the absolute knowledge the opposition between being and knowing is overcome once and for all. However, to say that in the absolute consciousness the knowing self and the objective truth become indistinguishable implies saying that knowledge has acquired the character of the *notion*. Accordingly, at the threshold of the absolute knowledge, the negative, the mediating, and the universalizing acts of consciousness suddenly cease to appear as distinct activities, but return into consciousness and remain one with it, thus fulfilling its intention of being perfectly unified and self-contained.

With the rise of the notional knowledge, then, the subjectivity has successfully completed the process of its embodiment. The problems of embodiment were fluid, and thus fluidity appeared as the distinguishing mark of the *Phenomenology*. Now, since at the terminal point of the phenomenological process the subject realizes that he is spirit knowing himself as spirit, he is in the position to envisage two possibilities at once : the prospect of watching how what is identified as distinct is moved by its immanent logic and returns again into its own unity, and the prospect of engaging in the investigation of pure notions, each of which would be considered by a fully constituted subject. The first project is the phenomenological science of the ways in which knowledge appears and gradually purges itself of its relative and apparent character. The second project is the philosophical science of notions, which is completely liberated from the burden of dealing with particular moments in a process toward a systematic and persistent overcoming of appearance, alienation, and restricted perspectives.

Thus we have before us two distinct projects in regard to the philosophical enterprise. The first one is an invitation to begin all over again the subject's formative itinerary, which, in virtue of its necessary and determinate progression, can be regarded as a rigorous discipline. The second project is also the work of the mature subject. It is a speculative inquiry, admittedly logical and apodictic, dealing with simple notions in dialectical isolation from one another, but in the light of the genuinely metaphysical import.

This twofold proposal is startling and intriguing, to say the least. One may wonder much about its feasibility and the difficulties it has to face. Of its inspirational value, however, there can be no question.

INDEX